the two-year college

PRENTICE-HALL SERIES IN EDUCATION
Dan H. Cooper, *Editor*

PRENTICE-HALL INTERNATIONAL, INC., *London*
PRENTICE-HALL OF AUSTRALIA, PTY., LTD., *Sydney*
PRENTICE-HALL OF CANADA, LTD., *Toronto*
PRENTICE-HALL OF INDIA (PRIVATE) LTD., *New Delhi*
PRENTICE-HALL OF JAPAN, INC., *Tokyo*

PRENTICE-HALL, INC.
Englewood Cliffs, N.J.

CLYDE E. BLOCKER
Harrisburg Area Community College

ROBERT H. PLUMMER
Flint College, University of Michigan

RICHARD C. RICHARDSON, JR.
Forest Park Community College

the two-year college: a social synthesis

Library of Congress Catalog Card No.: 65-19734

Printed in the United States of America   C-93514

The last quarter century has witnessed an educational movement unparalleled in human history. Never before has the concept that free or, at least, inexpensive higher education should be available to the masses been so boldly advanced.

The expansion of educational opportunities has been slow for many people. Its recent progress may be traced from the Morrill Act of 1862 through both the federal and state legislation of the early 1900's. The passage of the GI Bill of 1944 gave the nation its first opportunity to observe closely the results of increased emphasis on higher education. What began as a grateful nation's gesture to its fighting men and women became an economic and social change of unprecedented proportion.

The lesson of the GI Bill was not lost on the American public. If, through higher education, returning servicemen could increase their earning power, social mobility, and personal satisfaction, why could not other citizens have the same opportunity? The answer was obvious. Further, it was recognized that an almost unlimited number of highly educated individuals would be necessary if the United States was to sustain its domestic economy and its position in world leadership. The National Defense Education Act of 1958 represented a major attempt to extend educational benefits to the population as a whole.

While the general effect of popular sentiment and federal legislation has been to increase the universal availability of higher education, the vastly increased number of students has stimulated a countermovement in many four-year institutions. This reaction is evidenced by higher

foreword

21296

admissions standards, increased tuition charges, open acceptance of the necessity to eliminate large percentages of entering classes, and a resistance to broadening the curriculum of such institutions to include work not traditionally collegiate.

It is fortunate for both the American people and higher education that relatively new institutions—junior colleges, community colleges, technical institutions, and local college branches—were prepared to assume responsibilities eschewed by their more traditional counterparts. A phenomenon of the twentieth century, the two-year college grew slowly during the first forty years of its existence. In this period, certain concepts were advanced which provided the philosophical basis essential for the educational roles that the turbulent postwar period was to thrust upon these institutions. The belief that anyone could attend a two-year college counterbalanced the rising admissions standards of other institutions. The idea that these new colleges should include transfer and technical education, community services, and remedial educational activities provided the necessary framework within which flexible programs could be created to meet not only the needs of post-high school youth but also those of adults.

This happy combination of philosophy, situation, and institution has caused the two-year college to grow more rapidly than any other segment of American higher education. But growth is sometimes subject to growing pains, and these institutions have experienced such pains. There is a great urgency for study and evaluation of the two-year college as it has emerged.

The authors of this book are to be complimented for their critical analysis. For a long time writers on community colleges have sought refuge in the unique features of these institutions; by doing so, they have avoided facing certain harsh realities. It is also to the authors' credit that they not only have criticized, but also have sought to advance what may well be far-reaching concepts. Many readers may disagree with their proposals, but the resulting debate can only be beneficial.

In many respects, this book differs from previous works on the two-year college in that the authors have not been content simply to explore the status quo, but have sought to project new considerations by using existing practice as a point of departure. An effort also has been made to provide a theoretical framework within which the various functions of the two-year college may be related to each other and to the society from which these colleges draw their sustenance.

The comprehensive treatment of all facets of the two-year college will prove useful to those who are interested in learning more of its nature and operation. It will have particular value to those entering into or working in the two-year college. Hopefully, it will also create controversy among those who today chart the courses of the two-year college. New institutions demand creative thought and critical evaluation.

Frederic T. Giles
University of Washington

The two-year college may still be regarded among dowager circles as the "enfant terrible" of American education, but there can be little question that as an institution, it has arrived. Characteristic of any growing movement, however, particularly in its early stages, is a sensitivity to criticism, an unwillingness to admit that present philosophies do not represent eternal verities. The two-year college has seen its share of this point of view among the small band of pioneers who fostered and supported the institution in less affluent days.

With rapid expansion have come many able persons from the secondary schools and from the universities and colleges. The resulting influx of new ideas provides a challenge to the old guard to examine their positions, to defend them where facts permit, and to alter them when they are no longer applicable.

Change inevitably results in conflict between the defenders of the established order and those who see the need for new approaches to meet new problems. When the two-year college, as an institution, was required to struggle for its existence, little time was available for healthy controversy within the ranks of the faithful. All effort was required to sustain the organism. No one today, however, can claim that the existence of the two-year college as an important segment of American education is seriously threatened. The time has come to raise issues and to challenge relationships. Those within the field will raise no important questions that will not eventually come to the attention of those without.

There is yet another important reason for raising issue with certain

preface

of the presently accepted beliefs regarding the role and organization of the two-year college. Among many adherents, these beliefs are held with an emotional fervor analogous to that of the religious zealot. Such fervor is necessary during the early period of an organization's existence, but with age must come maturity. Emotional fervor must give way to reasoned consideration and a willingness to examine a variety of points of view, regardless of how heretical some may seem.

The writers of this volume have undertaken two major tasks. The first was to focus the viewpoint of the reader upon the relationship between the two-year college as an institution and the society which it was created to serve. Too frequently the temptation is to study the college as a reality in and of itself without stressing the essential relationships that exist between it and its environment and the effect this relationship has on evolution and change. It would be nice if it were possible to study institutions like chemicals, in isolation from contaminating external factors, but such an approach is neither feasible nor realistic with a dynamic element of society. Consequently, this work will stress relationships between society and education in an attempt to accurately chart the present location and future course of the two-year college.

In a like manner, every attempt has been made to inject controversial issues into the treatment of the various aspects of the institution. The writers, conceding a pragmatic outlook, are reluctant to espouse existing practices as absolutes. The continuum of events leading to the present moment may make certain of these approaches the best and truest practices, but in a rapidly changing society, these practices will not be true for all time. New approaches must be considered, for it is only through ordered change that the increasing responsibilities being assigned by society to the two-year college can be satisfactorily met.

C.E. B.
R.H.P.
R.C.R.

table of contents

the two-year college

The two-year college is receiving increasing recognition as the most significant development in American education in the past half-century. Despite this recognition, little attempt has been made to apply the unifying effects of theory to the confusion presently surrounding the concept of the two-year college. It will be the task of this book in general and this chapter in particular to develop a framework within which can be placed, with some degree of order, a series of facts and conjectures concerning this uniquely American phenomenon.

It should be the task of theory to advance and clarify the aims of the two-year college and, in so doing, to determine those roles it can fill and those it must eschew. In this way, a community faced with the choice of establishing a two-year college may know—in principle, at least—to what it is committing itself. By knowing this, the resources devoted to trial-and-error solutions may be reduced without impairing over-all organizational development.

The tasks of this chapter are threefold. First, it will be necessary to view the total range of functions which might be performed by the two-year college. (That is not to say that all—or even a majority—of these functions will be served by any given college.) Second, it will be shown

1

a theoretical approach

that the functions performed by a given college and the emphasis it places on a specific function will be largely determined by the sociopolitical viewpoints of those who are in a position to influence its development. Finally, an attempt will be made to identify the issues which presently confront the two-year college. The resolution of these issues within a framework of sociopolitical perceptions will set the stage for the remainder of the book.

The Two-year College in American Culture

The process of education can be viewed as the major influence on the socialization of the fledgling members of a modern society. With the decline in the influence of religion and the weakening of family ties, the schools—along with other social and economic structures—have consistently gained in influence and complexity. Today, there exists a variety of organizations seeking to fulfill what they perceive to be their distinct roles within the institutional context of education. Many of these organizations have well-defined objectives and have developed over an extended period. Others, like the junior high school, have only recently assumed their full responsibilities on the American educational scene. The two-year college, despite a history of more than half a century, has only within the last ten years emerged as a significant contributor to the educational process. This renaissance, stimulated by the fears and hopes attendant upon the increasing pace of automation, has found its greatest manifestation in the comprehensive community college. At the same time, as will be seen, its impact upon other two-year institutions has not been entirely lost.

Certain functions have been assigned to the institution of education, with concomitant expectations on the part of members of the society. Although these expectations are not always realistic and frequently may be contradictory, the fact that they exist has important implications for all strata in the educational process. How does the two-year college fit into the functional framework of education?

Definition of the uneducated

The first function that may be ascribed to education in general is that of defining the state of being uneducated as undesirable. Because education serves as a social mechanism to cope with the deficiencies of members of the society, it is by definition undesirable to be uneducated. It is interesting to observe that the level of education an individual must possess to escape the designation *uneducated* rises as the technological procedures of the society become more complex. At the turn of the century, for most purposes, an eighth-grade education was satisfactory to remove one from the category of the uneducated. As *uneducated* increasingly came to be associated with *unemployable,* the high school diploma assumed importance as the line of demarcation between *educated* and *uneducated.* Now, with the threat and the promise of automation, the college degree is gaining the significance once accorded the high school diploma. There has even been a phrase coined to describe the new generation of uneducated: *functional illiterates.*

The two-year college has been caught in the middle of this drive to increase the educational level of the population. The four-year college and the university are ill equipped to cope with the increasing hordes of education-minded individuals, particularly when so many of them lack even the most rudimentary requirements for baccalaureate courses. The comprehensive two-year college, with its willingness to offer courses of less than collegiate level, has been cited as the salvation of low-ability students. It must be pointed out, however, that if these courses do nothing more than promote a higher level of functional illiteracy, then the two-year college is not fulfilling its function.

The creation of a competent faculty

A second significant function of education is that of bringing together technically competent persons and those who have been defined as uneducated. As the categories of persons work together in complementary roles, the undesirable condition of the latter may be eliminated. As the agencies of education have increased in size and complexity, the number of specialized individuals required to permit these agencies to carry out their function has—of necessity—risen. Like any complex organization, the educational agency requires a staff to support and coordinate the activities of those engaged in the educational process. Many of these specialized staff members are not directly involved in teaching, a circumstance frequently criticized by individuals who misunderstand the complexities of modern education and wistfully remember the bygone days of the one-teacher school.

The modern two-year college has not yet acquired the multiple-level supporting positions to be found in the large university. This is owing, in large part, to its avowed disinterest in research. But the two-year college's increasing responsibilities in the area of diagnostic and remedial work and in the development of varied technical programs and an emphasis on counseling have produced far more complex staffs than those commonly found on the secondary school level. Although two-year colleges are often understaffed in terms of their avowed goals, the staffs that are available to them are not always organized for maximum effectiveness: many two-year colleges utilize secondary school patterns of organization.

The legitimation of ability

Yet another function of education is the legitimation of an individual's ability to perform a certain type of job. No longer can an office boy work his way to the presidency of a large manufacturing concern. The ranks of junior executives, from which future promotions will be made, are all but closed to those not possessing the seal of approval from an accredited institution of higher learning. Industries that formerly trained their own technicians now find it less costly to have this service performed by such institutions.

It is in this technical training that the opportunity so manifestly exists for the two-year college to make its unique contribution. For nearly every four-year professional program, a comparable two-year technical program can be found. These technical programs can be completed by students who do not have the ability required for the baccalaureate degree. Furthermore, the need for technicians is increasing more rapidly than that for professionals. Estimates of the technician-to-professional ratio vary from two-to-one to four-to-one or even six-to-one. In the future, requirements for technicians may increase geometrically as more and more highly skilled persons are graduated from the universities. No other agency of education is so well equipped as the two-year college to serve the function of legitimation with respect to technicians.

The transmission of culture

The fourth function—the transmission of culture—is so obvious as to require little elaboration. Historically, two-year colleges have concentrated on this function, often to the exclusion of all others. Up to the last decade, the main stock-in-trade of the two-year college was the respectable college-transfer program, with its nervous duplication of the general requirements of surrounding senior institutions.

Today, as in the past, the transfer program depends entirely upon the acceptance of two-year college credits by four-year schools. With this type of axe suspended above the two-year college, little latitude has remained for flexibility or innovation. Perhaps it should be pointed out that two-year colleges can provide the first two years of the transfer program somewhat less expensively than the four-year colleges. Whether or not this entitles the two-year college to particular distinction depends upon one's point of view.

In answer to those who would give this fourth function a more exalted position than that of the others, it should be pointed out that, although education is the main agency which has as its goal the preparation of individuals for effective functioning in an ongoing society, there are many agencies—the church and the library, to mention only two— which are concerned with the preservation of the cultural heritage. The responsibility of the two-year college in this area cannot be denied, but neither can it be argued, in a modern society, that this is the major reason for its existence.

In addition to transmitting the cultural heritage, the institution of education, primarily through its upper levels, attempts to develop new knowledge. Although education seldom benefits directly from the systematic exploration of the knowledge made available through research, those institutions of society which do benefit directly are predisposed, as a result, to provide more support for education than they might otherwise have done. As has been noted, the two-year college has made something of a fetish of not being research-oriented. If research is taken to mean the search for knowledge simply for the sake of knowledge, then it must be agreed that this role is more adequately performed on the university level. Aside from pure research, however, there is a serious need for applied or action research in all levels of education. The two-year college should not rely solely on the answers provided by senior institutions for the resolution of its unique problems.

The socialization of individuals

A final function of education involves the socialization of individuals. Although this is a crucial function, it is one that is extremely difficult to define. Depending upon the viewpoint that is held of society, various requirements may be seen as essential to the socialization process. Special-interest groups attempt to pressure legislative agencies into requiring that facts be taught as they (the groups) see them. Thus, a law may be passed requiring that a certain subject be taught in a manner favorable to the interests of a particular group. Pressure may also be brought to bear on administrators in an attempt to coerce them into deleting certain aspects of the educational process which are viewed by certain groups as inimical to attitudes they consider desirable. The most famous example of exclusion of a particular kind of knowledge from the curriculum is the prohibition of the teaching of the theory of evolution in Tennessee. In a very real sense, it is the essence of education to achieve an objective treatment of controversial areas free of the multitude of interests which intrude. And yet it is not desirable for the schools to achieve complete ethical neutrality, for this would be to neglect the function of the transmission of culture.

More than other institutions of higher education, the comprehensive two-year college, with its close community ties, is likely to become the focus of pressure groups. The more masters a given agency serves, the less freedom it is likely to have. A common pattern of financing and control for the two-year college involves dependence upon both state and local authorities. Unless the college seeks actively to preserve the academic freedom of its staff members, the slow erosion of intellectual freedom may make it quite as impotent in the shaping of social forces as the public secondary school.

The two-year college, then, is potentially capable of fulfilling a wide range of functions in contemporary society. It may provide the line of demarcation in certain areas between those who are and those who are not educated in a functional sense. It may establish an environment in which such barriers to education as retardation in reading, inability to communicate effectively in writing, inadequate financial resources, or immaturity may be overcome with the assistance of specialized professional persons. It can help reduce the number of functional illiterates in our society by stressing technical and specialized education for those students who lack the intellectual ability or other necessary requisites for baccalaureate work. It can provide the media for transmitting important aspects of the culture through a well-developed program of general education. It may develop new knowledge to cope more effectively with the problems imposed upon it by society. Finally, the two-year college— through the courses it teaches or fails to teach, through the manner in which it handles controversial areas, and through the emphasis and nature of the student activities it encourages—contributes to the concepts developed by its students concerning the duties of an adult citizen in a free society.

Sociopolitical Forces and the Two-year College

Basically, all institutions arise in response to certain needs that become evident within a society. Even when needs are clearly recognized, however, the action advocated reflects the social positions and backgrounds of the individual advocate. John Dewey said:

> All social movements involve conflicts which are reflected intellectually in controversies. It would not be a sign of health if such an important social interest as education were not also an arena of struggle, practical and theoretical. [3:v]

Individual perceptions of the two-year college are influenced by sociopolitical orientations. Consequently, the functions emphasized or ignored by a specific institution depend upon the social referents of those who are in a position to contribute to its development. Because institutions must always be certain that their image is acceptable to a majority of their constituents, certain patterns of control and organization will predictably develop where corresponding types of thought patterns prevail.

It is possible to categorize contemporary American thought into four basic positions: *reactionary, conservative, liberal,* and *radical.* Each position represents a point along a continuum. Each contributes, in its own way, to the continuing shifts and adaptations within the educational order.

The reactionary position

The reactionary position has been detailed with unusual lucidity by Mortimer Adler and Robert Hutchins. [1, 5] Their beliefs were essentially predicated upon the Greek ideal of rational humanism and a clear distinction between the liberal arts and vocational education. This point of view, based upon the Aristotelian concept of man as a rational being, considers the function of education to be the teaching of the classics and the development of the individual's ability to solve problems encountered throughout life. Popularized by Hyman Rickover during recent years, this concept has gained adherents among educators, members of boards of control, and laymen in various sections of the country. [7]

In spite of arguments to the contrary, the reactionary position involves three serious limiting factors. First, it ignores the body of knowledge in psychology and the social sciences. Most individuals cannot understand the complex concepts and content which are included in the classical studies; furthermore, they do not have the capacity to relate these principles to the realities of individual and group behavior. Second, there is a continuing need for vocational education in the new fields of knowledge which have developed within the last century. The assumption that the training received from studying the classics can be transferred to the problem-solving techniques has not been demonstrated by research. Current psychological knowledge indicates that the direct application of problem-solving methods to functionally related materials, situations, and concepts improves learning. Third, the traditional background of American education is essentially democratic, and movements toward the narrowing of educational content or opportunities meet effective resistance from those individuals and small common-interest groups within the community whose aspirations and opportunities are threatened. Thus, the forcing of all students into the same educational mold would generate reaction on the part of those who found themselves left out.

Two-year colleges heavily influenced by the reactionary position are likely to give scant attention to any function other than the transmission of culture. Perhaps the best illustration of colleges which stress closed, static systems of thought are certain denominational colleges controlled by fundamentalist sects. They do not accept ideas or knowledge which run counter to their own notions of what constitutes "proper" material for the minds of their students. The reactionary influence, however, is by no means limited to these schools. The dismissal of teachers for advocating political viewpoints opposed to those of the controlling group, the banning of books, and the overstress on liberal arts (even for those eminently unsuited for such training) in many instances represent the influence of reactionary thought.

The conservative position

The conservative position in American education is an eminently respectable one. It draws strongly upon tradition, but it is not entirely resistant to change when such change can be proved to be consistent with the accepted ideals of that tradition. The concept of general education is representative of the conservative position. The evolution of general education and its application in higher education demonstrates the mediating effects of liberal views upon the conservative position. James B. Conant is the chief spokesman for this point of view. He has recognized the need of vocationalism in higher education, but he also has pointed out:

> Unless the educational process includes *at each level of maturity* some continuing contact with those fields in which value judgments are of prime importance, it must fall short of the ideal. The student in high school, in college, and in graduate school must be concerned . . . with the words *right* and *wrong* in both the ethical and [the] mathematical sense. Unless he feels the import of these general ideas and aspirations which have been in a deep moving force in the lives of men, he runs the risk of partial blindness. [4:111]

Thus, general education represents the compromise between two extreme positions: that which would reconstruct education to conform with the Greek pattern, as at St. John's, and that which would eliminate significant attention to the transmission of culture (particularly with reference to ethical traditions and concepts). The Harvard Report represents the most comprehensive attempt to reconcile the theories of Adler and Hutchins with those of Dewey, but the attempt did not bring satisfaction to the proponents of either position. [2:294]

Since the publication of the Harvard Report, there has been sustained study and modifications of those college programs centered around the concept of general education. [8] Many colleges have re-examined their curricula and have attempted to achieve a balance by requiring students to take courses in the social sciences, the humanities, the arts, mathematics, and science, after which they would be free to pursue specialized studies in vocational courses. The pattern of general education during the first two years and specialized education during the last two years has become the *modus operandi* in most colleges and universities. It can be seen from the foregoing that the traditional four-year liberal arts colleges, as well as the majority of large universities, fit comfortably into the conservative niche. The private two-year college with its finishing school atmosphere, and the public two-year college which concentrates on a limited transfer curriculum, also represent logical concomitants of the conservative influence. There can be little doubt that, like the reactionary influence, the conservative position emphasizes the transmission of culture. Because the conservative view is less resistant to change, however, additional functions may receive attention where necessity dictates.

Because of the cultural lag between societal demands and institutional adaptation, it is quite possible that the conservative position is predominant in education today. Although liberalizing elements are clearly visible, education has yet to breathe the new wind deeply.

The liberal position

The liberal position grew out of the concepts set forth by Charles W. Eliot, William James, and John Dewey. Educational liberals recognized the changing needs of society, the need for egalitarian education, and the meaning of the new knowledge developed by psychologists between 1875 and 1925. The developments in higher education during the past fifty years have been, in large measure, the outgrowth of their thinking.

Higher education has not yet really accommodated itself to the liberalizing influence. Nevertheless, a liberal trend can be observed in a number of four-year colleges and universities which have departed in varying ways from traditional patterns. Team-teaching, independent study, the interdisciplinary approach, as well as the changing emphasis on the student personnel program, represent attempts to make the educational pattern more responsive to a changing society. It is interesting to note that public elementary and secondary schools, with their greater responsiveness to public pressures, have gone much further in implementing what they conceived to be the demands of the liberalizing influence. In fact, many of them went to such extremes that a reverse force has been generated, currently represented by certain conservative and reactionary interests, which is actively seeking to move the status of education back a full half-century.

In the two-year college, the liberalizing influence is best represented by the comprehensive community college with its emphasis upon educational programs designed to fit the needs of the majority of individuals without regard to tradition. The community college has been organized to provide flexible educational programs which recognize the limitations and needs of students rather than to seek students who fit the requirements of traditional curricula. Liberals, recognizing the need for broader educational programs, argue that the introduction of vocational courses adapted to individual and societal needs does not vitiate traditional college courses. This issue, which has been the focus of dispute between conservatives and liberals for the past seventy-five years, will be examined in detail in subsequent chapters of this volume.

It should be evident by this point that the educational liberal would emphasize a particular function of the two-year college in accordance with his perceptions of societal requirements. This pragmatic approach results in some attention being given to all the potential functions with stress on those that promise to provide the best solutions to imminent problems. Reduction of the number of functional illiterates through technical education and remedial work would be certain to receive primary emphasis. The transmission of culture would not be overlooked, but neither would it occupy the center of the stage. The liberal also recognizes the need for constant evaluation so that emphasis on various functions may be altered in terms of changing requirements.

The radical position

The function of the radical is to emphasize the need for change. Those who are considered radical by their peers are, in many cases, the innovators—the creators of human progress, rejected initially but eventually accepted because of the weight of evidence which slowly builds in support of their concepts. Their goals may not be realized during their own lifetimes, but ultimately their contributions are integrated into the accepted referents of society.

The radical position in American education is difficult to define because it represents the vanguard of the evolutionary process. At any given time, the radical position will be defined by the acceptance it receives from the conservative element. Best represented by the Reconstructionist position, the radical emphasizes—above all—the social nature of man. Accepting the concept of social determinism, the radical reasons that, if society is responsible for the way in which men develop, then it is also responsible for taking remedial action when the behavior of men becomes inconsistent with the perceived goals of the society.

The Reconstructionist position has been identified by Morris as having "much of the flavor of Marxism." [6:375] Perhaps this accounts for its present lack of verbal support. Yet few would disagree with the goals expressed by the radical. Believing, with Marx, that society has in some manner degraded the importance of work and turned it into a distasteful chore, the radical would alter the present leisure-oriented trend of society by restoring labor to its proper place of dignity in the scale of human values. The radical influence would add that, in order to accomplish this, the schools must become the agents of social change. Only the knowledge provided by science, and its use in consciously shaping human destiny, can save society from the inexorable fate to which it is slowly being pushed. This activist orientation constitutes a major distinction between the liberal and the radical. The radical does not share the liberal's belief that things are constantly getting better and require little or no attention; he believes that man must act to improve his situation and that his failure to do so invites disaster.

Just as the reactionary would subjugate all other potential functions of the two-year college to the transmission and conservation of culture, so would the radical subjugate all other functions to the socialization of the individual. The socialization process, as viewed by the radical, would not have as its goal the adaptation of the individual to existing society; rather, the socialization process would be an instrument of change through which the student would acquire the image of a better world and the desire to seek its implementation.

A few private institutions of higher education, primarily in the four-year field, have attempted to organize learning activities without regard for society as it exists today. These institutions see themselves in the vanguard of a movement which will revolutionize higher education and, ultimately, the society it serves. Too extreme to enjoy widespread acceptance from the more conservative elements of society, these colleges nevertheless focus attention on certain weaknesses in existing educational practices and, by so doing, become the catalyst which may bring about needed change.

Although there has been no active radical influence in educational content and method during recent years, the activities of government—particularly on the federal level—have induced violent shifts in educational programs and emphasis. Direct intervention in higher education, through a variety of federal programs, began during the Depression years. More recently, the Veterans' Rehabilitation Act of 1944 (P.L. 346), similar legislation designed to aid veterans of the Korean Conflict, and the National Defense Education Act, have induced massive changes in higher education which have had, and will continue to have, far-reaching effects on colleges and universities as well as on society in general. These programs are ultimately intended to safeguard national security, but they have had an almost revolutionary effect upon the number and kinds of educational programs in institutions of higher education. Thus, it is possible that sharp changes in educational practices will depend, to an increasing extent, upon the action of the federal government rather than upon that of lay or professional leadership at the state or local levels.

These, then, are the orientations of the four positions. The conservative and reactionary positions emphasize, in varying degrees, the concept of individual responsibility and appeal to past experience and tradition. The liberal and radical positions, having grown out of pragmatic concepts, stress that modern society has grown so complex that education must be constantly adapted to meet the widely varying needs of individuals and of the society in which they live. (Table 1-1 details the essential aspects of each position.)

This discussion will emphasize only the conservative and liberal positions, because most of the influences on the two-year college can be traced to one or the other. The reader should bear in mind, however, that extreme influences exist as a part of any organized movement and may, under certain conditions, exercise devastating impact.

Image of the two-year college

During the course of this discussion, it will become apparent that there are many images of the two-year college which grow out of the attitudes, values, and consequent perceptions of individuals and groups in society. Each perception of the college is the product of the values and needs of the individual or group at a particular point in time. The educator sees the college as one type of institution if he has a conservative orientation; his image is quite different if his ideas concerning education tend to fall within the range of any of the three other points of view.

At the same time, the layman, whether young or old, may see the college in an entirely different light—not necessarily because of his general orientation toward society, but because of his personal need for the services the college provides. Thus, one individual who does not see any direct profit to himself may think of the two-year college as a place where inadequately qualified students are ruthlessly weeded out so that public funds can be saved. On the other hand, one whose personal interests are not being served by the college, and who has a propensity for the reactionary position, might well see the college as an unnecessary organization threatening certain values he holds dear.

TABLE 1-1. Sociopolitical Positions:
Implications for the Two-year College

	Radical	Liberal	Conservative	Reactionary
Attitude toward change	Rapid change	Gradual change	Maintenance of status quo	Regression to the past
Attitude toward governmental action	Highly centralized	Centralized for specialized and necessary services	Decentralized essential services for selective groups	Laissez faire
Implications for education	Educational programs for social reconstruction	Educational programs for gradual change	Educational programs for preservation of the culture	Educational programs for preservation of absolute values
	Directed curriculum for social objectives	Curriculum adapted to current problems and needs	Curriculum centered upon traditional subject matter	Curriculum limited to immutable truths
	Selection of students for social purposes	Self-selection of students	Selection of students on academic basis	Selection of students on academic, social, and economic basis

The Two-year College: Nine Issues

It is evident that all the positions currently associated with the two-year college cannot be equally correct—except, perhaps, in the minds of those who advance them. The question is: Can the two-year college meet the expectations of educators, as well as those of society? There are both danger signals and developments which engender optimism about the future of this segment of higher education. As the images of the two-year college are examined from various points of view, it will become apparent that constructive resolutions of current problems are within reach, but that final success will depend upon social forces of the first magnitude. Only by analyzing the relationship between American society and the roles of the two-year college can an adequate image be developed.

Educational services

Can the ideal of the comprehensive community college be realized through the continuation of all types of educational services provided in response to apparent or assumed community, state, and national needs?

Organizations, both public and private, are created to perform one or more services of value to those who bring the organization into being. Even large organizations find it necessary to differentiate functions in order to achieve the intermediate and long-range objectives sought. Otherwise, there is a constant danger that none of the diverse goals will be attained. Generally, two-year colleges are not yet plagued with the problem of size. The allocation of emphasis to various programs and functions does, however, raise some question as to whether it is possible for a single institution to serve effectively so many masters at one time.

Students

Can the two-year college effectively serve the educational needs of unselected students of different ages, cultural backgrounds, abilities, levels of socialization, attitudes, and motivations?

The two-year college claims a unique place in higher education by attempting to serve educational functions which are not adequately met by secondary schools, four-year colleges, or universities. The public community college has adopted as its basic tenet the "open door" policy, whereby all high school graduates and adult citizens in the community who meet minimal educational requirements may be admitted. This policy, of course, encourages heterogeneity in the student body, which—

in most instances—includes individuals from every social and economic level. But it also raises a question: Can any college serve the best interests of all students when they have only a broad cultural heritage in common?

Institutional adaptation

Can the two-year college continue its adaptation to changing societal conditions and needs, or will it become a traditional and static institution with fixed and limited educational objectives?

The history of American higher education is replete with examples of colleges originally organized for specific purposes and later transformed into more traditional institutions conforming rigidly to the accepted patterns of the university. For example, the land-grant colleges were originally intended to provide instruction in agriculture and mechanics, and did so until the mid-1920's. During the past forty years, however, these colleges have been transformed into universities serving the same educational functions as the public and private institutions founded earlier. The same transition has taken place in teachers colleges within the last fifteen years. Having made the change from college to university status, their programs have come to mirror those typical of older universities. The two-year college confronts the same issue: Will it continue as an experimental college or will it, like many of its predecessors, adopt a more traditional pattern?

College-community relationships

Another problem of the two-year college concerns the degree to which it can achieve immersion in and interaction with the community while continuing to fulfill its educational objectives on a satisfactory level.

It has been said that the campus of the comprehensive community college is the community, and that such an institution should provide those educational and cultural services which are not made available by other agencies in the area. Ideally, such services include any program which contributes to the educational and cultural betterment of the community and its citizens. This concept further increases the responsibilities of the community college, for among its potential students must be numbered every citizen in the community; among its responsibilities must be included all activities which can be defined as *educational* or *cultural*. This concept introduces a question: Are there practical limitations to the services a single organization may effectively provide?

Delineation and stability

Can the two-year college develop a related cluster of roles which will make possible the achievement of its objectives? Closely related to this question is another: Will the two-year college continue in its present organizational form, or will it be divided into such institutions as vocational or technical schools, college-transfer institutions, or four-year colleges?

Although there is widespread support for the two-year college among various groups and locales within the United States, there is also energetic and continuing opposition to what many regard as a truncated and inferior version of the four-year institution. There is no substantive evidence that the two-year pattern is superior to other possible variations for its particular segment of post-high school education. There are those who would systematically convert two-year colleges into four-year institutions as the need for additional degree-granting institutions manifests itself. The argument has also been advanced that two-year colleges may best serve society by eliminating transfer programs and concentrating on vocational and technical training for those in need of such services. Issues relating to the stability of the two-year college will be examined in greater detail in the ensuing chapters, but it should be kept in mind that the survival of the two-year college in its present form is not necessarily assured for all time.

Post-high school education for all

Will society accept the principle that *all* individuals have a right to education, beyond the high school level, to the limits of their abilities and motivation?

This tenet has been accepted in some areas of the country and has been rejected emphatically in others. There is as yet no unanimity on the principle that *all* individuals in *all* parts of the country, regardless of class, economic level, or age, should be encouraged to improve themselves through post-high school education with generous assistance from public or private funds. There are those who believe strongly that responsibility for education beyond the high school is an individual matter; there are others who feel that educational opportunities should not be restricted on the basis of economic status.

Financial support

If the principle of higher education for all is accepted, will there be sufficiently broad acceptance of the financial responsibility for support of both public and private two-year colleges?

It is virtually axiomatic that Americans accept the concept of social responsibility for educational and philanthropic activities and organizations—until such responsibility is reduced to the problem of arranging satisfactory financial support. The difficulties of finding adequate financial support for education in the United States have been discussed in detail by many people and in every possible way; however, the addition of the two-year college to the educational system of the country introduces another dimension to this problem. Are there sufficient numbers of people willing and able to support more and larger two-year colleges, both public and private? Will these people be receptive to a level of support which will make it possible for such colleges to meet the expectations for educational services which have been enunciated by both lay and professional persons? Obviously, the maintenance of quality programs, whatever they may be, depends upon the availability of sufficient funds.

Educational leadership

Will there be adequate numbers of administrators and faculty members dedicated to the philosophy and objectives of the two-year college to make this institution a significant and indispensable part of post-high school education? Although there are outstanding exceptions, in general there has been a dearth of leadership in two-year colleges. The proponents of the two-year college have frequently been outnumbered and outvoiced by their opponents among university personnel, the very individuals who most need to accept the responsibility for providing leadership. There continues to be vocal and persuasive opposition to general post-high school education among laymen and educators alike.

There is also reason to question the general understanding and acceptance of the concept of the comprehensive community college even among those administrators and faculty members who have been associated with it. In many instances, a substantial number of such individuals have contributed far less than could reasonably have been expected of them. Thus, the question can be asked: Will educators on all levels provide the leadership necessary to the complete realization of the potentials of the two-year college?

Administrative organization

How can the two-year college be organized and controlled, internally and externally, in order to achieve its objectives most effectively and efficiently? Should the college follow the patterns of organization characteristic of four-year colleges or secondary schools, or should it develop its own patterns specifically adapted to its unique objectives? Can the college be structured so that a reasonable degree of efficiency may be attained without sacrificing effective educational services?

The external patterns of control and coordination of two-year colleges, both public and private, vary markedly from community to community and from state to state. There is no single pattern of control which dominates the national scene; however, some general trends have become apparent during recent years which indicate that certain types of external control are more effective than others. This issue is closely related to the further development of two-year colleges, and it will be examined carefully in later chapters.

Specific Questions Related to the Basic Issues

The two-year college is a creature of the twentieth century and, therefore, has not yet developed a great deal of insulation from the swiftly changing cross-currents of the society which gave it life. It is closely related to the social, economic, and political conditions which shape its character. Being young and relatively untried, it does not enjoy the stability of traditions generally associated with other institutions of higher education. But the fact that it is not fettered by tradition is a distinct advantage in that the college has the opportunity to develop in response to current needs and thinking; it is not circumscribed by ideas which have governed other colleges and universities over the past two hundred years. On the other hand, the very lack of stability that results from such a situation generates a multitude of problems with which the institution must grapple if it is to succeed in achieving its objectives. Thus, this young partner in education has both promise and problems of the first magnitude, and its future will depend upon the outcomes of its struggle toward maturity.

The major thesis of this volume is the examination of the problems which face the two-year college and the suggestion of possible solutions. Some of the questions to be examined are of immediate import; others are far more complex. The solutions suggested will be far-reaching and will impinge upon the cherished concepts of laymen and educators alike. The questions to be defined and discussed arise from both internal and external conditions and forces, and they contain within themselves political, social, and economic implications of major significance.

In general, the issues defined below can be classified under four general categories: educational roles, organization and control (internal and external), financial support, and general issues. It must be pointed out that these questions have varying degrees of relevance to all other segments of higher education; however, they are especially important to two-year colleges in view of the vastly increased responsibility they face in the immediate future. Furthermore, because the two-year college has not yet been fitted snugly into an unbreakable mold, there is still time for critical analysis and basic changes within such colleges.

Educational roles

(1) Should the two-year college retain the "open door" policy, or should it impose selective admissions policies, thus eliminating individuals of limited academic ability or inadequate academic background?

(2) Should the public two-year college attempt to develop more comprehensive educational programs serving many diverse educational needs and a wide range of individuals, or should it restrict its programs to traditional college-transfer programs?

(3) Can the college simultaneously provide college-transfer programs of high quality and vocational, technical, and community-service programs?

(4) How can the college stimulate status for and acceptance of vocational and technical programs in the face of the "halo" effect of transfer programs?

(5) Can the educational programs of two-year colleges be coordinated so that students have a meaningful four-year educational experience?

(6) What types of community-service programs can be provided by the two-year college which are compatible with other educational functions and of significant value to the community?

(7) What types of personnel services should be developed in order best to serve the needs of students and to facilitate the educational objectives of the college?

(8) How can the bifurcation of the student-personnel program and the academic program be transformed into a mutually supportive educational process for the benefit of students?

(9) How can the college adapt its programs to the wide differences in abilities, motivations, and ages of its students?

(10) Can the college continually adapt its programs to rapidly changing occupational and educational needs and, at the same time, retain order and stability within the institution?

(11) What are the distinctive roles of the two-year college which are not merely reflections of either the secondary schools or of four-year colleges?

(12) Can the two-year college develop educational leaders with the energy and foresight necessary to bring such colleges to their maximum potential?

Organization and control

Internal

(1) Is the generally accepted pattern of administrative organization of the two-year college appropriate to its educational mission?

(2) What is the role of the faculty, of the students, and of the board of control in the administration of the college?

(3) Can the two-year college retain internal flexibility of administration and programs in the face of increasing size and complexity in many such colleges?

(4) How can the principles of democratic administration be applied in the college in such a way that it will achieve its objectives most propitiously?

(5) What are the policies and procedures necessary for the orderly control and functioning of the college, and by whom should they be developed?

External

(1) What are the essential aspects of state legislation for the organization of public two-year colleges?

(2) Which of the following colleges has the most effective forms of organization and control?
 (a) Separate-district community colleges
 (b) State-controlled community colleges
 (c) College or university extension centers
 (d) Technical institutes
 (e) Colleges under the direction of the local school district

(3) What are the optimum state administrative organizations and services essential to the development of the two-year college?

(4) How much coordination is necessary for the rational development of the public two-year college which will render effective educational service while, at the same time, being efficient and economical?

(5) How can an optimum degree of control from both local and state levels be achieved?

(6) Can a level of educational statesmanship on the local level be developed to insure needed educational services to the area and while preserving acceptable academic standards in the college?

(7) Should the groups controlling two-year colleges restrain the impulse to adopt the four-year plan, or should a substantial number be encouraged to become baccalaureate degree-granting institutions?

(8) Can the college avoid domination by four-year colleges and universities and retain its freedom to experiment with different pro-

grams and organizational forms more appropriate to its educational purposes and organizational needs?

(9) Can and will the various states develop the machinery of coordination that will provide defined roles for the two-year colleges, four-year colleges, and private colleges, and generally eliminate costly competition and duplication in higher education?

Finance

(1) Can adequate financial support be secured to insure both high-quality educational programs and services and the necessary diversity of programs required to meet local and national needs?

(2) What is the minimum level of financial support necessary for sustaining the multiplicity of programs in the college?

(3) How should operating costs be distributed among students, local sources, and state and federal governments?

(4) How should capital costs be distributed among local, state, and federal sources?

(5) What is the optimum distribution of resources within the college to insure effective and balanced instructional programs and other educational services—i.e., guidance, counseling, and community services?

General issues

(1) Is the state responsible for the provision of equal educational opportunities for all citizens beyond the high school?

(2) What roles should business and industrial communities play in influencing the educational programs of the two-year college?

(3) Can the two-year college achieve effective interaction with special-interest groups—i.e., business, industry, and cultural groups—thus stimulating a variety of educational endeavors by the college while retaining institutional control of the philosophy, purposes, and programs of the college?

(4) Will the two-year college continue to exist in its present form, or will it prove to be a transitional institution destined to become a vocational or technical school, a college-transfer institution, or a four-year college?

(5) What are the general images of the two-year college held by its faculty and students, and by those in the community. How do these perceptions affect the functioning of the college as an educational organization?

(6) Can the two-year college attract and hold qualified faculty members who understand and accept the college's purposes and functions

and who will provide imaginative leadership and instruction within the context of the college?

Bibliography

1. Adler, Mortimer J., "Labor, Leisure, and Liberal Education," *Journal of General Education,* VI (October 1951), 35-45.
2. Brubacher, John S., and Willis Rudy, *Higher Education in Transition.* New York: Harper & Row, Publishers, 1958.
3. Dewey, John, *Experience and Education.* New York: The Macmillan Company, 1939.
4. *General Education in a Free Society: Report of the Harvard Committee.* Cambridge, Mass.: Harvard University Press, 1945.
5. Hutchins, Robert M., *The Conflict in Education in a Democratic Society.* New York: Harper & Row, Publishers, 1953.
6. Morris, Van Cleve, *Philosophy and the American School.* Boston: Houghton Mifflin Company, 1961.
7. Rickover, H. G., *Education and Freedom.* New York: E. P. Dutton & Co., Inc., 1959.
8. Thomas, Russell, *The Search for a Common Learning: General Education, 1800–1960.* New York: McGraw-Hill Book Company, 1962.

Origins of the Two-year College

The two-year college is an important segment of post-high school education in the United States, and it shows promise of becoming the largest and most important. In many respects, it has been the least well-defined aspect of the total educational system. Two-year colleges, for purposes of this discussion, can be defined as public or private junior colleges, comprehensive community colleges, college and university extension centers, two-year branch colleges, and technical institutes providing at least two—but less than four—years of college-level work. [11:1] The term *junior college* will be used to identify public or private two-year colleges whose primary emphasis is upon college-transfer courses and programs. *Community college*, as defined by the authors, is a comprehensive public two-year college which offers post-high school education programs to meet the needs of the community.

Influences

Two-year colleges, in their various forms, evolved from both conservative and liberal educational thought during the nineteenth century.

2

the two·year college: the educator's view

A brief look at some of the more significant forces from which they emerged will provide an understanding of their current problems and future potential.

The university leaders who called for the reform of the American college—while "liberal" in the eyes of traditional American educators—actually represented a conservative position, in that their frame of reference was the German university. The giants of this era who worked for the reformation of American universities were William Rainey Harper, of the University of Chicago; Henry P. Tappan, of the University of Michigan; William W. Folwell, of the University of Illinois; Richard H. Jesse, of the University of Missouri; and Alexis F. Lange, of the University of California. These university leaders were striving for the establishment of upper-division and graduate education as the ideal of higher education, and they conceived of the two-year college as a proper adjunct of secondary education. [10:594] They envisioned the shifting of the first two years of college study from the university campus to the high school, thus separating the freshman and sophomore years from the rest of the university program.

Many of the leaders of higher education in the late 1900's were educated in Europe, and their ideas of university development were in contradiction to established American tradition. They advocated the concentration, at the university level, upon highly specialized instruction in the subject-matter disciplines and the encouragement of intensive research by university faculty members.

A second force which impelled university leaders to encourage the development of junior colleges was the fact that many secondary school graduates were inadequately prepared for the rigorous demands of college study. The European concept of highly selective and limited enrollment in advanced study influenced American institutions to raise their academic requirements and to restrict admission to those students who fitted the academic patterns and expectations of the times. [28:46–47]

With the increase in the number of students seeking admission to four-year colleges, it was logical for these institutions to look for other outlets for those individuals who could not meet the exacting requirements resulting from the adoption of the German pattern. Nevertheless, public universities found it difficult to resist the demands of the taxpayers for the admission of large numbers of students.

Harper attempted to find a satisfactory compromise between the American four-year college tradition and the German ideal by establishing a lower division called a *junior college* at the University of Chicago in 1896. Subsequently, as he succeeded in influencing the establishment of junior colleges in the surrounding area, these colleges were established—the first at Joliet, Illinois, in 1901—as segments of secondary school systems.

The first two-year colleges

Even before the concept of the junior college had been developed on university campuses, a number of private two-year colleges had been established. The first of these was Monticello College (1835); the second, Susquehanna University (1858). [29] These colleges were organized to provide a type of post-secondary school education quite similar to that found in the first two years of the traditional American college. Their continued expansion grew out of the desire of various religious denominations to provide education for their young people which emphasized the tenets of their particular faiths.

The American secondary school was a natural outgrowth of the ideal of an egalitarian society in which the individual would be allowed to rise to the limits of his abilities. During the latter half of the nineteenth century, the secondary school was still a fluid concept, and, as such, was the object of conflicting views and the center of experimentation and controversy. The three- and four-year high school did not become a stabilized institutional form until the mid-1920's. At the turn of the century, the upward extension of the high school began in Michigan, Indiana, and Illinois. [12:24–28] The effort in Goshen, Indiana, was short-lived, but Detroit Junior College, in Michigan, continued to function and later became Wayne State University. Joliet Junior College is still a part of the public schools of that city. The first of California's now numerous junior colleges was established in Fresno in 1910. Legislation passed in that state in 1917 insured the future development of such institutions. [12:29–30] Missouri and Minnesota established public junior colleges in 1915; Kansas and Oklahoma, in 1919; Arizona and Iowa, in 1920; and Texas, in 1921. [31] These early colleges were true extensions of secondary education: they were housed in high school buildings, had closely articulated curricula, and shared faculty and administrative staffs. They encountered difficulty during their early years because, as a deviation from the trend toward the four-year high school, they were not recognized as an essential part of secondary education.

The development of public two-year colleges was sporadic at first, and a substantial number of those founded during the early twentieth century failed to survive. Others became four-year colleges or branches of state colleges or universities.

But the innovations which took place in education during the 1920's encouraged the further development of two-year colleges. The emergence of the concept of the comprehensive high school, the enactment of pertinent legislation (e.g., the Smith-Hughes Act), and later progress in vocational education provided the historical base for the broadening of the college curriculum. Furthermore, the acceptance of the principle of publicly supported secondary education for all stimulated new thinking about the needs of those students who could not or would not complete the conventional college preparatory program. As larger numbers of students completed four years of high school, increasing numbers sought admission to college. Although many states attempted to provide more adequate opportunities for these high school graduates, it became apparent that something other than the traditional college campus educational plan would have to be developed.

Another force contributing to the development of adaptations of college education was the ferment resulting from the advent of pragmatism between 1900 and 1930. This major philosophical shift from realism and idealism had far-reaching effects on public education, and gave the two-year college the intellectual support it needed for sustained expansion during this period. [2:289–95]

The public school system was finally stabilized as a twelve-year program in most states by 1940, although California continued to maintain a few high school-junior college organizations. [27] The effort to establish the German university system was not successful, and colleges and universities continued to admit freshmen and sophomores. Later developments indicated, however, that many such institutions retained their lower divisions reluctantly and for reasons having little to do with educational considerations. Some of these were the need for larger numbers of students to obtain larger state appropriations, intercollegiate athletic programs, and the insistence that public institutions serve the sons and daughters of the parents who paid for their operation.

The achievement of stability, however, left a void within the educational system. Four-year colleges never perceived themselves as responsible for the education of the majority of high school graduates. Their educational programs were, at least in theory, based upon restricted admissions and restricted curricular offerings designed to prepare students for professional occupations and scholarly pursuits. Furthermore, such colleges were, in many instances, beyond the reach of a large number of potential students who simply could not find the money for college expenses. The two-year college filled this void.

During the same period, state colleges and universities began to extend off-campus services to the community as a whole through extension centers and branches. The services rendered by these centers varied markedly, ranging from noncredit adult-education courses through undergraduate programs and even graduate study. Many of them were integrated into comprehensive state systems of two-year colleges such as those found in Pennsylvania, Indiana, and Wisconsin. [14:178, 384, 477] The process of extending the services of the universities began during the period 1900–30; it was stepped up during the 1930's, and accelerated most rapidly during the years immediately following World War II. [25:14–22]

A corollary development, beginning in 1895, resulted in the emergence of the technical institute. [30] These institutions grew out of the need for specialized educational programs which would prepare students for specific occupational requirements, programs which were not then available on either the secondary or college levels. Although the number of technical institutes has fluctuated over the years in relation to changes occurring in secondary and higher education, the institutes appear now to be an established part of the total framework of two-year colleges.

Legal developments

The first legislation, passed in California in 1907, emphasized that the secondary schools should be permitted to extend their programs for an additional two years and/or provide college-transfer programs at their discretion. By 1961, twenty other states had passed similar legislation. Connecticut passed a law in 1959 which stated that courses were to be "those customarily provided during the first two years of college." [6] These laws illustrate Holmes's contention that legal action follows closely "the prevalent moral and political theories, intuitions of public policy. . . ."

The broadening of the concept of the two-year college was relatively slow in coming. California again led the rest of the country by passing new legislation, in 1917 and 1921, which provided for vocational and technical courses in two-year colleges. [5] Mississippi also passed such legislation during the 1920's, and three other states made similar provisions in laws passed during the 1930's. The Mississippi law of 1928 is unusual in that it greatly expanded the concept of the college by spelling out the need for the correlation of the work of high schools and junior colleges. Furthermore, the law specified the courses which might be offered to implement the concept.

> These courses shall consist of agriculture, including horticulture, dairying, animal husbandry, and commercial gardening; domestic science and the household arts; commercial branches, including banking, accountancy, and transportation; and the mechanical arts, such as carpentry, masonry, painting, shopwork in iron and wood and repairing and constructing of motor vehicles. Wherever it is practical, instruction shall be given in teacher training, music, and public speaking. Insofar as possible, junior colleges shall offer a complete course of instruction so that their graduates may immediately thereafter enter professional schools if they so elect. [23]

TABLE 2-1. Legislative Activity for the Establishment and Expansion of Public Two-year Colleges

State	1900–9	1910–19	1920–29	1930–39	1940–49	1950–59	1960–62
Alabama							1961 1962
Alaska						1953	1962
Arizona			1927	1931	1947 1949	1953	1960 1961 1962
Arkansas							1962
California	1907	1917	1921 1927	1931 1935 1937	1943 1945 1949	1953 1955 1957 1958 1959	1960 1961 1962
Colorado				1937		1957 1959	1960 1961 1962
Connecticut				1937		1959	1962
Delaware							
Florida				1939	1947 1949	1953 1955 1957 1959	1961 1962
Georgia						1958	1962
Hawaii							
Idaho				1939		1953 1955 1957	1961 1962
Illinois				1937	1945	1951 1953 1955 1957 1959	1961
Indiana							1962
Iowa			1927	1931 1935	1941 1943 1949	1957	
Kansas		1917	1923	1931 1937	1941 1947	1957	1961
Kentucky				1936	1946		1960 1962
Louisiana			1928				
Maine							1961
Maryland							1960 1961 1962

28

TABLE 2-1. *(Cont.)*

State	1900–9	1910–19	1920–29	1930–39	1940–49	1950–59	1960–62
Massachusetts					1947 1948	1957 1958	1960 1962
Michigan		1917	1929	1931 1935	1947	1951 1955 1957	1960 1961
Minnesota			1925 1927	1939		1957	
Mississippi			1928 1929	1930 1932 1934 1936 1938	1940	1950	1960
Missouri			1927				1961
Montana				1939	1947	1953	
Nebraska				1931	1941 1943 1947	1955 1957	
New Hampshire							1961 1962
New Jersey					1946		1962
New Mexico						1957	1962
New York					1948 1949	1953 1955 1957	1960 1962
North Carolina						1957	1961 1962
North Dakota				1931	1941 1949	1957 1959	1962
Ohio							1961 1962
Oklahoma				1939	1941		1962
Oregon					1949	1951 1957 1959	1961 1962
Pennsylvania							1963
Rhode Island							1960
South Carolina				1935			
South Dakota							
Tennessee							
Texas			1929	1935 1936 1937	1941 1945 1949	1955 1957 1958 1959	1961 1962

29

TABLE 2-1. *(Cont.)*

State	1900–9	1910–19	1920–29	1930–39	1940–49	1950–59	1960–62
Utah							1962
Vermont							1962
Virginia							1962
Washington					1941		1961
					1943		
					1945		
West Virginia							1961
							1962
Wisconsin				`			1962
Wyoming					1945	1951	
						1953	
						1955	
						1957	
						1959	
Total legislative activity	1	3	13	29	36	54	60

Legal provisions for the inclusion of general education for citizens; adult education; occupational, vocational, and recreational programs; terminal courses; and community services first appeared in California in 1921; in Nebraska, in 1931; and in Wyoming, in 1945. Similar legislative action was taken during the 1950's and 1960's. It is apparent that progress toward the comprehensive two-year college began rather hesitantly about 1920 and continually gained more adherents and attention as the needs of society became more apparent to the people and their representatives during the succeeding forty years.

Two events, the Great Depression and World War II, stimulated rapid implementation of the concept of the comprehensive community college. Although there were legal provisions for programs in areas other than college-transfer work, the essential stimulus for activation on a broad basis was lacking until the mid-1930's, when federal funds became available, and the 1940's when the war emergency created unprecedented needs for educated and trained personnel. The momentum generated by the problems of the 1930's and the war years was further accelerated by the return of veterans and the increasing educational demands of a technical economy.

The educational purposes of the two-year college, as set forth in the legislation, were originally based upon the concept that it was to provide either an extension of high school educational programs or a limited number of college-level courses within the existing high school organization. Early laws did not spell out specifically that the two-year college was a distinct entity, or that its educational program was to be clearly collegiate in kind and quality. The language of the laws implied that the program of the two-year college was to serve as preparation for college work—as a basis for further academic study—but there was no clear-cut indication as to whether the program was to be collegiate or secondary school in nature and organization.

The fact that two-year colleges grew from the college-transfer program has important implications for their condition today. The transfer function is the oldest and most revered of the educational services which the two-year colleges provide, and the latecomers—technical, vocational, and guidance programs—are still having to justify their value and continued existence in such colleges.

The history of legislation shows that the transfer program was established in California in 1907, in two more states in 1917, in seven during the 1920's, in six in the 1930's, in two in the 1940's, and in three in the 1950's. In contrast, mention of technical and vocational education appeared in the law in California in 1917, in two more states in the 1920's, in three between 1930 and 1939, in seven during the 1940's, in six in the 1950's, and in five states after 1960. [31:274–75] Thus, courses which were not designed to provide transfer credit lagged behind college-transfer programs both as to time of adoption and the number of states which recognized the need for them.

Adult education, guidance, and other educational services had an even slower rate of acceptance. California again led the rest of the nation by adding provisions for such services to existing laws in 1921. Nebraska passed a law providing such services in 1931—the only such act passed during that decade. Wyoming took action in 1945, but the most active changes have taken place since 1950. Since that time, fifteen states have amended their laws to include broad educational responsibilities for two-year colleges.

The concept of the comprehensive community college has been outlined in the laws of the various states from 1907 to the present; however, the prototype was contained in the laws passed in California and Mississippi between 1907 and 1928. Thus, the ideal of broad educational services—neither secondary nor collegiate—came into being as a legally recognized aspect of public education. There was, however, a significant time lag between the statement of the concept in the law and its implementation—a lag caused by the lack of adequate state financial support for comprehensive community college programs and the inability of local districts to add such costs to their already underfinanced local school programs.

Summary

The two-year college might be considered an historical accident growing out of the struggle between conservative thought and liberal thought during the first half of the twentieth century. University leadership appealed to an older educational tradition, the German ideal, which was held in higher esteem than the younger four-year American college pattern. This concept, envisioning the highly specialized education of an intellectual elite, did not entirely succeed because it ran counter to previous tradition and custom. The university remains an inconsistent amalgamation of the four-year college and the German university pattern.

Liberal thinking insisted that public education be expanded to provide equal opportunities for all. This ideal was the driving force behind the creation of the public elementary and secondary schools. It also stimulated the response of the secondary schools to extend their work beyond the fourth year in response to the demands of the universities for students of higher quality. The continued expansion of secondary education into the thirteenth and fourteenth years was not universally accepted in all sections of the country or by all segments of the educational community. Thus, the two-year college remained, for the most part, an unstable appendage of secondary education until recent years.

The Public Community College

Having entered the educational scene at the turn of the century, the public two-year college set forth upon its development as an extension of free public education beyond the high school. During the last sixty years, its organization, purposes, programs, and financing have changed but its growth has been continuous. There were seventy such colleges in 1921, 258 in 1938, 363 in 1955, and 403 in 1962. [22:41; 13:28] Enrollments had increased to a total of 644,968 full-time and part-time students in 1961.

The public two-year college is the outgrowth of a philosophy of education which believes that:

> The American way of life holds that all human beings are supreme, hence of equal moral worth and are, therefore, entitled to equal opportunities to develop to their fullest capacities. The basic function of public education then should be to provide educational opportunity by teaching whatever needs to be learned to whoever needs to learn it, whenever he needs to learn it. [34:1]

In order to make this philosophy operational, an ideal image of the community college must also be stated. Gleazer enunciates one concept of this ideal when he says:

> A good community college will be honestly, gladly, and clearly a community institution. It is in and of the community. The community is used as an extension of classroom and laboratory. Drawing upon the history, traditions, personnel, problems, assets and liabilities of the community, it declares its role and finds this accepted and understood by faculty, administration, students, and the citizenry. [15:1]

These assumptions are made on the basis that there will be unanimity among the various individuals and groups in the community as to the educational and social validity of the two-year college, as contrasted with other types of institutions of higher education, and that this support will make for a free interchange and mutual strengthening of the social fabric of the community. That these assumptions are unrealistic can be clearly demonstrated by reference to the available literature which presents, in marked contrast to the happy unanimity suggested by Gleazer, a picture of confusion among both professional and lay thinkers.

Purposes

The purposes of the community college have been restated many times during the last forty years. Such statements buttress the ideology of an ideal type of educational institution standing between secondary schools and four-year colleges and universities. One such statement by Crawford makes apparent the comprehensive view of the educational missions of the community college in terms of the purposes it should serve:

> . . . it is appropriate for community colleges to provide, for all persons above the twelfth-grade age levels, education consistent with the purposes of the individuals and the society of which they are a part, subject only to the restrictions in the state statutes. . . . The educational needs appropriate for community colleges to fulfill *at this time* include:
> (1) The need for programs of liberal arts and science courses, usual to the first and second years of college, which will provide sound general and preprofessional education of such quality that credits may be transferred to a nationally or regionally accredited four-year college or university and applied towards degrees of the baccalaureate level or higher
> (2) The need for vocational and technical programs in the trades, industrial, agricultural, and semiprofessional fields. Such programs may be of long or short duration, depending on the amount of time needed by the student to complete the requirements for entrance into the occupation
> (3) The need for programs of courses for adults and other community college students, for which credit may or may not be given, designed to provide general education and to improve self-government, healthful

living, understanding [of] civic and public affairs, avocational growth, constructive use of leisure time, personal and family living satisfactions, cultural depth, and to facilitate occupational advancement

(4) The need for individual services to students including guidance and counseling, assistance in career selection, removal of deficiencies in preparation for college programs, personality and health improvement

(5) The need for programs and services for individuals and groups interested in cultural, civic, recreational, or other community betterment projects [7:1-2]

This list of purposes concisely illustrates the uniqueness of the community college as compared with the secondary school and the university. Because the community college stands between these two segments of the public educational system, it must—and does—face simultaneously in both directions, serving the needs of students who intend to complete the requirements for a baccalaureate or higher degrees and, at the same time, providing other needed educational services to a complex society. These purposes can be viewed in a number of different ways. First, the college provides educational services for young people who will eventually transfer to four-year colleges as well as for those who will terminate their formal studies at the end of one course, one semester, or the two-year period. Second, the college makes available various adaptations of standard courses and sequences of study for specific individual and societal needs. These adaptations include seminars, conferences, short courses, or occasional meetings and programs which contribute to the general welfare and improvement of the entire community.

These purposes are consistent with the ideal concept as stated by Gleazer: the community college is a functioning segment of the community, and its mission centers around the education of the young, the continuing education of older citizens, and the general improvement of the community through beneficial and appropriate educational and cultural services.

The claim is made that one of the most important functions of the community college is to make available to students comprehensive counseling and guidance services. [20:191-212] The community college is the center within which students make far-reaching decisions regarding their educational and occupational futures. These choices are substantially more complex and difficult than those which they made in secondary school. Furthermore, their decisions have far-reaching effects upon their long-range future. They need, therefore, extensive professional help from mature and sensitive adults who have a deep understanding of individuals as well as an extensive knowledge of the world as it is today and as it may be in the future. Does the community college fulfill this function? How adequately does it meet this responsibility?

Characteristics

One of the striking characteristics of American higher education is its diversity. Direct comparisons among institutions, state plans of higher education, or various types of two-year colleges are nearly impossible. Diversity, to a certain degree, is an advantage, but it can also make difficult an understanding of the functions of higher education and, by so doing, weaken the relative position of post-high school education in our society.

The two-year college is probably more diverse in defined functions, programs, clientele, and philosophical bases than any other educational institution in existence.

Fields, in his analysis of community and junior colleges, identified five fundamental characteristics which he thought clearly established the uniqueness of this institution. [12:63–95]

(1) *Democratic*—low tuition and other costs; nonselective admission policies; geographically and socially accessible; and popularized education for the largest number of people

(2) *Comprehensive*—a wide range of students with widely varying abilities, aptitudes, and interests; a comprehensive curriculum to meet the broad needs of such students

(3) *Community-centered*—locally supported and controlled; local resources utilized for educational purposes; a community service improving the general level of the community

(4) *Dedicated to life-long education*—educational programs for individuals of all ages and educational needs

(5) *Adaptable*—to individual differences among students, differences in communities, and the changing needs of society

Thus, we see that the comprehensive community college is an organization of and for the people it serves. Its services are not confined to the traditional functions of the four-year college, but include activities which contribute to the general upgrading of society as a whole. In essence, it provides those services which are not made available by the high school or by other institutions of higher education.

The administrative organization of community colleges follows a number of patterns. First, there is the one sometimes called the *public school college*, which is a part of the public school organization. In the second form, a common pattern in California, the public schools are included within a district, and the community college is under a separate legal district, but both are under the same board of control. The third type is the *independent college*, which has a separate board of control and legal powers of control and taxation for its support. The fourth type is the *state community college,* one of a state system of colleges centered in a state policy and administrative body which directs the operation and development of all the colleges within the system.

The students who attend community colleges represent a cross section of the general population being served. They are generally from middle-class and blue-collar families, and their educational achievement tends to exceed that of their parents. Some of the students in these colleges come from professional and managerial groups, but the percentage is small. The students represent all age groups in the community. Their academic ability varies widely, and their attitudes and motivations cover the entire span of a typical population. The majority attend college part-time because of financial and family responsibilities.

Financial support for community colleges comes from a variety of sources. Of the forty-two states having publicly supported colleges, nineteen have specific formulas for state financing, twenty-six appropriate funds annually, and thirteen share support with the local district. [24:7–14] In general, community colleges derive their operating funds from state appropriations, local taxation, tuition and fees, and gifts and donations from private sources. Furthermore, the cost per student in such colleges is generally lower than that in four-year institutions.

There is no consistent pattern for capital financing in community colleges. States deal with this problem in three ways:

> [First,] . . . those having stipulations in the law dealing specifically with the provision of capital funds for two-year colleges, either with respect to the State's or locality's responsibility and authority to provide such funds; second, those with no specific reference to capital funds in the law but providing capital funds in their appropriation acts; and third, those which have neither formula provision for capital funds in the law nor appropriation acts to serve this purpose. [24:21–22]

University Extension Centers

Since 1900, two-year colleges have grown apace. Resident extension centers were first established just before the turn of the century: thirteen universities had such centers in 1920; nineteen, in 1930; twenty-five, in 1940; and thirty-eight, in 1950. [25:15] There are currently seventy-three institutions which are members of the National University Extension Association which have the following numbers of students in formal extension classes: [26:88]

Academic degree credit	325,760
Graduate degree credit	58,928
Technical institute and certificate credit	25,600
Noncredit courses	150,826
Total	561,114

Purposes

Extension centers and, in some cases, branch colleges have as their central purpose the provision of educational services to the population which supports the parent institution. They provide a way of taking educational resources to the people who could not otherwise take advantage of the educational institutions they support with their taxes. The Oregon Extension Division states its responsibilities as that of "filling off-campus educational and cultural needs . . . ," and sees its role as that of "an innovator, expediter, and developer. . . ." [13:2] Another purpose which is served is that of economy to both student and state. Branch campuses, such as those in Pennsylvania, take the first two years of collegiate study closer to the students' homes, thus saving the expense of building additional residential facilities on the central campus and eliminating excessive room-and-board costs to students.

Characteristics

Extension systems are organized in a number of different patterns. They may be under the direct supervision and control of a campus administrative officer or exist as a part of a state system of extension services within which all state colleges and universities cooperate. [1] Their facilities may consist of full-time and part-time instructors, or primarily part-time personnel who serve in one center.

There are a few branch colleges—as in Wisconsin and Michigan—which are functional administrative units having organizational status equal to that of other colleges allied to the parent university.

The student clientele of extension centers have the same wide ranges in age, ability, educational objectives, and socioeconomic origins as does the community college. [25:86–95] The differences among students are reflected in the type of program they pursue. Thus, those students who are enrolled in college-level courses which can be transferred to the central campus must meet admission requirements similar to those required of students on the main campus. Various methods of selection may be used with students who are enrolled in other types of courses or programs.

The educational programs of extension services include college-transfer courses, graduate courses, technical programs, nursing programs, drafting, civil defense, citizenship training, language courses for non-English-speaking people, and conferences and short courses for business and professional groups. For example, Purdue University provides extensive technical programs throughout the state. [9] On the other hand, Wisconsin's branch colleges are primarily college-transfer-oriented. [32:1–2]

Most financial support for extension centers comes from their users. Morton found that more than 60 per cent of the operational costs were paid through fees and tuition. [25:96] Off-campus services of public colleges and universities remain a peripheral part of their programs; their main attention continuing to be focused upon conventional college teaching and research.

Morton found that there was general satisfaction among students with respect to the services they received from extension centers. He found, however, that the extension center had not succeeded in effectively relating itself to the community. Students indicated that there should be greater attention to guidance services, more adequate library materials, more satisfactory physical facilities, and a broader course offering. Furthermore, and perhaps most significant, 80 per cent of all respondents said that they had no voice in determining the services made available or the conditions under which they might be used. [25:94–95]

The Technical Institute

The technical institute constitutes the smallest numerical grouping among two-year colleges in the United States. Henninger identified 144 technical institutes in his 1958 study. [19:4] These institutions have as their central purpose the education of individuals in technical engineering fields, thus qualifying them for work at a skill level between that of the engineer and the skilled engineer craftsman. [16:544] These post-high school institutions may be parts of universities, colleges, community colleges, or independent entities, as in New York State. Examples of the technical institute include the Milwaukee Institute of Technology, Erie County (New York) Technical Institute, and Ohio Mechanics Institute.

Characteristics

Administratively, the independent two-year institution resembles the junior and community colleges, but when such specialized technical programs are found in four-year colleges and universities their administrative relationships may take almost any imaginable pattern. In general, the organization of both the two-year and the four-year technical institutes resemble that of a similar conventional post-high school institution.

The most meaningful study available is that done by Brunner and Morrison. [3] They found that 30.3 per cent of 264 institutions offering engineering-related curriculums were four-year colleges and 69.7 per cent were two-year colleges. Approximately two thirds were public and one third private.

The majority of students in technical programs attended part-time and were enrolled in programs ranging in length from one to three years. [3:24]

Analysis of these programs is more meaningful in terms of curricula rather than the institutional structure itself, owing to the mixing of such programs with two-year and four-year colleges and true technical institutes. Accreditation by the Engineering Council for Professional Development is based upon specific curricula rather than upon institutions per se. Thus, a college might have six or seven technical programs of which only one or two were accredited by the Council. [4:725] Thirty-four institutions had Council-accredited curricula in 1958.

The educational programs offered by technical institutes include technical (engineering) and nonengineering related occupational curricula as well as craftsman-clerical curricula. Engineering technologies are classified into nine major groups, and nonengineering related curricula are listed in six major categories. The craftsman-clerical programs include those courses which are commonly considered to be of less than college grade. There were 24,488 students enrolled in these programs in 1958, while there were 206,374 individuals enrolled in all organized occupational curricula that year. [3:25–29] Of course, there is no single pattern of financial support for the technical institute, as it does not exist within a single administrative pattern.

Private Junior Colleges

The private two-year college, as previously pointed out, made its appearance on the educational stage seventy years before the publicly controlled college. In 1900, there were eight such colleges, and their number steadily increased until 1947, when they reached their largest number: 323. [21:41] Since then, the number of private colleges has declined to 273; they now account for about 50 per cent of all two-year colleges listed by the American Association of Junior Colleges.

Purposes

Private junior colleges are generally organized for the purpose of providing a particular emphasis within the scope of narrow and specific educational objectives. Such colleges attempt to develop a distinctive image which will be attractive to those students they plan to serve. Furthermore, the emphasis of the college will faithfully reflect the ideas and desires of the sponsoring body. Colleges with a religious affiliation function within the precepts laid down by the parent group; thus, the educational objectives of colleges affiliated with the Lutheran Church

(Missouri Synod) are outlined in the functions of the Church's Board of Higher Education.

> The Board of Higher Education shall strive to maintain the educational institutions of the Synod at a high level of efficiency and generally promote, improve, supervise, and direct adequate education for the preparation of its ministers and teachers, and to assist, encourage, and advise with regard to means and objectives of higher Christian education, always keeping in mind the specific religious, spiritual, and professional ideals and objectives of our whole educational system. [18:6–63]

Church-related colleges are organized and operated with the avowed purpose of propagating the faith and preparing future leaders for the organization. The educational programs which these colleges provide are the logical continuation of parochial education on the elementary and secondary levels, thus supplying a comprehensive educational experience for the members of the church. Many denominations maintain institutions of higher education, including both two- and four-year colleges, intended primarily for the members of the sect.

Characteristics

Enrollments in private colleges have fluctuated in relation to general economic conditions and the availability of students over the last sixty years. Also, the percentage of the total number of two-year college students enrolled in public colleges has been increasing. Thus, in 1961, 13.9 per cent of all such students were in private colleges; 86.1 per cent were in public colleges [22:30–32]

Private colleges have tended to remain small, in keeping with their limited objectives. Two other factors militating against their growth are their high cost to students and the competition for students engendered by both two- and four-year public institutions. Only one private two-year college had an enrollment in excess of 3000 students in 1962; 211 had enrollments of less than 500 students. [22:33]

In general, private junior colleges have well-defined educational objectives and programs. A typical statement of purposes might include: emphasis upon religious conviction, critical thought, cultural development, a high level of scholarship, and good mental and physical health. [17:20]

The most pervasive problem faced by the private junior college is the finding of adequate financial support. The costs of both capital construction and operation have risen dramatically during the last twenty years, and many such colleges have found it difficult to compete for qualified faculty, to maintain their physical plants, and to provide the supplies and equipment essential to their educational programs. Their primary sources of support are tuition, other student fees, and gifts from alumni and friends.

These colleges, like the public colleges, do provide programs other than college-transfer courses. Although their technical and vocational curricula are more limited than those of public institutions, the colleges do render valuable services in some types of nontransfer programs. Their most important contributions to junior college education were outlined by Tead as: reduced class size, individualized guidance, social education in intimate dormitory living, more homogeneous curricular offerings, and closer association with selected faculty members. [33:249–53] Whether the private colleges can continue to lay legitimate claim to these advantages will depend, to a large extent, upon their ability to find strong administrative leadership and adequate and increasing financial support in the future.

The Two-year College in American Higher Education

Two-year colleges, classified as *private junior colleges, public comprehensive community colleges, technical institutes, extension centers,* and *branch colleges* (of four-year colleges and universities) are essential segments of American higher education. A student graduating from high school (or one who has obtained an equivalent level of competency) may choose among the two-year college, the specialized professional school, and the four-year institution. He may move on from any one of these to professional education after one or more years, depending upon the requirements of the college, the state, or the professional school he enters. Thus, he can take a variety of paths to reach his educational objectives (see Fig. 2-1).

There is, of course, no single image of the two-year college. These educational organizations include comprehensive public community colleges, public colleges offering only college-transfer studies, private sectarian and nonsectarian colleges, technical institutes, extension centers specializing in freshman and sophomore courses for transfer to the main campus, extension centers which also provide vocational and technical programs, and branch campuses of colleges and universities. Each of these types of institutions purports to fulfill a defined list of educational functions to satisfy the needs of an almost unlimited variety of students.

The comprehensive community college

The comprehensive community college reflects the pattern of the comprehensive secondary school and, in some instances, is simply an upward extension of secondary education into the thirteenth and fourteenth years. Its avowed purposes include providing all the post-high school educational services—from cultural activities of general community interest to college-transfer programs. Its students come from all age

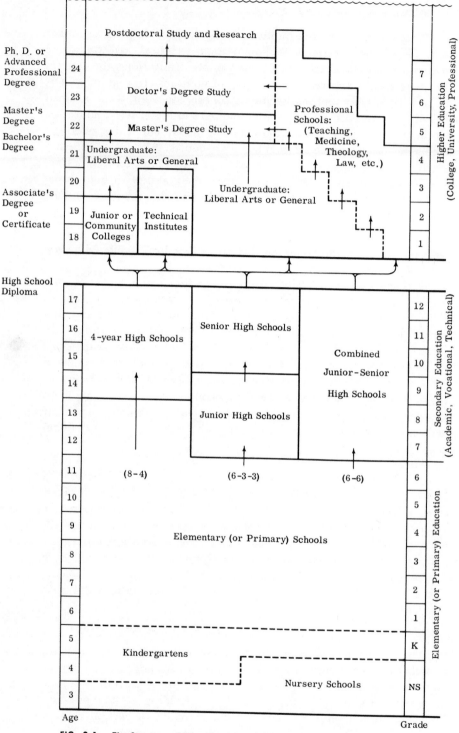

FIG. 2-1. The Structure of Education in the United States [8:xiv]

groups and socioeconomic backgrounds and bring with them an infinite variety of abilities, motivations, and attitudes. The community college, then, is the medium through which the educational services which society must have can be extended to all. Its programs must reflect the needs of the local community as well as the more generalized and shifting needs of a technological and scientific society. By its very breadth and lack of selectivity, it can provide educational services beyond the high school for all those who want to take advantage of such opportunities.

The private two-year college

The objectives of private two-year colleges are more limited, more closely related to their original purposes and to the objectives of the individuals or groups which founded or continue to support them. Their purposes, in the main, center around the college-transfer program or denominational objectives, appealing to particular social and economic groups interested in the cultural and social development of their children. The image of this type of college is traditional: the ivy-covered walls and the quiet and refined campus life.

The technical institute

Technical institutes present an entirely different pattern of educational services. They are the educational resource for the vocationally orientated student who is interested primarily in acquiring knowledge and skills which will be immediately useful and which will allow him to enter a recognized occupation. The image of this college is one of learning the applications of specific kinds of knowledge and skills which are necessary to the vocational preparation of the individual, but which lack status in contemporary society.

The extension center

Extension centers present another variegated picture of educational services ranging from formal courses of "collegiate grade" through audio-visual services, conferences, seminars, correspondence courses, radio and television classes, and all kinds of short courses designed for occupational or professional groups. Within such extension programs are branch colleges which have complete resident programs, as well as divisions of the parent institution carried on in high school buildings. Extension programs in most colleges and universities remain peripheral to the central concerns and attention of these institutions, with the result that their image is not clear either to the supporting institution or to their students.

From the educator's point of view, the two-year college continues to occupy a tenuous position between secondary education and higher education. There are limitations to the continued expansion of the services of secondary schools in view of the extensive expectations to which they have already been subjected by the society which supports them and the refusal of that society to provide adequate financial support for them. Above the two-year college, colleges and universities are still struggling with the definition and delineation of their roles within the expectations of society and space, faculty, and financial limitations. The development of two-year colleges, in many different forms, has been the result of the continuing process of role definition by high schools and colleges.

Bibliography

1. Blocker, Clyde E., and Henry A. Campbell, Jr., *Administrative Practices in University Extension Centers and Branch Colleges.* Austin, Tex.: University of Texas, 1963.

2. Brubacher, John S., and Willis Rudy, *Higher Education in Transition.* New York: Harper & Row, Publishers, 1958.

3. Brunner, Ken A., and D. Grant Morrison, *Organized Occupational Curriculums in Higher Education.* Washington, D.C.: USGPO, 1961.

4. _____, and D. Grant Morrison, "Engineering Technical Institute Enrollments and Graduations in ECPD-Listed Institutions: 1958," *Journal of Engineering Education,* LI (May 1961), 725–49.

5. California Statutes 1907, c. 69, p. 88; 1921, c. 477, p. 724.

6. Connecticut Public Acts, 1959, c. 232, p. 554.

7. Crawford, Ferris N., "A Twentieth Century Institution: The Community College." Address delivered at Southwestern College Agreement Conference, Battle Creek, Michigan, November 16, 1961.

8. *Digest of Educational Statistics.* Washington, D.C.: USGPO, 1963.

9. *Division of Applied Technology, Announcements for the Year 1962–63.* Lafayette, Ind.: Purdue University, 1962.

10. Eby, Frederick, *The Development of Modern Education.* Englewood Cliffs, N.J.: Prentice-Hall, Inc., 1952.

11. *Education Directory, 1961–62, Higher Education.* Washington, D.C.: USGPO, 1962.

12. Fields, Ralph R., *The Community College Movement.* New York: McGraw-Hill Book Company, 1962.

13. *General Extension Division.* Salem, Ore.: Oregon State System of Higher Education, 1962.

14. Gleazer, Edmund J., Jr. (ed.), *American Junior Colleges.* Washington, D.C.: American Council on Education, 1960.

15. _____, *A New Social Invention: The Community College*. Washington, D.C.: American Association of Junior Colleges, n.d.

16. Good, Carter V., *Dictionary of Education*. New York: McGraw-Hill Book Company, 1959.

17. *Green Mountain College Catalogue*. Poultney, Vt.: 1961–62.

18. *Handbook of the Lutheran Church*. St. Louis: Missouri Synod, 1963.

19. Henninger, G. Ross, *The Technical Institute in America*. New York: McGraw-Hill Book Company, 1959.

20. Henry, Nelson B. (ed.), *The Public Junior College*. The Fifty-fifth Yearbook of the Society for the Study of Education, Part I. Chicago: The University of Chicago Press, 1956.

21. *Junior College Directory*. Washington, D.C.: American Association of Junior Colleges, 1961.

22. *Junior College Directory*. Washington, D.C.: American Association of Junior Colleges, 1964.

23. Mississippi Law 1928, c. 283, s. 308.

24. Morrison, D. G., and S. V. Martorana, *State Formulas for the Support of Public Two-year Colleges*. Washington, D.C.: USGPO, 1962.

25. Morton, John R., *University Extension in the United States*. Birmingham: University of Alabama Press, 1953.

26. *Proceedings* of the 46th Annual Meeting of the National University Extension Association, 1960–61.

27. Reichert, Stephen B., Jr., "The End of the Four-year Junior College in California," *Junior College Journal*, XIX (February 1959), 307–12.

28. *Report of the Committee of Ten of Secondary School Studies*. Washington, D.C.: USGPO, 1893.

29. Sack, Saul, "The First Junior College," *Junior College Journal*, XXX (September 1959), 13–15.

30. Smith, Leo F., and Laurence Lipsett, *The Technical Institute*. New York: McGraw-Hill Book Company, 1956.

31. Struthers, Frederick R., *The Development of Community Junior College Legislation in the United States to 1961*. Unpublished doctoral dissertation presented at the University of Texas, Austin, Texas, 1963.

32. *Student Handbook*. Madison: University of Wisconsin, University Extension Division, 1962–63.

33. Tead, Ordway, "Why the Independent Two-year College?" *Junior College Journal*, XXX (January 1960), 249–53.

34. *The Philosophy of Education of the Joliet Township High School and Junior College*. Joliet, Ill.: Board of Education, 1950.

The fundamental unity and interdependence of American society is apparent to all who have more than a superficial acquaintance with the social sciences. American society, like other societies, is an organized structure within which the members share the basic elements and conditions of a common life. In its largest context, a society is both international and national in scope, but the frame of reference can be reduced to consist of a group of individuals related by common interests and needs.

The warp and woof of society is made up of the individuals within it and of the institutions they have created to insure the continuity and stability of the group and the achievement of goals perceived to be in its best interest. The generally accepted societal institutions are economy, education, government, health, family, religion, and recreation. [14:43]

Although the various components of society are broken down into such classifications for convenience of study and analysis, the very complexity of the social order and the infinite number of simultaneously interacting variables require analysis in the form of a multifactor matrix. It is the purpose of this volume neither to attempt a definitive

3

the social milieu
and the two-year college

analysis of all forces within a society nor to assess their relative importance in the development and functioning of the two-year college; rather,
attention will be focused on the identification and description of those
aspects of the social order which clearly have a direct bearing upon
post-high school education. Broad and pervasive social changes are
ultimately implemented on the community level, there being a general
cause-and-effect relationship between major social change and the behavior, attitudes, and expectations of individuals living in a social
microcosm: the local community. Thus, the sweeping changes in society
shape and direct the two-year college as it, in turn, attempts to meet
changing community needs.

Some Basic Societal Trends

The twentieth century has been marked by more basic and more
rapid social change than any other period in history. The commonplace
and the "permanent" have given way to concepts, processes, and attitudes totally unacceptable a few decades ago. Fundamental to such
change has been the economic revolution which has taken place over the
past forty years. Change in the economic system promises to be even
more startling and rapid during the next twenty or thirty years. These
changes have been the result of a number of new factors: the accumu-
lation of large amounts of capital for industrial expansion, scientific
discoveries, applications of new technological developments, and a rapid
broadening of consumer demand for goods and services. The change, in
effect, has been from an economy of limited consumption to one which
makes available goods and services to a large majority of citizens. Low-
cost production has, therefore, raised the general standard of living for
most Americans while it has raised labor costs and reduced the hours of
work required.

Rapid growth

The twentieth century has been a time of ferment in all spheres of
man's social and physical environment. It contrasts sharply with the
stability and the unquestioning acceptance characteristic of the Victorian
era. The pillars of Western culture—religion, politics, economics, science,
and philosophy—have disintegrated under the impact of rapid and widespread advances in the sciences and the social sciences. The ever-acceler-
ating expansion of man's knowledge has provided solutions to many of
his historical problems, but it has created a multitude of perplexing new
dilemmas which seem more inscrutable than any of the unsolved riddles
of the past. Progress is now so complex that it may bring a mixture of

good and bad, impediment as well as improvement. For example, metropolitan growth, which should be controlled by human, aesthetic, and civic standards, is in actuality governed by a crass commercialism. The diminution of institutionalized standards has caused man to lose the absolute values which gave him a sense of security and confidence, the immutable truths which guided and sustained him. In their place he has built a materialistic society based upon an empirical frame of reference and a relativistic system of ethics.

Man's reaction to the problems he has created with his vastly expanded knowledge has been to organize institutions of increasing size and complexity through which to improve his own and the group's responses to challenges that cannot be met individually. The results of basic research of the first four decades of the twentieth century were ripe for engineering development and exploitation with the advent of World War II. The combatants seized upon this knowledge in their struggle for survival. Consequently, there was a concentrated and unprecedented application of intelligence and manpower to the sciences and engineering. The immediate result was military victory, but the long-range implications have proved to be of greater significance than anticipated. The long shadow of these scientific and technical developments have colored and dramatically altered the two decades since the war. The continuing struggle between the Communist bloc and the West has, if anything, intensified the emphasis upon scientific and technological advance. It has been estimated that four million pages of new scientific research are being published throughout the world each year. This new knowledge is bound to change our lives, and some of the biggest changes are being made in the ways man makes his living.

The application of research findings to the further exploitation and control of the environment has affected all fields of intellectual inquiry and has vastly expanded knowledge in almost every area of study. This geometric increase of knowledge has forced a continuous and penetrating examination of the functions of the school, from the kindergarten through the graduate school.

Technological change

The most apparent trend during the first half of this century has been the development of a more complex and interdependent technological-industrial organization geared to produce unlimited quantities of material goods and designed to meet man's physical, mental, and social needs. Technological change has brought about the automation of production: now fewer persons can control a larger number of operations through increasingly complex electrical and electronic machines. Mechanization of production has created a society rich in material goods, but it has also created new and perplexing social problems which threaten concepts fundamental to Western civilization.

Chief among these is the problem of the worker displaced by automation. For example, a large, mass-production industry was able to reduce its work force from 28,000 in 1955 to 17,000 in 1961 (see Table 3-1), while producing the same number of units per hour. This drastic reduction in workers and the continued high levels of hourly production have been reflected in the continuing hard core of unemployment which has plagued the country since the early 1950's. [20:219]

TABLE 3-1.   Employment and Unemployment in the United States, 1950–63

Year	Employed (in millions)	Per Cent	Unemployed (in millions)	Per Cent
1950	59.748	94.7	3.351	5.3
1955	52.944	95.6	2.904	4.4
1960	66.681	94.4	3.931	5.6
1961	66.796	93.3	4.806	6.7
1962	67.846	94.4	4.007	5.6
1963	67.148	93.7	4.501	6.3

The problem of unemployment is particularly serious among the unskilled and among minority groups. They are the last to be employed and the first to be displaced by production cuts or by the introduction of automation. The problem is also costly for both state and federal governments which paid out $3.5 billion in direct relief and unemployment benefits during the fiscal year 1961. [20:302] The federal government, having recognized that chronic unemployment is detrimental to the economy as well as to the morale of the nation, passed the Manpower Training Act in 1962, thus making it possible for those without adequate education or training to receive the necessary help to qualify for jobs demanding specialized skills.

Technological change is inexorably linked to the welfare of the economy and the well-being of the individual. Thomas J. Watson, Jr., states the goals for technological improvement in these terms:

Technological change should be used to improve men's lives. We have seen that it brings both progress and problems. Our goal must be to apply new technology so that it will improve the way men live and work. Necessary adjustment to an accelerating technology must be planned and carried out with human considerations paramount.

Technological change should be encouraged to meet our own increasing industrial needs, to stimulate our social and economic progress, and to face successfully the long-term challenge of international Communism.

Technological knowledge should be shared so that people through-out the world, particularly in the underdeveloped countries, may improve their lives and benefit from up-to-date technology. [22:196]

Changes in the work force

Technological change has been instrumental in several significant shifts in the occupational patterns of the work force. Although such oc-cupations as farmer and farm manager, operator, farm laborer and fore-man, and nonfarm laborer have consistently declined in proportion to the total work force, there have been concurrent increases in professional, technical, clerical, and service occupations. Other occupational groupings have tended to remain relatively stable.

TABLE 3-2. Distribution of Population by Occupational Classification, 1950–61 [20:231]

Occupational Group	1950	1961
Professional and technical	7.52%	10.50%
Farmers and farm managers	7.36	4.10
Managers, officials, and proprietors	10.77	10.00
Clerical	12.79	14.70
Sales	6.45	6.60
Craftsmen and foremen	12.85	13.10
Operatives	20.36	17.50
Private household workers	3.15	3.10
Service workers	7.80	9.60
Farm laborers and foremen	5.05	4.90
Laborers (nonfarm)	5.90	5.90

Clark identifies two trends in the occupational identification of the work force in the United States. First, there have been, and will continue to be, declines in the primary industries (agriculture, lumbering, and fishing) and the secondary industries (mining, building, and manufac-turing), but a marked increase in the service industries (finance, insur-ance, government, and the professions). Second, there has developed a small but influential group of "producers of ideas and technological inno-vation." He expects that almost half the total work force will be in white-collar jobs by 1970. [5:45–48] His forecast is substantiated by the estimate that 200,000 individuals will be displaced by automation each year dur-ing the 1960's. [3]

Another trend of major significance has been the rapid increase in the number and percentage of women in the work force. There were 12.574 million women employed in 1940, constituting 24.3 per cent of the work force. By 1961, this number had increased to 22.533 million, or 32.8 per cent of the work force.

Technological advances have been the basis for almost unbelievable increases in the gross national product and marked increments in per capita income. Personal income increased 233 per cent, and the gross national product 136 per cent, from 1945 to 1960. These vast increases in productivity have made possible the expansion of such public service institutions as colleges, public schools, and hospitals, and have provided a higher standard of living for a larger segment of the total population. [7]

The constantly increasing need for highly educated and skilled manpower in the immediate future cannot be overstated. Wolfbein puts it this way:

> The first [factor] is the overriding factor of change, whether it be in factory-systems management, weaponry and space research, medical diagnostics, economic and statistical computations, or teaching techniques. In these fields theory and practice have been subject to radical and frequent changes and will surely continue to be.
>
> Under these circumstances, whether one talks of demands or needs, the critical factor is the great necessity for more professional personnel who are endowed with the maneuverability, the flexibility, the adaptability to respond with creativity to the changes to which we have referred. This is the second key.
>
> These two keys will open the door to an educational policy directed to flexibility in training professional and technical personnel and to a labor-management policy directed to efficient utilization of such manpower. These policies, in combination, will enable us to match "demands" and "needs" for such personnel. [24:46]

Three professional groups provide revealing information relative to the growing shortage of qualified professional and technical personnel needed to sustain an expanding and increasingly complex economy. These fields are: health service, science, and engineering. It is apparent that none of these classifications is finding sufficient numbers of educated personnel to meet adequately the demands of the future. This serious lag in supply has aroused concern both in government and in business and has stimulated some effective if spotty reactions intended to diminish the problem. [4; 19]

Social Change and Education

The strong currents of social change are the result of interactions among public and private educational institutions, business, industry, government, and the attitudes and needs of the general population as shaped by historical precedent, tradition, and a changing environment. It is impossible to say which force has been most influential in inducing such changes. It is safe to say that the total contribution is undoubtedly greater than the sum of the parts, and education has contributed to these developments in its response to changing demands and its subsequent impact upon society through the development and spread of knowledge.

Despite the resistance of educational conservatives, it is apparent that comprehensive public education is an essential part of the American social system, and this system cannot escape its responsibility for providing those services necessary for the well-being of its citizens. Institutions of higher education, which depend upon public support, cannot continue to be isolated from the mainstream of the social and economic system. These institutions, a part of the public domain, must respond to the needs of society in such a way as to preserve the best of the past and to contribute in every possible way to the solutions of today's problems.

General concepts of higher education have been shifting with the changing patterns of the social order. Some trends are discernible which indicate a change in the direction of—or at least in the expectations for—post-high school education in the United States. These changes arise from the perceptions of individuals as they are filtered through to educational leaders, members of Congress and state legislatures, and the members and leaders of power groups in the community.

How are these changes in attitude manifested? There are a number of indications that the United States has a clear commitment to the extension of higher education and to the expansion of educational programs.

The burgeoning enrollments in higher education show both a gross increase in numbers of students and the relative increase as compared with the general college-age population. [8:59]

TABLE 3-3.   Enrollment in Institutions of Higher Education
Compared with Population Aged 18–21 (Fall 1946–Fall 1962)

Year	Population Aged 18–21	Enrollment	Per Cent of Age Group Enrolled
1946	9,403,000	2,078,095	22.1
1950	8,945,000	2,281,298	25.5
1953	8,441,000	2,231,054	26.4
1956	8,701,000	2,918,212	33.5
1959	9,182,000	3,364,861	36.6
1962	10,745,000	4,174,936	38.9

The increases in enrollments during this period have significance beyond the mere increase in the number of individuals in colleges and universities. They indicate that a substantially larger proportion of the total number of families in the United States are willing—although not necessarily able—to pay at least a portion of the direct cost of college attendance—room, board, tuition and other expenses—for their children. Furthermore, the increase in enrollments, and the consequent increase in the number of post-high school institutions needed to accommodate additional students, have resulted in substantially larger public expenditures for higher education. These expenditures have been approved by local, state, and national governments and supported by the taxpayers upon whom the additional costs ultimately fall. Public expenditure for colleges and universities increased from $2.26 billion in 1949–50 to $5.628 billion in 1959–60. This is an increase of approximately 250 per cent in the cost of higher education during this period. [8:76] There is probably no better evidence of the desire for a public service than the willingness to pay the ensuing costs.

Other changes with regard to education include the expansion of curricula to meet changing scientific and technological needs. New courses have appeared in colleges and universities over the past twenty years. The vast increase in the amount of subsidized research and consultative services required and financed by government and business is also a response to basic social and scientific trends. And the introduction of mechanical teaching machines and techniques is a direct educational adaptation to broad societal trends.

Internal population migration

Major shifts in the socioeconomic levels of the population have resulted in the migration of large numbers of people from one geographic area to another. There have been declines in the population of a number of states (e.g., Arkansas, Kansas, Mississippi, North Dakota, and West Virginia) and burgeoning increases in the populations of others (e.g., California, Florida, Illinois, and New York). At the same time there has been a consistent movement of population from rural areas to urban centers. The urban population nearly doubled between 1930 and 1960, while the number of people living in rural areas remained constant. The country-to-city trend followed the shift in occupational patterns from primary to service industries. For example, 43.5 per cent of the country's population was classified as rural in 1940, 37.5 per cent in 1950, and only 30.1 per cent in 1960. [20:4] The population of the country has become more concentrated in urban areas, creating a number of major social, economic, and political problems.

A serious implication resulting from this shift of population has been the breakdown of small, well-knit, mutually interdependent communities in which individuals tended to have clear personal roles and the advantage of psychological support from the community and from subgroups within that community. [18] This gives rise to two important effects. The individual loses, to a large extent, a psychological referent necessary for personal security. He becomes isolated in a mechanistic environment which severely limits the integrity of his individual personality and his worth as an individual. Second, the mass migration to urban centers tends to sap the strength and leadership of rural areas and small towns. [10:103–30]

These, then, are some of the major forces which are constantly interacting and bringing about a fundamental metamorphosis in our society. They are sweeping changes, but their real meaning and translation into reality take place on the community level.

The Community

The environment of the two-year college includes, in the broadest sense, a wide range of individuals, groups, and agencies—all impinging, in varying ways, on the college's organization and operation.

TABLE 3-4. Extralegal Groups and Agencies
Influencing and/or Controlling Two-year Colleges

Level	Public	Professional
Local	1. Community residents 2. Alumni 3. Civic groups 4. Religious organizations 5. Labor groups 6. Business groups 7. Political groups 8. Philanthropic organizations 9. Advisory committees 10. Farm organizations 11. Students	1. Teachers' and administrators' associations 2. Public and private school teachers and administrators 3. Educational advisory committees
State	1. General population 2. Associations of members of boards of control 3. Advisory committees 4. Taxpayers' associations 5. Religious organizations 6. Political groups 7. Business groups 8. Labor groups 9. Farm organizations	1. Teachers' and administrators' associations 2. Four-year colleges and universities 3. Two-year college associations 4. Athletic associations
National and regional	1. General population 2. Special-interest groups	1. Accrediting associations 2. Professional and academic associations 3. Philanthropic foundations 4. Regional two-year college associations 5. American Association of Junior Colleges

The parents of college students influence programs by their close association and willingness to provide financial support. On a higher level, the state government may require all two-year colleges to be branches of the state university. Federal legislation can put special emphasis on one part of the curriculum, or may insure an abundance of instructors in one area while creating shortages in others.

The interactions of these groups with the college and among themselves make up the environment in which the college functions as an organic social institution. Misunderstanding or misinterpretation of the functions and needs of the institution by one or more such groups can create dislocations in college programs and policies that complicate the whole course of institutional development. On the other hand, widespread support and understanding by these groups can stimulate rapid and healthy growth of the college and its services to the community.

The complexity of the environment in which social institutions exist has been clearly stated by Monypenny:

> For the political scientist, any policy-making structure may be viewed as having three related elements. One is the formal structure itself as one finds it set out in law and practice. Another element is constituted by the groups in the population which have an interest in the policies which are determined throughout the structure. A third element is the goals which are sought by groups in the population and by their representatives in the policy-making structure. The structure itself may be viewed as the outcome of group activity in the pursuit of objectives which are to be realized through the structure. Any structure, therefore, has to be understood in terms of goals toward which it is directed, the competition of various groups with respect to those goals, and the predominance of groups in the structure of decision.
>
> The second major viewpoint which a political scientist brings to the study of any political situation is that there are not one but many goals which are simultaneously sought by any population. Any structure, therefore, necessarily is a structure for recording the predominance of certain goals and for effectuating adjustments between goals in conflict which are capable of mediation, For the political scientist, therefore, every study of policy-making is a study in conflict and the adjustment of differences through a political structure. No one goal is ever assumed to have such overwhelming support that it is likely to be realized in the form in which it is originally presented. Nor is it assumed that any single goal is likely to be dominant in any structure over a period of time. Rather, structure is the means whereby a variety of goals, sometimes logically incompatible, [are] realized. [17:1]

Differences exist not only among groups impinging upon the two-year college, but also within given groups.

Professional organizations

Colleges are also members of a broad, but well-organized, professional community in which both individuals and institutions share common interests and problems. Such organizations are one of the significant hallmarks of a profession, whether it be education or any other recognized specialization. The relationships of the two-year college with other institutions within the profession are important, for without satisfactory identification with other educational institutions the two-year college would have no accepted identity or purpose.

The most important of these organizations are the six regional accrediting associations for colleges and secondary schools. Although voluntary, these organizations exert more control over education than any other group: their approval insures qualitative and quantitative minimums in educational programs and insures the acceptance of transfer credits among all accredited institutions. In addition to the six accrediting associations, there are specialized accrediting groups—such as the National League of Nursing and the Engineers Council for Professional Development—which develop and apply standards to the programs provided by two-year colleges. Such organizations shape the organization and programs of colleges into a generalized mold, but—at the same time—they permit variations relevant to the philosophy and objectives of the individual college.

The general objectives accrediting associations seek to achieve are illustrated by the common denominators set forth by the Middle States Association:

> Curricula which provide, emphasize, or rest upon general or liberal education.
> Objectives and programs which develop [the] power to form independent judgments to weigh values, and to understand fundamental theory, rather than solely to amass facts and acquire skills.
> An atmosphere which stimulates the student to continue and broaden his education beyond the point he must reach to obtain his credits, certificate, or degree. [12:19]

In order to implement standards, accrediting associations analyze the organization, resources, programs, and outcomes of the college's work with students.

There are innumerable professional groups which also exert influence upon colleges. Among them the most important are probably state, local, and national faculty and administrator groups such as the National Education Association, the American Association of School Administrators, and the American Association of University Professors. These organizations, through their local and state groups, provide guidelines for the improvement of the profession and of educational programs. On the state and local levels they also provide checks and balances for state legislative and administrative bodies, boards of control, and administrators, thus restraining capricious and irresponsible decisions that might be detrimental to the profession or to the educational process.

Professional groups serve a useful function in that they tend to diffuse decision-making on educational policies among those best qualified to fulfill this responsibility.

The Community Power Structure

Closely related to the development, progress, and continuing operation of the two-year college is the community power structure. If the two-year college is truly a community-oriented institution, it must continually interact with its environment in responding to community attitudes and needs. The principles of the community power structure apply significantly to the public, private, and technical colleges which have either a limited clientele (religious group or economic level) or limited geographic service area.

Dahl, in his study of New Haven, has distinguished between actual and potential influence:

> One of the most elementary principles of political life is that a political resource is only a potential source of influence. Individuals with the same amount of resources may exert different degrees of influence because they use their resources in different ways. One wealthy man may collect paintings; another may collect politicians. [6:271]

He continues his analysis by differentiating between the influence of a collectivity as opposed to the influence of a single person, and then cites reasons for which individuals use their potential influence in differing degrees. These include varying access to resources, varying estimates of the chances for success in influencing decisions, varying opportunities for use of resources, and varying estimates as to the degree of satisfaction to be obtained from influencing a specific decision.

If Dahl's point of view is accepted, it becomes possible to explain the failure of many administrators to mobilize community support for educational objectives. There is a propensity on the part of many such individuals to operate on the basis of the much more simplified, and therefore more appealing, theory of a power elite. According to this concept, all the administrator need do is convince the "right" group of people that an educational need exists and this group will pass the word on to the rest of the community.

It cannot be denied that within any community there are some individuals who have more influence than others. These so-called opinion-molders can certainly be extremely helpful in presenting an issue favorably. What is frequently overlooked is that the opinion-molders may have only a peripheral interest in the issue and will consequently devote only a small amount of their potential influence to promoting it.

Within the same community, there may be many small or large

groups with little potential influence who may be vitally concerned about the same issue. Because they are concerned, they may—if properly approached—be willing to throw all their potential influence behind the issue. This will have a far greater impact than the desultory actions of a few opinion-molders.

Education, in particular, offers many examples. A small and normally impotent organization such as a local PTA has been successful in shaping the course of events for an entire city because of its members' persistence and willingness to devote their entire potential influence to an area in which the opposition was only peripherally concerned.

It is quite probable that within any community power structure there will be some influential individuals antagonistic to public education in general and vocally reluctant to support any program that extends beyond the bare legal minimum. This group is likely to be extremely concerned over financial issues and, hence, willing to muster all its actual influence in opposition—if it perceives its chances of success as reasonably good. There will also be within the community a group of public-spirited influentials who can generally be counted upon to support issues involving increased financial support for education. But because most of the members of this second group will have the means and the motivation to send their offspring to private colleges, their concern will be peripheral in nature; generally, they are unwilling to devote the same proportion of their potential resources as the first group.

Finally, there may be a small group of influentials whose vital concern with educational issues arises either from idealistic commitment or from personal involvement. The members of this group will be willing to devote their potential resources to an issue in accordance with their perceptions of its chances for success. The issue may then emerge as a power struggle between the first and third groups, with the second group occasionally lending verbal support first to one, then to the other.

The college administrator who is satisfied to concentrate his efforts solely on these three groups is doomed to achieve, at best, half a program, for the reactionary-conservative influentials outnumber their liberal opponents in most communities. The secret in combating the unusual influence of small but powerful special-interest groups lies in expanding and strengthening the base of support for the college.

If a majority of the smaller, less influential collectivities that exist within any community are courted assiduously by the college and lend their aggregate support to it, the conservative influentials will realize that their chances for success are diminished and, accordingly, will devote less vigor to the struggle. Conversely, the more liberal forces will be prepared to exert increased efforts. Vacillating influentials will sense the prevailing trend and lend their support.

Assume the existence of a community facing a specific bond issue, as represented by the large circle in Fig. 3-1.

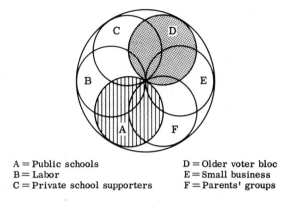

A = Public schools   D = Older voter bloc
B = Labor   E = Small business
C = Private school supporters   F = Parents' groups

FIG. 3-1. A Community Power Structure

Within this community are six organizations, all with the same degree of potential influence (the six inner circles are all the same size and equidistant from the center of the large circle). For individuals, as for groups, proximity to the center of the large circle represents potential influence; thus, it becomes obvious that within each organization, some individuals will be capable of greater potential influence than others. Finally, as demonstrated by the overlap, some individuals may have the capacity for considerable potential influence with several organizations, but no single individual is likely to exercise considerable influence in all organizations.

Although the six organizations represent loosely knit collectivities of individuals with varying interests, social relationships, and political ties, each has one area in common. It is through this bond that any organization realizes its potential for exercising influence. Appeals for support must, therefore, be directed toward this common interest. It should be noted that the pattern of organizations represented by Fig. 3-1 may very well hold true only for issues involving increased taxes for support of education. For other issues, a very different coalition might occur.

Organization *A* represents the public schools, vitally concerned (implied by the heavy shading) and exercising all their potential influence in support of the issue. Organization *D* is a group of older voters confronting the problem of fixed incomes and increasing costs. As such, they are vitally concerned and exercising all their potential influence in opposition to the issue. Organizations *B* and *F*, representing labor and parents' groups, respectively, are favorably disposed toward the issue;

but within each group, wide ranges of opinion exist. In like manner, Organizations C and E are composed of private school advocates and a coalition of small businessmen, respectively. Each is interested in keeping taxes low for reasons that may cover a wide range of opinion.

It can be concluded that the value of any influential to either side of this controversy depends to a considerable extent upon the organizations within which the influential is capable of exercising his resources and also upon his willingness to do so. It is possible, too, that a fiercely committed subcollectivity in any one of the four organizations peripherally involved in this controversy might use its aggregate influence to swing the issue in either direction.

Parental influences

The attitudes of parents toward the two-year college are conditioned largely by perceptions of or location within the class structure of the community. In a like manner, the level of aspiration which parents hold for their children is related to the status level they consider themselves to hold within the community. Thus, the potential achievement of individual goals bears closely on the perceptions of the college as a social institution.

The parents of two-year college students are primarily from a lower-middle-class or lower-class (blue-collar) background. The most significant data available, those developed by Clark [5:68], indicated that in the San Jose area 77 per cent of the students in junior college came from lower-white-collar, upper-blue-collar, and lower-blue-collar backgrounds. Other studies have substantiated these findings. Although various socioeconomic levels are represented among the students in two-year colleges, the preponderant group is from the lower socioeconomic section of the community being served.

The administrative officers and faculty of the college are not isolated from direct contact with parents. They meet them in the community, and find it necessary to deal with the very real problems that parents can, and sometimes do, introduce into the campus situation. Student failure is not always understood by parents, especially if such failure affects their expectations for a son or daughter. The two-year college must cope with the irrational parental reactions which grow out of such situations and must assist in offering acceptable substitute goals.

There are also direct implications for course content and for the curriculum in general. Faculty behavior perceived as unrealistic or erratic can create immediate and serious reactions among parents. The introduction of new ideas and concepts can lead to conflicts and misunderstandings within the family if such ideas are contrary to the internalized beliefs of parents. Parents may find it difficult to adjust to having their fundamental beliefs questioned by their children. If parents feel that the faculty is aiding and abetting students to reject deeply imbedded and emotionally based beliefs, there is a possibility of serious conflicts between the college and the parents.

Despite the problems created by conflicting ideas, parents who can be broadminded enough to accept and understand their children as adults may be richly rewarded by the experience.

Parents, in many of their roles, constitute one of the potentially most important segments of citizen support of the college and its programs. They can make the difference between adequate and inadequate financial and policy support. The presence of satisfied parents throughout the community can be a critical factor in bond or tax elections, elections of board members, and other activities which have direct impact upon the operation and improvement of the college. Their satisfaction with the services afforded them and their children provides a broad base of support for the college within the immediate service area.

The public schools

One of the most important organizations bearing upon the operation of the two-year college is the secondary school. Public community colleges draw the majority of their students from nearby high schools, and private two-year colleges spend much time and effort maintaining close relationships with the personnel of the schools from which they draw their students. Because a primary function of the guidance program in the high school is to aid students in selecting a college, the attitudes of school administrators and faculty members toward the two-year college must, of necessity, be shared by the students. The perceptions of secondary school professional personnel vary widely, depending upon the age, the quality of work, and the effectiveness of the liaison provided by the two-year college.

Many secondary teachers and counselors see the two-year college as an opportunity for students of limited economic means but adequate academic ability. In general, secondary school teachers are inclined to encourage those students able to do college work to attend some kind of post-high school institution. The two-year college appears to be an obvious choice for those students who cannot possibly afford to attend a four-year institution. Furthermore, some students may be too immature to compete with individuals of the same age in large, complex institutions; these students are urged to experience higher education in the two-year college first.

The two-year college is often regarded by secondary school personnel as an opening for personal professional advancement. As a matter of fact, a large proportion of junior college instructors have had experience in secondary schools. [15:172] Teaching in a collegiate institution has consistently offered greater status and higher prestige than teaching on either the elementary or secondary levels. It is also true that many junior college salary schedules are higher than those commonly available in the surrounding secondary schools.

Public school personnel also harbor certain negative feelings about two-year institutions. First, lack of knowledge concerning the educational purposes of such colleges hinders their acceptance by public school personnel. Except in a few states, the number of two-year colleges has been limited until recent years; thus, public school personnel have not had an opportunity to become acquainted with or to study at community colleges. Their perceptions of such institutions are consequently generated from the knowledge and values regarding higher education acquired during their own years in college and through their subsequent professional experiences. Lack of knowledge of two-year institutions on the part of college professors contributes to public school teachers' lack of understanding of this institution. The value judgments acquired in college may obscure or distort their attitudes when they are placed in the position of having to evaluate the potential of the two-year college.

Another problem relevant to high school personnel is the criticism of the preparation of students by members of the college faculty. The "pecking order" of criticism begins with the university and extends downward through the junior college, the high schools, and the elementary school. Each level sees itself as competent in the tasks assigned, but tends to rationalize any failures by charging that the students' previous educational experiences have been inadequate. The close relationship which must exist between the community college and the secondary school requires that there be mutual understanding between the personnel of the two institutions.

Perhaps the most serious problems experienced in the relationship between the personnel of the two-year college and that of the public school develop in those districts which have a combined public school-junior college system under one administration and board of control. The secondary schools have historically been underfinanced. Teachers have been required to work with an excessive number of students in classes. When the two-year college is a part of such a district, public school personnel find it difficult to accept the fact that college personnel may not be required to carry an equally heavy teaching load. For example, high school teachers may have thirty or more contact hours per week, while college personnel teach from fifteen to twenty-two. In addition, the college's financial demands can become a real threat to the economic security and the financial and professional aspirations of public school personnel. Because the college is an additional drain upon the resources available to all schools, the cost of its program may well mean the difference between adequacy and inadequacy in salaries, working conditions, and teaching equipment in the secondary schools. When such circumstances exist, the basic conflict of interest makes it difficult, if not impossible, for public school personnel to accept the importance of the two-year college and to promote it as essential to the community.

The argument that the image of the college is blurred and its potential inhibited was set forth in a Florida newspaper, which stated that, because public two-year colleges were organized under the county public school districts, the teachers were underpaid (in spite of having to meet higher educational and experience requirements for employment) and the colleges were underfinanced. [7]

Additional conflicts between the two-year college and the secondary school grow out of the need for clearly defined roles among college and public school administrators. The superintendent of the largest public school system in the area is generally recognized as the educational leader by teachers and the lay public. The introduction of a junior college president clouds the role of the superintendent and confuses those associated with both levels of education. Role definition in the community is important to the individual as well as to the institution he represents. Competitive attitudes among administrators do not contribute to a clarification of the situation. This problem is particularly acute in districts which have unified K–12 and junior college programs. [13] A frequent solution is to avoid using the title *president* for the chief college administrator, referring to him instead as *dean*. Confusing as such a device may be to administrative structure in the college, it helps to define the supremacy of the superintendent.

There is less than complete unanimity on the question: Should two-year colleges be a part of the local public school system? Those who support the continuing amalgamation of K–12 and two-year colleges contend that such an arrangement holds advantages for faculty recruitment, in-service staff training, curriculum development, financial and housekeeping services, articulation of educational programs, and physical plant development and utilization. It is also pointed out that the gains made by the personnel of colleges independent of public school districts are often without regard for and at the expense of teachers and students in elementary and secondary schools. [9]

The university

A close relationship generally prevails between four-year colleges and universities and two-year colleges—for at least two reasons. First, the majority of students in two-year colleges plan to complete work for a four-year degree—and many do eventually transfer to a four-year college where they pursue upper-division academic work. Second, transfer curricula in the junior college are designed to meet the requirements of four-year institutions and these programs are quickly modified when changes in entrance requirements for transfer students are made by four-year institutions.

The attitudes of university personnel may be discussed in two frames of reference: the personal and the educational. As a general rule, university administrators consider junior colleges to be a necessary adjunct to the educational system of the state. They have reservations, of course, if a two-year college system is set up at the expense of state-supported four-year institutions. However difficult the problem of finances might be, many college and university administrators recognize the two-year college as an essential factor in meeting the future educational demands of society. There are some notable exceptions to this position. Wisconsin, Indiana, and Georgia stand out as examples of statewide systems in which there is no provision for publicly supported community colleges independent of public four-year institutions. In these three states, all public higher education is dominated by four-year institutions, with branches or "satellite campuses" distributed over the state. A study of 102 extension centers and branch colleges undertook to ask directors of such organizations their opinions of the advantages and disadvantages of the two-year college. Respondents felt that the organization of post-high school education within a state college or university system was superior to the public community college in that it offered guaranteed accreditation. In addition, it was felt that the status and prestige of the university met the needs of a larger number of students, attracted more serious students and instructors with better academic qualifications, and maintained generally higher academic standards. [1]

University personnel are generally not familiar with—nor do they understand—the need for technical, vocational, adult-education, and community-enrichment programs carried on by public community colleges. They focus on the transfer program which the majority of them believe can be effectively carried out only on the college or university campus. Many college and university faculty members are quite dogmatic in their rejection of junior college transfer students, charging that they are "inferior" to students of similar levels who entered the university as freshmen. In general, their attitudes indicate that they feel the junior college is a second-rate institution, staffed by less-qualified faculty members, and providing an educational experience inferior to that available in four-year institutions.

A statement by a former university professor, growing out of a local election for the financing of a public junior college, vividly illustrates this hostility toward the two-year college:

> By way of summary, to establish an inferior institution whose faculty will be composed of high school teachers, because no first-class scholar will teach in a junior college when he can secure employment in a first-class college or university, and whose courses of study will not prepare anyone to enter the University or fit him for life will not solve any of our problems.
>
> Businessmen will not employ incompetent people. What is needed is for parents to send their boys and girls who have failed in high schools back to school to make up their deficiencies. [1:11]

The difficulties experienced by two-year colleges in projecting a satisfactory institutional image to university personnel result from a number of factors: the prejudices of the faculty members of the four-year colleges, the inferior academic preparation of students in some two-year colleges, and the belief of university faculties that a public two-year institution offering comprehensive curricula which include work other than "collegiate" courses *must* be inferior to the traditional four-year institution.

The attitudes of university personnel toward the two-year college may be explained in part by Galbraith's concept of conventional wisdom:

> To a very large extent, of course, we associate truth with convenience—with what most closely accords with self-interest and individual well-being or promises best to avoid awkward effort or unwelcome dislocation of life. We also find highly acceptable what contributes most to self-esteem.... Therefore we adhere, as though to a raft, to those ideas which represent our understanding. This is a prime manifestation of vested interest. For a vested interest in understanding is more preciously guarded than any other treasure. It is why men react, not infrequently akin to religious passion, to the defense of what they have so laboriously learned. Familiarity may breed contempt in some areas of human behavior, but in the field of social ideas it is the touchstone of acceptability. [11:8–9]

The admissions policies and procedures for transfer students constitute another important area of potential difficulty. Registrars of four-year schools are sometimes overly exacting in their analyses of transcripts from community colleges. Unless the course descriptions in the two-year catalog correspond exactly to those of the courses in the university, there is a good possibility that the student may lose credits or be required to take additional courses which include knowledge already mastered. The need for close articulation of programs intended to lead to a baccalaureate degree is too obvious to require further elaboration. Arbitrary and unannounced changes in course requirements result in hardship for transfer students and inevitably damage the reputation of two-year college programs.

Lack of cooperation between universities and two-year colleges is detrimental to both because of the negative responses it evokes from students and parents. In some states, legislative action has been taken to insure that the work completed in public two-year colleges will be accepted by publicly supported universities. It is unfortunate that such legislation should be necessary, but the lack of clear-cut administrative controls and the imposition of unrealistic requirements leads inevitably to legislative attempts to coordinate the total program of higher education.

Labor organizations

Organized labor has demonstrated a continuing interest in all levels of education. A powerful force in many industrial communities, the traditionally liberal labor movement has advocated increased financial support as well as adequate vocational and technical programs. The working members of unions have long viewed formal education as the means through which their children may rise above the position of their parents. With the advent of evening programs and the increasing emphasis on adult education, union members have found that education can assist them in improving their own status.

It is interesting to note, however, that the viewpoint of the working-class persons is somewhat ambivalent. They may strongly support the concept of technical and vocational education and even seek to improve their own status through such courses, but they may also insist upon the prestige of liberal arts courses for their children. As the technical program comes into its own, and as improved methods for distributing wealth provide working-class people with an increasing share of the fruits of production, the tendency to overidealize the professional person, who is not dependent upon an hourly wage, may fade and with it the emphasis upon liberal arts.

Because organized labor does not have nearly the cohesive force in political matters that it exercises in collective bargaining, it is difficult to evaluate how much reliance should be placed upon its support. Individually, working-class people lack education and influence; they are not likely to be active in policy-making groups. Although labor leaders are eager to offer verbal support, they may be unwilling to make the sustained effort necessary to inform and educate the rank and file to the point where the entire group can bring its full weight to bear.

In general, the labor movement has made, and is continuing to make, important contributions to the public two-year college. It should be pointed out, however, that certain problems can arise. If the antagonisms and unrealistic demands frequently associated with union-management relations is carried over into the educational arena, the board of control may be split between the two groups. Such a conflict would be detrimental to both and not in the best interests of the college. Furthermore, labor representatives may view the administrative staff of the college as management-oriented and, through their actions, encourage a division between faculty and administration. Such a division would make healthy development of the college difficult, if not impossible.

Business and industry

The two-year college has historically enjoyed the abiding friendship of business and industry. It is true that this friendship has not been entirely altruistic on the part of either the college or business; both have recognized the advantages to be served by a close association.

From the point of view of business and industry, the two-year college serves a number of important functions. One of the first questions likely to be raised by any potential employee of a company will concern the quality and extent of educational facilities within the community. The existence of public higher education contributes to the ease with which qualified personnel may be recruited. The community college, with its emphasis on technical education, provides training for skills critical to industry. It has been demonstrated that the two-year college can furnish superior training at reduced costs. This is particularly true when industrial leaders serve on advisory committees and qualified employees of the concern are retained by the college to assist in the development and teaching of courses.

In addition to guaranteeing a pool of trained manpower, the college may also furnish retraining opportunities for workers whose skills have become technologically obsolescent. By raising the educational level of the community, the college helps to increase the purchasing power of potential buyers. And the college itself is an important consumer of goods and services within the community.

Although certain advantages accrue to business and industry from the services of a comprehensive community college, these advantages are by no means one-sided. Business and industrial concerns contribute heavily to the financial support of the college by enlarging the tax base. The managerial elements furnish the leadership for college boards and for mobilizing community support on important issues.

Many business concerns emphasize the need for additional education as a primary requisite for advancement. In this way, large numbers of adult students are encouraged to seek the services of the college. Not only are employed persons motivated to attend college by desire for advancement, but new high school graduates come to view the college as an avenue to steady employment. The relationships mentioned above are further strengthened by the presence of industrial leaders on technical advisory committees. Through this association, the college is provided with invaluable free assistance in developing and evaluating programs as well as in placing graduates.

One further contribution needs to be mentioned. Industrial and business leaders have increasingly come to recognize the role played by higher education in developing the skills and climate necessary for their continued success. With this recognition has come a desire to contribute to higher education: foundations have been established and scholarship funds provided. These voluntary donations have frequently been responsible for the more rapid development of specialized programs than would otherwise have been possible.

It would not be entirely satisfactory to leave the reader with the impression that no problems exist in relationships between the two-year college and business and industry. Although most business leaders have a strong sense of social responsibility, there are some who seek to escape their fair share of the cost of education. For example, some attempt to obtain unfair tax advantages by resisting equitable evaluation of holdings. Nor is it unknown for businesses to seek independent political subdivisions in close proximity to educational facilities so that they may enjoy all the enumerated advantages with none of the responsibilities. Smaller businesses not infrequently unite in ultraconservative types of associations which seek militantly to resist any tax increase regardless of the validity of the purpose.

A 1963 stand by the U.S. Chamber of Commerce serves as a refreshing alternative to the problems outlined above. Recognizing the contributions made by community colleges, this organization clearly outlined the values of such institutions to the business community and urged members to work actively for the formation of new colleges and to support those already in existence.

Implications for the Two-year College

The changes taking place at an ever-increasing rate in our society will have profound effects upon all aspects of higher education, but particularly upon the two-year college. As these changes take place, pressure will be exerted upon existing educational institutions to provide new and better solutions to the unique educational problems of the individual, who must continually adapt to social and economic change or become a civic and economic liability. There will be resistance to change, as there always is, but change will take place nevertheless. The college which does not seek to make sound and logical adjustments to such change will soon be bypassed or replaced by institutions that do respond to current needs. A number of direct implications of importance to the two-year college are growing out of today's social and economic changes.

Maintenance of fluidity

First, the community college must remain fluid in its educational objectives, programs, and administrative organization in order to respond effectively to new conditions and demands as they arise. This does not mean that the college must be a potpourri of responses to real or imagined needs; there must be reason and logic behind changes and additions to college programs lest the stability and integrity of the institution be eroded. Clark points out the danger of unbridled program expansion when he says:

> Security is the prime prerequisite for responsibility in education, in the sense of consistent, goal-directed behavior. Marginality, as a prime source of insecurity, tends to undercut the autonomy of administration, and to render decision-making more susceptible to external influences. Administrative action is then judged to be irresponsible, inconsistent in terms of goals, and overly responsive to immediate desires. [4:149]

Reasoned change which is consistently relevant to the college's needs while protecting its integrity is essential if the organization is to succeed in meeting its responsibilities and adapting to a changing environment. The transfer program will tend to remain relatively stable (with only minor adjustments as changes move down from four-year colleges and universities). The technical, vocational, and guidance phases of the college, however, will be the targets of societal pressures as attempts are made to find solutions to the increasingly complex problems of society. If the two-year college is to provide the services society will insist upon, it must do so within an institutional framework strong enough to resist expediency and opportunism.

It is apparent that the central problem facing the two-year college is the maintenance of a balance between the extremes of complete fluidity and rigidity. The college is drawn in two directions at once; toward experimentation, which is the outgrowth of changing social and economic needs, and toward adherence to traditional patterns of education which have high status value. The dilemma is intensified by the fact that social and economic needs are not necessarily equatable with the values of individuals or groups in society. The two-year college finds itself in the position of having to strike a balance between societal requirements and the very personal and individual needs of its students. Having only a tenuous footing in post-high school education and a short history, the college tends to gravitate toward postures which insure status and acceptance based upon symbolic values rather than upon observable results as reflected in the achievements of former students and direct contributions to the economic and social order.

Meeting community expectations

In order to function within the framework of the immediate community, as well as within the larger environment, the college must be cognizant of the values of society and of the implications these values have among its immediate clientele. Values are of importance to the college because they are the central beliefs of individuals and society which set the general limits of thought and behavior. Williams has defined them as ". . . modes of organizing conduct—meaningful, affectively invested principles that guide human action." There is no clear line between group and individual values, for there is a strong overlap and interdependence between the two categories. But there are certain societal values which the two-year college must keep in mind. [23:388–422]

The American culture is marked by a stress upon personal success. This means that the individual is expected to achieve occupational competence and recognition. Students and their parents look upon post-high school education as a tool which can be used for the development of skills and knowledge in an occupation which provides material and status rewards.

Americans also have a strong orientation toward work and activity in which they seek to dominate the environment rather than place importance upon intellectual pursuits of no immediate value. Closely coupled with activity is the emphasis upon efficiency and practicality—the hallmarks of a technological society. Williams points out:

> The elevation of sheer technique into something closely approaching a value in its own right involves the familiar tendency to turn mean values into goal values through a gradual withdrawal of attention and affection and affect from the original ends—a development that is reinforced insofar as immediate interests and short-run goals are stressed. A culture that in the first place tends toward an unhistorical and utilitarian orientation would be especially likely to encourage just those behavior patterns in which technical efficiency can become valued for its own sake. [23:397]

Other identifiable values include moral orientation, humanitarian attitudes, material comfort, and external conformity. Each of these contributes in its own way to the influences on the community college. They are translated into the interactions between the community and the college campus, with direct and powerful influences upon the behavior of administrators, faculty members, and students.

The community expects the college to provide cultural leadership through faculty participation in community groups and through programs initiated by the college. In recent years, having a college in the locality has become a mark of status much sought after by chambers of commerce, business and industrial leaders, and others interested in encouraging community improvement and expansion. The economic contributions of college expenditures and the college population is not unimportant in the eyes of the community leaders, especially those individuals whose businesses may be directly related to supplies, equipment, and services needed both by the institution and the students.

The community expects the college to provide educational opportunities for those students, regardless of age, who seek them. Education is the key to social mobility and to occupational competence; the denial of educational opportunities, particularly to individuals of the middle class, is contrary to individual expectations and values.

Another primary expectation of the community is that the college will provide transferable credit leading the student toward the bachelor's degree. This function of the college enjoys acceptance by nearly all individuals in society. The college must, therefore, provide courses which are acceptable to four-year institutions with a minimum of credit loss. If the two-year college fails to meet this primary expectation because of the policies of four-year colleges or their changing requirements, or because of lack of accreditation or insufficiently high academic standards, it will find itself in a difficult position. The loss of credit is a serious problem when students transfer to other colleges. It may arise from the student's own deficiencies or lack of planning, but the blame falls upon the college itself. It is necessary to carry on a continual program of information with each generation of students and parents, explaining the intricacies of transfer of academic credits from one institution to another.

Another community expectation concerns the freedom of the individual to choose his course of study and to be admitted to such programs with minimum institutional requirements. Thus, many students come to the two-year college poorly prepared for the work they must do and with little or no understanding of the requirements they must meet before being admitted to advanced study in the professions. The lack of a logical relationship between aspirational level and demonstrated ability is one of the most serious problems facing the college. As is shown in Chapter 5, the academic ability of junior college students is significantly lower than that of four-year college freshmen in high-grade colleges and universities. The stimulus of status, as it attaches to professional occupational goals, is central to the personality needs of many students. Merely being identified as a premedical student has its rewards, and this need for identification with a status objective results in irrational decisions by many students.

The primary drive of both parents and students in relation to college education is occupational competence. The individual who is capable of holding a job only on the unskilled or semiskilled level is a problem—not only to himself, but to society in general. The knowledge that students come to college to assure themselves a secure niche in an occupation will make it easier to judge their behavior and to develop programs and teaching methods relevant to this vital objective.

Last, the community expects the college to perform these multitudinous tasks in an economical fashion. There continues to be consistent underevaluation of the cost of superior education. The layman equates educational production with the techniques associated with business and industry, not recognizing that there are significant differences between an educational organization and a business enterprise. The values of education have always been elusive and difficult to define. In general, the public approves of education as a social necessity, but there is a striking difference between this general belief and the willingness to provide the financial resources necessary to achieve it.

Given these interdependent and often conflicting attitudes, the junior college must, like all other organizations, have definite but flexible perimeters if it is not to lose itself in a welter of competitive and conflicting objectives. At present, there seems to be more danger of excessive rigidity than of excessive flexibility.

The establishment of federally sponsored area vocational schools is a case in point. Before this legislation was passed, the Manpower Retraining Act was passed for the purpose of making educational opportunities available to individuals who had been displaced by automation. Some of the public community colleges reacted promptly and organized training programs suited to their industrial needs. But most of them did not respond quickly or effectively. Why did this occur? The obvious conclusion is that boards of control and administrators saw the Manpower Retraining Act as unrelated to the objectives of their colleges. The addition of such programs apparently did not contribute to the image of the college as an academic institution. On the contrary, the addition of skill-oriented programs for the training of lower-class and lower-middle-class persons contributed only to what Clark has termed *precarious values*. Such values are the antithesis of those attitudes and symbols which contribute to high status in our society. Rather than further depreciate its image by the addition of skill courses and students from the lower socioeconomic levels of society, the community college did not make the necessary adaptations—and another type of institution came into existence.

Some Essentials of College-Community Relationships

There are at least five essential elements which must be present if the college is to establish institutional stability and make effectual adaptations to changing societal needs. First, the college must have a carefully defined philosophical position inclusive enough to embrace multiple objectives while concurrently setting limits within which the college can effectively perform its missions. Generally speaking, the philosophical statements appearing in two-year college catalogs are poorly written and incomplete. Worse, they are not necessarily understood or accepted by administrators, faculty members, or laymen. The development of a philosophical statement is not a minor assignment which can be completed by any individual on the college faculty. It requires a thorough explanation of values and the translation of these concepts into a statement which squares with immediate and long-range aims. As has been pointed out in Chapter 2, it is doubtful that the two-year college can successfully perform its manifold functions without a philosophy of experimentation which is accepted both by educators and laymen.

Second, the college itself must have strong administrative leadership intellectually and emotionally committed to multivariant educational objectives. If the president and his subordinate administrators have no basic belief in the value of guidance and technical and vocational education, these feelings are transmitted to the faculty and students with the result that the "halo" effect of transfer programs grows stronger and the students and faculty may even become hostile toward courses in other areas. The importance of the attitudes and expectations of college staff members is stressed in Chapters 6, 7, and 8.

The college has a definite responsibility to develop, among board members and citizens in the area, attitudes favorable to programs specifically adapted to individual needs and to the social and economic characteristics of the community being served. The new two-year college does not enjoy broad understanding and acceptance; until it does, it will find itself in a disadvantageous position as it attempts to interpret the value of new and experimental courses.

A fourth element which must be present for the broad development of the two-year college includes not only the attitudes of faculty members and administrators but the implementation of these values in financial support for courses and guidance services essential to a heterogeneous student population. Technical education is expensive. If, when available resources are distributed, a disproportionate amount is channeled into transfer programs, the comprehensive development of the college will be seriously impeded. Financial support is one of the primary observable criteria of the values of the administrator.

Last, and perhaps of most importance, is the need for a clear definition of functions of all segments of post-high school education. The competition between four- and two-year colleges is unconscionable in terms of achieving imperative educational goals and providing efficient and effective educational services to the state and local community. Many states have made efforts in this direction through state surveys and the organization of coordinating bodies on the state level. There has been resistance to this movement among both two-year and four-year colleges, some of which is based upon the fear of nonprofessional political domination from the state level. This fear may be justified in some instances. On the other hand, comprehensive planning of educational services is an inevitable outgrowth of an increasingly complex society and it is not beyond the capabilities of educational leaders, in cooperation with political figures, to develop effective coordination and economy of operation in all segments of higher education. Role definition on this level, and acceptance of such definition by the individual institutions, is imperative for the best interests of the students, the college, and society at large.

Bibliography

1. Blocker, C. E., and H. A. Campbell, Jr., *Administrative Practices in University Extension Centers and Branch Colleges.* Austin, Tex.: University of Texas, 1963.

2. Letter appearing in *The Austin American,* December 10, 1963.

3. Clague, Nuan, and Leon Greenburg, *Bureau of Labor Statistics.* Speech before Twenty-first American Assembly, Arden House, New York, May 1962.

4. Clark, Burton R., *Adult Education in Transition: A Study of Institutional Insecurity.* Berkeley, Calif.: University of California Press, 1958.

5. ————, *Educating the Expert Society.* San Francisco, Calif.: Chandler Publishing Company, 1962.

6. Dahl, Robert A., *Who Governs?* New Haven, Conn.: Yale University Press, 1961.

7. *Daytona Beach Morning Journal and Evening News,* August 3, 1963.

8. *Digest of Educational Statistics.* Washington, D.C.: USGPO, 1963.

9. Dotson, George E., "Advantages to the Junior College of 'Common Administration' School Districts," *Journal of Secondary Education,* XXXVIII (March 1963), 148–50.

10. Fromm, Erich, *The Sane Society*. New York: Holt, Rinehart & Winston, Inc., 1955. Pp. 103-30.

11. Galbraith, John K., *The Affluent Society*. Boston: Houghton Mifflin Company, 1950.

12. Gleazer, Edmund J., Jr., *American Junior Colleges,* Washington, D.C.: American Council on Education, 1963.

13. Hall, George L., "Confusion in the Control of the Junior College," *Junior College Journal,* XXXII (April 1962), 432-36.

14. Hertzler, J. O., *Social Institutions*. Lincoln, Neb.: University of Nebraska Press, 1946.

15. Medsker, L. L., *The Junior College*. New York: McGraw-Hill Book Company, 1960.

16. Mills, Thomas J., "National Requirements for Scientists and Engineers: A Second Illustration," in S. J. Mushkin (ed.), *Economics of Higher Education*. Washington, D.C.: USGPO, 1962. Pp. 58-66.

17. Monypenny, Phillip, "A Political Analysis of Structure for Educational Policy Making," in W. P. McLure and Van Miller (eds.), *Government of Public Education for Adequate Policy Making*. Urbana, Ill.: University of Illinois, 1960. Pp. 1-21.

18. Reisman, David, *Faces in the Crowd*. New Haven, Conn.: Yale University Press, 1952.

19. Rossiter, Clinton, "The Democratic Process," in *Goals for Americans*. Englewood Cliffs, N.J.: Prentice-Hall, Inc., 1960. P. 64.

20. *Statistical Abstract of the United States*. Washington, D.C.: USGPO, 1963.

21. Stewart, W. H., "Health Manpower: An Illustration," in S. J. Mushkin (ed.), *Economics of Higher Education*. Washington, D.C.: USGPO, 1962. Pp. 47-57.

22. Watson, Thomas J., Jr., "Technological Change," in *Goals for Americans*. Englewood Cliffs, N.J.: Prentice-Hall, Inc., 1960. P. 196.

23. Williams, Robin M., *American Society: A Sociological Interpretation*. New York: Alfred A. Knopf, Inc., 1951.

24. Wolfbein, S. L., "The Need for Professional Personnel," in S. J. Mushkin (ed.), *Economics of Higher Education*. Washington, D.C.: USGPO, 1962. Pp. 43-46.

The control and financing of both public and private two-year colleges is a direct outgrowth of customs, traditions, and legislation. Elias has pointed out that the confused image of the two-year college appears to be related to state and regional differences in legislation and to the historical development of the institution. If there is one outstanding characteristic of all higher education, it is the wide range of purposes and objectives among colleges, reflecting the particular history from which they have grown. [12:23]

The fact is that the historical antecedents of both public and private education, as well as the social and political aspirations of the people of various sections of the country, differ markedly. Thus, colleges with some aspects in common—curriculum, instruction, and educational purposes—differ in patterns of control and financial support. Each college is designed to serve its purposes successfully, but under different conditions.

Perhaps the lack of a monolithic system of higher education can best be clarified in a statement by Oliver Wendell Holmes:

> The life of the law has not been logic: it has been experience. The felt necessities of the time, the prevalent moral and political theories, intuitions of public policy, avowed or unconscious, even the prejudices which judges

4

control and financing
of the two-year college

share with their fellow men, have had a good deal more to do than the syllogism in determining the rules by which men should be governed. The law embodies the story of a nation's development through many centuries, and it cannot be dealt with as if it contained only the axioms and corollaries of a book of mathematics. In order to know what it is, we must know what it has been, and what it tends to become. We must alternately consult history and existing theories of legislation. But the most difficult labor will be to understand the combination of the new products at every stage. The substance of the law at any given time pretty nearly corresponds, so far as it goes, with what is then understood to be convenient; but its form and machinery, and the degree to which it is able to work out desired results, depend very much upon its past. [17:4]

In the following pages we will analyze the control and finance of both independent and public two-year colleges in a frame of reference encompassing three categories: (1) establishment, (2) control, and (3) finance. These are the foundation upon which all colleges are built. They provide the basis for the initial legal acceptance of the college and for its continuing existence. Although the antecedents of the formal legal framework are custom and tradition, a legal structure formally accepted by the majority of the electorate became necessary for the implementation and perpetuation of the institutional form known as the two-year college.

The Change Process

The American society is a pluralistic society in which multivariant values find expression in the acts of private and public agencies. In private colleges, control is vested in a formally organized group or groups in which the needs and wishes of the members are translated into specific policies and procedures. There are provisions for the communication of these wishes to the elected or appointed members of the governing groups, and these recommendations, in turn, are implemented as the framework within which the college functions.

The same general principles of interaction prevail in government at all levels. The needs that arise in a changing society are translated into laws or administrative regulations which make provisions for the meeting of these needs. Educational policy, like all other group activities of central importance to a majority of citizens, results from a process consisting of stimulus, reaction, and response. This is not necessarily a logical sequence, and the reactions to new demands resulting from changing conditions, therefore, do not necessarily produce logical responses. But there is, for the most part, a cause-and-effect relationship between the educational needs of society and the policies and practices which characterize the two-year college.

I
Educational
policy results   II
from...........Basic social, economic,
                political, and techno-
                logical forces, often
                national and worldwide   III
                in scope, which provide ....Political activity extra-
                                            legal in nature. Many
                                            groups debate and seek
                                            information, and school
                                            leaders exert influence.
                                            These activities, usually
                                            interrelated at local,
                                            state, and national levels,   IV
                                            culminate in ....Formal, legal
                                                                        expression of
                                                                        policy which
                                                                        represents the
                                                                        value choices
                                                                        of influentials
                                                                        who partici-
                                                                        pated in the
                                                                        process.

FIG. 4-1. A Flow Chart of Policy-making in Education

Campbell has outlined the process of change in Fig. 4-1. [8:73]

As will be shown later, checks and balances are built into both private and public organizations. Characteristically, organizations have a number of executive, legislative, and administrative branches which perform related but discrete tasks designed to synthesize the activities of the organization. The principle of separation of powers (with its frequent results: conflict and inefficiency) is well entrenched and will continue to prevail. Decisions are, thus, the outgrowth of compromises rather than the expression of the will of a single individual or group. The filtering process has been aptly illustrated by Russell in Fig. 4-2. [35:77–89]

FIG. 4-2. The Change Process in State Government

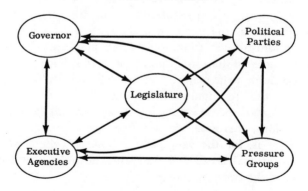

Public Two-year Colleges

The legal development of public two-year colleges began in California in 1907. Since that time, there has been continual legislative activity on behalf of the concept, establishment, control, and finance of the two-year college. The legislation which recognized and encouraged the origin and continuation of two-year colleges can, of course, be understood only in the light of the history, mores, and traditions of a particular state or region. Public community colleges are a part of state systems of education; the speed of their development depended on the basic attitudes of the populace as well as on the absence or presence of numerous and strong four-year colleges, both public and private. Thus, the public community college enjoyed its earliest and most rapid development in the West, while the private junior college grew with most vigor in the Northeast. The past has left its imprint upon the legislation being considered and passed in the state legislatures today.

The development of community college legislation was relatively slow in the early part of this century; however, there has been continual acceleration of legislative activity in every decade since 1900. California was the only state to recognize the two-year college before 1910; and Michigan and Kansas followed suit in 1917. Seven additional states— Arizona, Iowa, Louisiana, Minnesota, Mississippi, Missouri, and Texas —passed similar laws during the decade 1920–29. The trend continued through the 1930's and 1940's, but the most aggressive action has occurred since 1950: fifty-four legislative acts or amendments to existing acts were passed between 1950 and 1959, and sixty from 1960 through 1963.

The state legislatures' rapidly increasing interest and activity on behalf of the two-year college are in direct response to the changing needs of society and the growing demand for the extension and enrichment of educational services. As has been pointed out in Chapter 3, the economic and social pressures generated since World War II have made the expansion of higher education inevitable. Appropriate legislation has been passed at different speeds in the various states, but there has gradually emerged in most states a discernible pattern for the role of the two-year college, and the requirements for its establishment, control, and finance.

Establishment

Legal procedures for the establishment of community colleges first appeared in the California law of 1907:

> The board of trustees of any city, district, union, joint union, or county high school may prescribe postgraduate courses of study for the graduates

of such high school, or other high schools, which courses of study shall approximate the studies prescribed in the first two years of university courses. The board of trustees of any city, district, union, joint union, or county high school wherein the postgraduate courses of study are taught may charge tuition for pupils living without the boundaries of the district wherein such courses are taught. [5:88]

This act was permissive only in that it did not set requirements for the size of the district, provide for state agency approval, or mention financial support. The only requirement for establishment was action by the board of education of the district (there was no reference to approval by the electorate or any other legal body). It was not until the act of 1917 that a minimum tax valuation of $3 million was required for the establishment of a college. A Kansas law of 1917 required, for establishment, both board action and a local election. In 1921, California amended its law to require tax valuation of $10 million for districts made up of one or more high school districts or a county, a minimum of 400 high school students, and approval by a state agency. [7]

The criteria for the establishment of community colleges continued to develop and expand, for by 1929 the following conditions were considered essential for the successful organization and operation of such colleges: [24:118–20, 133–34]

(1)   An enrollment of at least 150 students
(2)   A high school enrollment of at least 900 students
(3)   A district population of at least 17,000
(4)   An assessed valuation of at least $30 million
(5)   A minimum of a two-mill levy on an assessed valuation of $15 million
(6)   A minimum of 50 per cent (or at least $30,000) of the cost of operation supplied by the local district
(7)   A per-student cost of at least $400

The criteria currently advocated for the establishment of colleges are substantially more comprehensive than those of thirty years ago. The criteria now applied on the state level include: [30:12–25]

(1)   General legislative authorization of two-year colleges
(2)   Local action by petition, election, or action by local board of control
(3)   Approval by a state agency
(4)   A minimum assessed valuation considered adequate for sound fiscal support of the college
(5)   A state or local survey to demonstrate the need for the college
(6)   A minimum population of school age
(7)   A minimum total population of the district
(8)   A minimum potential college enrollment within a specified number of years after establishment of the college
(9)   Types of educational programs (curricula) which will be offered

(10) Availability and adequacy of physical facilities
(11) Compliance with state operating policies
(12) Proximity of other institutions

The establishment of a two-year college is no longer a simple and uncomplicated process, particularly in states which have developed a systematic and complete plan for higher education within their boundaries. If educational opportunities are to be made available to all on an economical basis, statewide coordination and planning are essential. The ideal development of two-year colleges—and, for that matter, all institutions of higher education—within a state should follow the steps outlined by the American Association of Junior Colleges (see Fig. 4-3). This

FIG. 4-3. Summary of Steps Leading to the Sound Establishment of a Community Junior College [33:9]

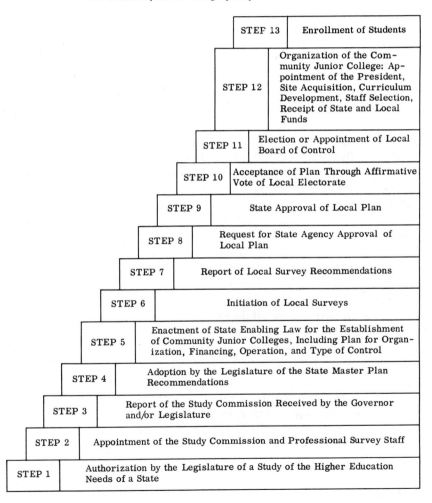

procedure takes into account the many factors which must be considered when the educational resources of the state are expanded in response to changing needs. Each step in this process contributes to the soundness and rationality of new or expanded colleges which will effectively serve the people of the community. This method also has the advantage of developing complete information as to the feasibility of expanded services, as well as that of providing concrete information to individuals and groups concerning the benefits and responsibilities entailed in such expansion. Furthermore, the method clearly fixes the responsibility and authority for support and control of such colleges *before* they are established. It thus eliminates the problem too often encountered among publicly supported services—a desire to have the service but an unwillingness to foot the bill.

Control

Control of the public two-year college rests firmly in the hands of the state. A significant portion of this control, however, is delegated to local boards of control; therefore, both levels must be examined in some detail.

Martorana found that, in the thirty-eight states having two-year colleges, control is implemented through five types of organizations: "(1) the state department of education, (2) the state department or superintendent of education, (3) the state board of higher education, (4) the board of a four-year university, or (5) a separate state junior college board or commission." [23:36] His analysis, which appears in Table 4-1, shows that twenty states control two-year colleges through the state board of education. The second most popular pattern of control (eight states) is through the state board of higher education. Five states channel control through the boards of four-year universities, and six have separate state boards or commissions for community colleges. The majority of states, twenty-six in all, have placed community colleges under the control of the superintendent of education or the state department of education, which is also responsible for all public schools from the first grade through the fourteenth. This indicates that the image of the two-year college as a collegiate institution is not clearly delineated, at least insofar as agency control is concerned. In most instances, however, the department of education usually has a division which is specifically charged with the supervision and control of community colleges.

Table 4-2, on page 84, illustrates significant differences in control of the five types of two-year colleges. Initial control over the private junior college is exercised by the legislature, in that it decides if the college is to be issued a charter and what the conditions in the charter are to be. Fur-

TABLE 4-1. State Agency Responsible for Supervision and Coordination of Junior Colleges

State	State Board of Education	State Department or Super-intendent of Education	State Board of Higher Education	Board of Four-year State University	Separate State Junior College Board or Commission
Alabama	x				
Alaska				x	
Arizona					x
California	x				
Colorado	x				
Connecticut	x				
Florida	x				
Georgia			x		
Idaho	x				
Illinois		x			
Iowa		x[1]	x[1]		
Kansas	x				
Kentucky				x	
Louisiana		x			
Maryland	x				
Massachusetts					x
Michigan	x				
Minnesota	x				
Mississippi					x
Missouri	x				
Montana	x				
Nebraska		x			x[2]
New Hampshire	x				
New Jersey	x				
New Mexico			x[3]	x	
New York			x		
North Carolina			x		
North Dakota	x[1]		x[1]		
Ohio				x[4]	x[2]
Oklahoma	x[1]		x[1]		
Oregon	x				
Rhode Island			x		
South Carolina		x			
Texas		x			
Washington	x				
West Virginia	x[1]			x[1]	
Wisconsin	x[5]				
Wyoming					x
Total number of states	20	6	8	5	6

[1] Responsibility between two state agencies
[2] For area community colleges only
[3] For fiscal matters only
[4] For two-year branch colleges only
[5] State board of vocational and adult education

TABLE 4-2. Levels and Types of Control of Two-year Colleges

Level	Private Junior College	Public Community College	University Branch and Extension Center	State Community College	Technical Institute (Public)
Federal	No direct control	No direct control	No direct control	No direct control	No direct control
State legislature	Grant charter	Enabling legislation	Enabling legislation	Enabling legislation	Enabling legislation
State administrative office	Standards of minimum quality	Establishment and state regulations	No direct control	Establishment and state regulations	Establishment and state regulations
State board of control	No control	Promulgates regulations	No control (regents of university)	Direct control	Varies
Local board of control	Direct control	Direct control within legal limitations	None	None	Varies
Local administration and faculty	Supervised control under board	Supervised control under board	Little control (policies formulated by the university)	Supervised control under state board	Varies

thermore, the legislature can revoke the charter if the college violates the provisions therein or refuses to abide by its legal acts. Some states also impose educational requirements on the college, although such regulations are limited in scope and do not infringe upon the right of a private school to impose requirements upon students according to its stated objectives or denominational biases.

Public community colleges are under the direction of a number of state bodies and the local board of control. In contrast, branches and extension centers of state colleges and universities are directly controlled by the institution's board of regents. The same general pattern of control is found in state community colleges, whose policies and procedures are established by the state board of control. There is no clear pattern for the control of technical institutes in those states in which such institutes exist. Some are partially controlled by local boards while others are under the direct supervision of the state.

These differences in control are important, in that change and adaptation to shifting local requirements and conditions can take place more rapidly and effectively when local boards and administration and faculty are closely related to policy formulation and implementation. The further removed the controlling group, the slower the process of change and the less responsive the governing group to the needs of the students and the community.

The kinds of external legal control upon colleges have no consistent pattern among the states, in that the legal framework and administrative powers delegated to state agencies range widely from state to state. Nevertheless, there are some aspects of college control that are general and widespread. They include:

(1) Conditions for the establishment of the college
(2) Prescription of courses to be offered
(3) Operation and control of the college by a state agency
(4) Certification of faculty members and administrators
(5) Prescription of fiscal procedures and policies
(6) Standards for accreditation
(7) Controls over budgets, admissions policies, tuition charges, physical facilities, educational standards

The actual operation of a state board of control for a two-year college does not necessarily meet the ideal patterns laid out in the policy statements defining its areas of responsibility. A representative group of board members had this to say about the problems of state control of two-year colleges:

(1) The state board has responsibility for interpreting junior colleges and their needs to the legislature and the people of the state.

(2) The board should make certain that their activities stimulate [the] confidence of professional educators and the public in junior colleges and their programs. Unless the board develops an image of fairness and leadership in the eyes of those working within colleges and those supporting the colleges, there is little chance of developing an outstanding state program and widespread support from the public.

(3) There is difficulty in persuading the junior colleges in a state that they should conform to general policies and direction from the state level, and that they must be responsive to the changing needs of society. The enactment of policies and procedures on the state level does not necessarily assure the compliance of individual institutions with such policies with reasonable consistency.

(4) Too many junior colleges have aspirations to become four-year institutions, with the result that they give the impression that they do not believe in the essential value of two-year educational programs.

(5) There is little agreement [about] the "best" type of organization of junior colleges—e.g., K–14 districts, independent districts, or state junior colleges. It was pointed out that the traditions of a state will determine, to a large extent, the type of organization which will become the pattern for that particular state. Whatever pattern is adopted should encourage maximum continuity of educational programs from the secondary schools through the junior college and on into the four-year colleges and universities. [2:93]

There were some sharp contrasts between the opinions of local board members and those of representatives of state boards. The most important differences centered around the concept that the state board, or an administrative branch of state government, should codify and enforce policies and procedures with regard to finance, buildings, curricula, personnel, and other administrative matters. Members of local boards maintained that the duly elected representatives of the local district should have latitude in the development and supervision of such matters. Furthermore, local board members felt that there could be more flexible programs and more appropriate institutional responses to community needs if there were a minimum of control from the state level.

The advantages of state direction, as enunciated by state board members, included a more consistent statewide pattern of educational opportunities, more consistent quality of programs and teaching faculty, more economical operation and capital construction programs and more adequate articulation of educational programs on all levels.

Controlling groups and agencies

Legal controls are not confined to the state legislature and the administrative agencies primarily concerned with this responsibility. Depending upon the structure of local and state government, there are several agencies which impose direct or indirect controls and influences upon the college. In some states, there are direct relationships among municipal or county governmental units regarding finance and other aspects of college operation. In Texas, for example, the county government may be responsible for the collection of local taxes levied by the board of control. In New York, the local share of financial support must be approved by the county board of supervisors as a part of the county budget.

**TABLE 4-3.   Legal Groups and Agencies
Influencing and/or Controlling Public Two-year Colleges**

Level	Legal	Policy and Administrative
Local	Board of control Municipalities The courts County government	Board of control College administration Faculty

State	The legislature
	The executive
	The courts
		State department of education
		Board of regents
		Superintendent of public instruction
		State junior college board
		Four-year state university:
		  Executive departments
		  (Budget, Health, and so on)

National	The Congress The executive The courts	Executive departments

The executive branch, on both the state and national levels, influences the activities of the college through policy and procedural decisions. Thus, the attorney general of the state might decide that community college programs are of secondary school, rather than collegiate, level—a decision that would determine for which kinds of federal financial support the programs are eligible. Court decisions also have a direct bearing upon the work of the college: they determine the legality of the institution's existence and of those of its practices and procedures that might be questioned by other organizations or by individual citizens.

The influence of the federal government, because of Constitutional limitations, is indirect, but this is not to say that federal influence is unimportant. First, the federal interest in education has been rapidly widening in scope, particularly since 1940. This interest grew out of war needs during the early 1940's, and has been stimulated further by national scientific and technical demands in recent years. Second, federal influence has been exerted through the government's financial support of specialized programs such as the Veterans' Rehabilitation Act, the Manpower Retraining Act, student grant and loan programs, distribution of surplus property to colleges and universities, direct aid for construction and equipment, direct aid for language and science programs, and vocational programs.

Federal aid to two-year colleges is significant in that it has made possible the implementation of programs beyond the scope of available local and state support; however, such aid can be criticized on the basis that it is too specific and has a tendency to distort college programs and curricula. The untoward emphasis upon languages and sciences is a case in point. Other subject-matter areas need assistance, too, but they have not had adequate financial backing and attention. On the other hand, legislation for the expansion and improvement of technical and vocational education has moved many two-year colleges into programs which they should have developed before federal support was made available.

Control is not the only function carried on by state agencies on behalf of two-year colleges; equally important are the coordinating functions which integrate and relate the functions and services of educational institutions above and below the level of the community college. Such coordination is important both for economic and for educational reasons and is receiving increasing attention from the colleges as well as from state agencies.

Such coordination can be of major importance with regard to: [24:17–29]

(1) Coordination of curriculum with both secondary schools and four-year colleges
(2) Extension of college guidance services to area high school students
(3) Participation in the development of clearly defined roles for two-year colleges in order to insure more effective liaison and cooperation between two- and four-year colleges
(4) Stimulation of interinstitutional coordination among two-year colleges:
    (a) Development of standards for the establishment of two-year colleges within a statewide plan
    (b) Supervision of colleges' fiscal management
    (c) Stimulation and coordination of program development
    (d) The staffing of two-year colleges
(5) Coordination of colleges with agencies of the federal government

The local board of control of the public college has complete authority and responsibility—within the legal limits drawn by the state—for the organization and operation of the institution. The duties and responsibilities of the board are usually spelled out in detail in legislation, in administrative directives from governmental agencies, and in court decisions. The private college board enjoys greater latitude in its responsibilities and activities; however, it, too, must adhere to the limitations imposed through its state-issued charter.

The responsibilities of the board are: [11:53–57]

(1)   To select the president
(2)   To oversee and approve the educational program
(3)   To protect and promote institutional public relations
(4)   To acquire, conserve, and manage funds and properties

It has often been said that the most important of these four functions is the selection of the president, for he is the professional educational leader of the college and his success or failure will largely determine the future of the college. Although the college needs the services of the right kind of president at the right time, it would seem that the other three responsibilities of the board are of equal importance: their neglect endangers the quality of the educational program and the relationships between the college and the community.

The local board members themselves hold a somewhat different perspective. They recognize the breadth of their responsibilities, but their understanding of their roles in relation to the college is somewhat different from the perceptions of the administration and faculty.

Members of community college boards defined the functions and responsibilities of the board as: [2:92]

(1)   To select the college president
(2)   To create a favorable public image of the college in the community
(3)   To establish cooperative relations between the administration and the board
(4)   To work toward more adequate support of the college through local and legislative action
(5)   To provide a bridge between the college and the community
(6)   To approve clear-cut policies for the operation of the college, which are developed, recommended, and implemented by the president
(7)   To protect the administration and the college from unreasonable pressures from the community (the protection of academic freedom is a primary responsibility of the board)
(8)   To develop and maintain faculty morale and quality teaching through the development of fiscal policies, salary schedules, fringe benefits, and personnel policies which attract and hold outstanding teachers
(9)   Periodically to review and approve the philosophy and objectives of the college, and to make certain that the philosophy is flexible and that the institution is moving toward its objectives
(10)   To control the college—a function that should not be transferred to a state or higher body

The members believed the board should not appoint any college personnel other than the president. The responsibility for choosing all subordinate personnel must lie with the president, for he must have an administrative and academic team with which he can successfully work.

There was a lack of unanimity among board members regarding the question of having the junior college as a part of a K–14 organization. Opinion seemed to be split between those who worked with independent junior colleges and those whose colleges were a part of unified districts.

Some faculty members would confine the responsibilities of the board to the selection of the president and the over-all supervision of fiscal affairs, maintaining that laymen should not have extensive control of or contact with the educational program of the college. This attitude is substantiated by a study of seven community colleges, in which the relationships among faculty members were analyzed. The study showed that members of the boards of control were not involved or influential in curriculum development and change. The faculty members considered the members of the board to be influential in general policy development, but not important in the educational affairs of the college.

This point of view seems quite unrealistic when one considers the legal responsibilities of the board. The issue here is whether the board should function as the bridge between the college and the community, or whether such interactions should be the exclusive province of administrators and faculty members. The board of control occupies a strategic position between the external forces which make demands upon the college and the need of the college for stability and integrity.

Perhaps the most important function of the board is to mediate the conflicting and often contradictory expectations of external groups:

> ... board members should be sensitive to the desires, aspirations, and judgments of the people, recognizing that after all the conversation, comments, commendations, and complaints have been heard, they themselves must ultimately serve as umpire[s] and resolve the arguments, because it is their responsibility to do so. [37:7]

The most persistent problem with regard to the role of the board of control is the development of policies which encourage excellence in administration and teaching. There is no clear-cut line separating policy decisions from the implementation of those decisions. Thus, there is always the possibility that board members will intrude upon the responsibilities of the college administration rather than confine their attention to the development of over-all policy and the evaluation of the organization as a whole. The intrusion of the board into routine administrative decision-making could destroy the effectiveness of the organization more quickly than any other factor. The board's attention to the minutiae of administration will undermine the morale of the chief executive officer, subordinate administrators, and the faculty, and eventually lower the quality of the educational program.

Finance

The pattern of financial support of two-year colleges varies, both among the different states and among the colleges within certain states. Operating funds are derived from three sources: state aid, local taxes, and tuition fees. A few colleges also derive income from endowment funds, gifts, and auxiliary services; however, such income sources are enjoyed by a relatively small number of institutions and are not a significant factor nationally. One of the exceptions is Flint Community Junior College which has a permanent endowment in excess of $5 million.

State aid for operating costs varies from none to 100 per cent. In their study of forty-two states, Morrison and Martorana found three internal and comparative differences in the amount of state support to two-year colleges (see Table 4-4). Morrison and Martorana conclude that:

> In general, the extension centers, branches, and state two-year colleges, whether junior colleges or technical institutes, receive a higher percentage of support from state sources than do the local or municipal junior colleges. This is especially evident in those states in which there is more than one type of two-year college.
>
> Excluding the seven . . . states with no tuition and the two with no specific patterns, therefore, with varying levels of tuition requirements, there are a total of forty-eight different state patterns showing some support received from student tuition. Approximately three fourths of these, regardless of type, receive one half or less from tuition; approximately two thirds receive one third or less; and 40 per cent receive less than one fourth from tuition. [31:19]

State funds for operational costs are supplied in two ways: by formula or through grants. The formula method is generally based upon student attendance, minimum foundation principle, instructional units, academic hours taken or completed, or the number of full-time equated students enrolled.* Grants are based upon the appropriation of funds by the legislature and divided among the colleges on the basis of the administrative regulations imposed by the controlling state agency. Twenty-three states use a formula for state aid; five use the grant method. Eight states provide no aid of any kind. [23:39–40]

Local support is derived from local funds appropriated by school districts or county government, or from tax levies authorized by state

---

* The minimum foundation program in most states provides a predetermined number of dollars for each student. Full-time equated students are defined as units obtained by dividing the number of academic hours taken by part-time students by either 12 or 15.

TABLE 4-4. Per Cent of Operational Costs Derived
from State, Local, and Tuition Sources,
by Number of States, 1960–61 [31:16–19]

Source	Type of Institution	100	75–99	50–74	25–49	1–25	None
State	Community college (local control)			3	14	4	8
	Community college (state control)		6	4			
	Junior college (private)				1		
	Two-year branch of college or university	1	4	3	1	1	1
	Technical institute	2		2			
	Two-year county teachers college			1			
	Extension center of college or university						
Local	Community college (local control)	2	2		12	7	
	Community college (state control)						
	Junior college (private)						
	Two-year branch of college or university						
	Technical institute						
	Two-year county teachers college				1		
	Extension center of college or university						1
Tuition	Community college (local control)		2	3	14	7	3
	Community college (state control)				4	6	
	Junior college (private)			1			
	Two-year branch of college or university	1	1	2	1	4	1
	Technical institute			1	1		2
	Two-year county teachers college					1	
	Extension center of college or university						

law or local election. Only four states use the appropriations method for the acquisition of local funds; twenty-eight states authorize local tax levies. Three states have no local taxes earmarked for the support of the two-year colleges.

Capital outlay

Provisions for state aid for capital expenditures are somewhat more clear-cut than provisions for support of current operational expenses. Most states either supply all the funds for campus construction and equipment, or none at all. Support patterns vary within particular states according to the type of two-year college. Some receive substantial state aid; others, little or none. Support of capital expenditures is not as firmly established a state responsibility as is aid for current operations, in spite of the fact that physical facilities are essential to the proper and effective functioning of the colleges. The history of two-year colleges appears to have given rise to the assumption that they can function effectively in physical facilities which include high school and elementary school buldings and similar structures formerly used for other purposes. This assumption is, of course, erroneous.

Table 4-5 demonstrates that, with only a few exceptions, states have not assumed responsibility for the provision of physical facilities for local junior colleges. The contrast among the local colleges, state junior colleges, technical institutes, and branches is most striking. It is apparent that state legislatures have been more favorably disposed to providing capital outlay funds to state-controlled two-year colleges, technical institutes, and university branches and extension centers. In twenty-two states, all the capital funds for these colleges are supplied from the state level. In only one state is 100 per cent of these funds supplied to locally controlled colleges. In contrast, twenty states supply no capital outlay monies to locally controlled colleges, one supplies 14 per cent; three, 50 per cent; one, 76 per cent.

TABLE 4-5. State Patterns for the Provision of Capital Outlay Funds for Two-year Colleges [31:27]

State Aid (Per Cent)	Local Aid (Per Cent)	Local Junior College	State Junior College	Technical Institute	Branch, Extension Center	Other	All Two-year Colleges
None	100	20			4	5	29
14	86	1					1
50	50	3					3
76	24	1					1
100	None	1	9	5	8		23
Variable by years		1					1

These practices account for the wide differences of physical plant values per student among four-year colleges, private junior colleges, and public two-year colleges. In 1960, public two-year colleges had $1817 in physical facilities for each student; public four-year institutions had $4815; and private two-year colleges had $4507. [13:79] It is doubtful that community college programs can be substantially improved and expanded to meet current and future demands for post-high school education if the colleges continue to depend upon local financial resources for the replacement and expansion of buildings and essential instructional equipment.

The Independent Junior College

Independent two-year colleges, as classified by the American Association of Junior Colleges, include church-related, proprietary-nonprofit, and proprietary-profit institutions. These colleges may be traditional transfer institutions with comprehensive programs, or they may have a particular social or occupational emphasis. In 1962, there were 278 such colleges, with a total enrollment of 105,535 students. [1:30] Born during the first third of the nineteenth century, the independent junior college was a natural outgrowth of the pressures created by the westward migration and joined the large number of nonpublic four-year colleges already in existence.

The private college won legal acceptance early in the history of this country. Court decisions and constitutional law emphasize the right of any group or individual, within certain broad limitations, to establish and operate colleges dedicated to advancing the purposes and objectives of that individual or group.

Establishment

Independent colleges may be established under the statutes of the various states. Generally, an authorized executive office of the state receives the application for the charter for the college—an application which must meet the legal requirements outlined in the statute. If the group has indicated legally acceptable purposes, the charter is granted without question. At the time the college is organized, a corporation is established, thus making it possible for the board of control to hold and convey property and to make contracts with individuals and business organizations.

An example of a state charter granted to a denominational institution is that of Mars Hill College, North Carolina. This charter was originally passed by the state legislature in 1859. [26:266–69] The charter, as amended, contains these principal statements:

(1)   The college is a corporation.
(2)   The property of the college shall be exempt from taxation.
(3)   The number of trustees shall not be less than a certain minimum or more than a certain maximum.
(4)   The faculty has the authority to confer degrees, with the consent of the trustees.
(5)   The college may hold and convey property.
(6)   The trustees have the authority to appoint, direct, and remove the college president.
(7)   At least twenty-one of the twenty-five trustees must be members of the Baptist denomination.
(8)   Hazing in any form is prohibited.
(9)   The trustees shall "conduct the affairs of the college in the best manner possible for the promotion of scientific and literary research, moral and Christian education, as fostered by the Baptist denomination. . . ."

Control

Church-related colleges are ultimately controlled by the governing board of the church itself. In the case of Mars Hill College, final control of the college rests with the Baptist Convention of North Carolina. Such a pattern of control is typical of Baptist colleges in other states, also. The colleges under the auspices of the Roman Catholic Church may be under the control of a bishop or of the leader of a particular order; however, these individuals are responsible to higher councils within the Church on matters of central significance to the Church.

The organization of the Lutheran Church, Missouri Synod, provides another typical example of the national organization of a church-related and church-controlled system of higher education. The organization and functions of the various levels of the Church with respect to higher education appear in Fig. 4-4. [16: Sec. 6.01–6.169]

It should be noted that this particular organization insures a broad base of lay and clerical participation in the operation of the colleges. There is sufficient breadth of power in both groups to assure an effective response to changing needs and conditions which impinge upon the colleges within the system. The relative autonomy of the boards of control within the broad purposes and objectives laid down by the related church makes it possible for them to evolve policies and approve administrative procedures which are relevant to the needs of a particular institution. This distribution of power among many individuals, groups, and committees is the very antithesis of monolithic control by an entrenched bureaucracy.

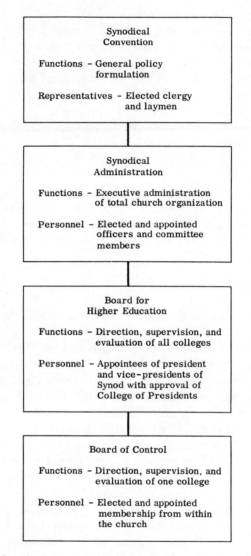

FIG. 4-4. Organization and Control of Lutheran Colleges

The controlling boards of nondenominational colleges function under a charter or articles of incorporation granted by the state, and they are usually self-perpetuating (that is, new members are selected and appointed by the existing members). Thus, the board of control has continuity in terms of the kinds of individuals who are members and the socioeconomic levels from which they come. Such boards range in size from fewer than ten to more than thirty-five.

The boards of control of such colleges have broad powers of policy-making and control. They are responsible for finance, faculty policies, educational programs, student welfare, the physical plant, and the over-all supervision of the affairs of the college. Within broad legal limits, the board of control can develop and implement any policy requirement consistent with the purposes of the college. In this way, it shapes the college with respect to educational programs, types of students, and the orientation of faculty members.

Independent two-year colleges select board members with several important objectives in mind. The attitudes of these individuals toward the college and its educational purposes must be such as to foster the continuation of its basic philosophy and purposes and engender broad understanding and support for them both within and outside the institution. Denominational colleges generally have boards made up both of clergymen and of lay members of the church. Such a variety insures communication and continuity of church doctrine between the mother church and the college. Both denominational and nondenominational colleges select board members who can provide high-level leadership, add status and prestige, and provide strong financial support.

Board members of private colleges come from upper socioeconomic levels and are characterized by extensive education, high personal income, and a high status. Many colleges make it clear that board members must be able and willing to contribute money to the college and also to spend some time encouraging others to support either the annual budget or the capital development program of the college.

One of the more significant implications of board membership is the congruence of the values professed by the college and those of board members. Thus, board members should have a commitment to the values of private education. Furthermore, the college must create a frame of reference or climate for students and faculty which is consistent with the values and mores of the members of the board. In this way, both the board members and the college are assured of the perpetuation of attitudes and values which both hold important. Such values may not be consistent with those of the society as a whole, but they constitute the justification for the continued existence of private colleges.

Such boards can control the educational environment of the colleges they serve much more completely than can the boards of public institutions. The legal basis for the private college, the charter granted by the state, provides that the board will have complete powers of management, will have the authority to appoint administrators, and will not be subject to the checks and balances which are imposed upon public boards. [34:15] Because it has such broad powers, the board of a private college can control the curriculum, the instruction, student-personnel services, finance, and all the other manifold functions and activities in which the college is involved. This control is exerted, for the most part, through the appointment and supervision of the president and administrative staff.

Finance

Independent colleges have three major sources of income: tuition fees, endowment income, and annual gifts. A high proportion of the total current expenditures of private two-year colleges comes from tuition charges and other student fees. The average sum paid for tuition and fees by full-time students in 1961–62 was $542. [4:5] These colleges held total endowment funds of $42.097 million in 1960. [13:80] It is apparent that the endowment income for these colleges, in most cases, is not sufficient to provide more than a small percentage of the total funds necessary to meet annual operating expenses. The third source of income—current gifts—is used to supplement other sources of income in the private college. Approximately one fourth of the colleges solicit gifts from alumni and friends each year. [32:91]

Timmins has pointed out that private colleges depend heavily upon gifts from many sources. [37:3–6] These sources include corporations, religious denominations, alumni, members of governing boards, friends of the college, and foundations. These colleges also benefit from a variety of state and federal programs; e. g., loans for construction of dormitories.

Gifts for capital purposes are extremely important to independent two-year colleges. These institutions are subject to more restrictions in attempts to borrow money and to float bond issues than are public colleges. It is necessary, therefore, for them to raise funds for buildings and campus development from private sources. In some instances, the college will amortize buildings by issuing bonds, pledging the income from the buildings (usually dormitories) for a designated period of years. Some colleges also use a portion of the tuition paid by students to pay for new construction. It is difficult, however, for a college to complete extensive construction projects without support from gifts. The success of private colleges in obtaining capital funds is indicated by their total physical plant value: $251.514 million—or $4507 per student. [13:79]

The significance of income from gifts has been pointed up by Floyd Elkins of Hinds Junior College, who analyzed the amount of support given to denominational and nondenominational junior colleges. He found that 87 denominational colleges received a total of $30.073 million during 1960–63. Fifty-four nondenominational colleges received $13.890 million in gifts during the same period.

Church-supported colleges received from $391 to $1443 annually per student during the three-year period. Colleges not related to churches did not enjoy quite as much support per student—from $56 to $334 annu-ally—but these amounts made the difference between financial solvency and program retrenchment.

Widespread interest in the welfare of private junior colleges is dem-onstrated by the sources of gifts to these institutions. Religious denomina-tions, of course, contributed heavily to the colleges existing within their particular organizational framework. In the over-all picture, however, private institutions received generous and sustained support from alumni, individuals, business and industry, foundations, and other sources. Indi-vidual contributions accounted for the largest gross sum received, business and industry made the second largest contributions, and foundations ranked third in their support of private colleges.

Trends in Legal Control

The pace and content of legislative activity during the last decade has wrought many changes in the public two-year college. The mere fact that legislators are paying greater attention to the needs of these colleges indicates the quickening interest in and the more enthusiastic response to broader concepts and services in post-high school education. Thus the first trend discernible in the legal status of two-year colleges is a more comprehensive definition of the relationships between such institutions and the state. As has been shown, interest in the two-year college developed slowly during the early decades of this century. But since 1950, there has been a marked acceleration in the study and develop-ment of public community colleges.

In many states, recent legislation has not only dealt with specific problems of control, administration, and finance, but has also included a more comprehensive and clear delineation of the educational role of the two-year college. Although this trend is somewhat uneven, there is evidence that most states are looking to the two-year college as a compre-hensive institution which will make available a wide range of educational services to individuals of all ages. The roles of the secondary schools and of the four-year colleges and universities, while still flexible, have been reasonably well established in past years. And state legislation and regu-latory statements bear out the fact that the two-year college, too, is be-ginning to be accepted as a state responsibility and as an essential part of the total public educational system.

The attention which has been focused upon higher education in recent years has also stimulated a trend toward statewide study and planning of public educational institutions—from the elementary through the graduate levels. Surveys of state educational needs are now readily accepted as an essential part of the over-all development of education.

Such surveys provide the basis for definitive legislative action in the establishment, support, and direction of two-year colleges. The results of such surveys have also demonstrated that the two-year college is essential as a part of the over-all state system of post-high school education.

In the area of finance, there has been a discernible trend toward increased state financial support of the operational costs of two-year colleges. Furthermore, such increases have also been made in funds for capital expenditures. Although this pattern is not clear and uniform among the various states, the trend appears to be toward the state's providing the largest share of operational costs, local taxes supplying the second largest share, and tuition bearing the smallest share of such expenses. State support for capital outlay has been somewhat slower in developing. Nevertheless, consistent progress has been made toward the sharing of these costs by local and state sources.

Federal agencies have displayed far more interest in the problems and potential of two-year colleges during the past fifteen years. The U.S. Office of Education has recognized the importance of community colleges in many published studies and by the inclusion of relevant statistical information in other publications concerned with higher education. In the past, federal statutes classified two-year colleges as part of secondary education. In contrast, recent federal legislation has recognized the two-year college as an essential part of higher education. Furthermore, there have been specific provisions for federal aid to two-year institutions within the same general principles which previously had been applied only to four-year colleges and universities.

There has been a continuing trend toward more complete state control and coordination of all higher education, and this development has had important implications for two-year colleges. State legislation has become more specific and prescriptive and the regulations promulgated by state administrative agencies have further restricted the flexibility of community colleges in many states. Such activity has, as its purpose, the development of a more efficient and effective state system of post-high school education—a system which avoids overlapping, duplication, and the unnecessary dispersion of financial resources.

Problems

Despite the great progress which has been made by many states in the encouragement of public two-year colleges, there remain several important problems, some of which exist because of the absence of needed legislation and some of which have grown out of the limited perceptions incorporated into state laws. In the area of finance, one of the most important continuing problems is the equating of junior college costs with those of elementary and secondary schools. Although there are exceptions, many states continue to provide funds on the basis of formulas and grants equivalent to those of the public schools. This method of financing tacitly implies that the cost of junior college education should be equal to that of elementary and secondary education. This assumption is erroneous: the community colleges are expected to provide transfer courses of a quality comparable to that of courses offered in four-year colleges, and also technical and vocational courses which require expensive equipment and low student-teacher ratios. Two-year colleges will continue to be handicapped as long as they do not receive —from state aid, tuition, and local taxes—financial support equivalent to that accorded the lower-division baccalaureate program in a four-year college.

Many states continue to use awkward and complicated formulas as a basis for providing state funds. The average-daily-attendance method is both time-consuming and expensive, and it is not generally used as a basis for providing funds for state colleges and universities. There is little justification for this method in post-high school education. The savings which would result from a simple count of full-time equated students three weeks after the beginning of each semester could be used to improve the educational programs of the colleges. The situation is complicated further by peculiar aspects of some state laws. In one state, for example, funds are provided on the number of academic hours completed by each student rather than on the number of hours undertaken. In another, legislation prohibits the payment of state aid for part-time students. Still another imposes complicated restrictions upon the application of state funds for educational programs.

Another serious weakness is the lack, in twenty states, of any state support for capital outlay purposes. Physical facilities and equipment are used for the education of individuals who may eventually live in any portion of the state or the United States. Campus development requires large outlays of funds which, in many instances, are beyond the scope of the local community. The unfairness of such laws is even more clearly demonstrated when local community colleges are compared with state colleges, technical institutes, branches, and extension centers, which for the most part build their campuses entirely with state monies. This seems to be clear discrimination between local two-year colleges and those controlled from the state level. The authors can only conclude that, in the absence of effective state-level remedies, colleges will have to depend upon large federal grants for buildings and equipment.

There has been an unjustifiable amount of legislative and administrative intrusion into the curriculum. There must be some very general state control of course work and curriculum patterns. On the other hand, the prescription of specific courses and the arbitrary exclusion (by law) of other courses tends to stultify and to inhibit the two-year college. In one state, for example, two-year colleges cannot receive state funds for courses which do not appear in the catalogs of four-year colleges or universities. Furthermore, a sequence of social science courses is prescribed by law, and students who do not complete the sequence may not be granted a degree or certificate. Curriculum construction and the delineation of course content, within certain broad limits, should be the prerogative of the local board of control, the administration, and the faculty of the college.

There has been a discernible trend toward more stringent administrative direction and control at the state level. Some of this control is the outgrowth of legislation, but a large part of it appears to have its genesis in Parkinson's Law and the lack of a clear distinction between state and local responsibility for two-year colleges. For example, in those states which make provisions for capital outlay, there has been a mushrooming of rules and regulations regarding instruction, the design of buildings, and the kinds of equipment which can be placed in them. In at least one state, all courses must be submitted to the state governing agency for approval before state funds will be authorized for annual operating purposes. Agency approval must be obtained for the title of the course, a description of its contents, and a detailed statement of its purposes. This trend seems to indicate that state administrative groups have misconstrued their obligation for educational leadership, taking it to mean responsibility for control and direction of colleges in the most minute detail.

Another weakness in state legislation is the lack of a decision regarding the transformation of two-year colleges to four-year colleges. This is a continuing problem in states which have not taken definite action on this question. It results in political maneuvering at each legislative session, with consequent debilitation of all two-year colleges within the state.

Last, federal legislation for specific educational programs has tended to distort and unbalance the curricula in two-year colleges. The financial support of foreign languages and sciences has been beneficial in a narrow sense, in that these areas needed additional financial support. However, the over-all effect of such support has been to weaken other essential sectors of the curricula. Thus the achievement of the ideal of the general education for all students can become an acute administrative and educational problem for two-year colleges.

In summary, it is apparent that there are numerous cooperating and competing legal bodies on the local, state, and federal levels which affect the development and functioning of two-year colleges. Historically,

Americans are unwilling to define authority relations for decision-making in their organizations. The two-year college is no exception. There are conflicts between the proponents of local control and those advocating state-level control, and both groups feel the impact of federal direction—however indirect it may be—through financial aid. There are decided differences among groups with respect to the values and objectives being sought, and these differences lead to power struggles within the system. In many instances, such struggles seriously reduce the productivity of the educational institution, distracting the energies and attention of educational personnel from the primary purposes of the college. Although there seems to be some progress toward a more rational and mutual coordination of effort, much remains to be done to improve the effective cooperation of authority groups on all three levels and to guide them toward the development of generally acceptable educational goals.

Bibliography

1. Barnett, W. H., *Qualifications and Philosophy of Education of Public Junior College Board Members.* Unpublished doctoral dissertation presented at the University of Texas, Austin, Texas, 1953.

2. Blocker, C. E., "Role of the Board of Control: A Summary," *Selected Papers,* 43rd Annual Convention, American Association of Junior Colleges, Seattle, Washington, 1963. Pp. 91–93.

3. _____, and H. A. Campbell, Jr., *Administrative Practices in University Extension Centers and Branch Colleges.* Austin, Tex.: University of Texas, 1963.

4. Bokelman, W. R., and L. A. D'Amico, *Higher Education: Basic Student Charges, 1961–62.* Washington, D.C.: USGPO, 1962.

5. California Statutes 1907, c. 69, p. 88.

6. California Statutes 1907, c. 69, p. 88, and 1921, c. 477, p. 724.

7. California Statutes 1921, c. 477, p. 714.

8. Campbell, Ronald P., "Processes of Policy-making Within Structures of Educational Government: As Viewed by the Educator," in W. P. McLure and Van Miller (eds.), *Government of Public Education for Adequate Policy-making.* Urbana, Ill.: University of Illinois Press, 1960. Pp. 59–76.

9. Clark, Burton R., *Educating the Expert Society.* San Francisco: Chandler Publishing Company, 1962.

10. Connecticut Public Acts 1959, c. 232, p. 554.

11. Corson, J. J., *Governance of Colleges and Universities.* New York: McGraw-Hill Book Company, 1960.

12. Elias, Lloyd J., "Suggested Research Related to 'The National Image of the Public Community Junior College,'" *Conference Proceedings,* State Directors of Junior Colleges and Coordinators of State Systems of Two-year Colleges. Washington, D.C.: USGPO, October 1961.

13. *Digest of Educational Statistics.* Washington, D.C.: USGPO, 1963.

14. Galbraith, John K., *The Affluent Society.* Boston: Houghton Mifflin Company, 1958.

15. Hall, George L., "Confusion in the Control of the Junior College," *Junior College Journal,* XXXII (April 1962), 432-36.

16. *Handbook of the Lutheran Church.* St. Louis: Missouri Synod, 1963.

17. Holmes, Oliver Wendell, Jr., *The Common Law.* Boston: Little, Brown & Co., 1881

18. Hyman, Herbert H., "The Value Systems of Different Classes: A Social Psychological Contribution to the Analysis of Stratification," in Reinhard Bendix and S. M. Lipset (eds.), *Class, Status, and Power.* New York: Free Press of Glencoe, Inc., 1953. Pp. 426-41.

19. Iffert, R. E., *Retention and Withdrawal of College Students.* Washington, D.C.: USGPO, 1957.

20. Jensen, Gale, "Power Struggles in Educational Systems, *The University of Michigan School of Education Bulletin,* XXXIV (October 1962), 2-6.

21. *Junior College Directory.* Washington, D.C.: American Association of Junior Colleges, 1963.

22. Kansas Laws 1917, c. 283, p. 410.

23. Martorana, S. V., "The Legal Status of American Public Junior Colleges," in *American Junior Colleges.* Washington, D.C.: American Council on Education, 1963. Pp. 31-47.

24. _____ (ed.), *Coordinating Two-year Colleges in State Educational Systems.* Washington, D.C.: USGPO, 1957.

25. McCabe, Robert H., *The Influence Structures in Curriculum Matters Within Six Southwestern Junior Colleges.* Unpublished doctoral dissertation presented at the University of Texas, Austin, Texas, 1964.

26. McLeod, John A., *From These Stones.* Mars Hill, N.C.: Mars Hill College, 1955.

27. Medsker, L. L., *The Junior College.* New York: McGraw-Hill Book Company, 1960.

28. Mississippi Law 1928, c. 70, p. 86.

29. Monypenny, Phillip, "A Political Analysis of Structure for Educational Policy-making," in W. P. McLure and Van Miller (eds.), *Government of Public Education for Adequate Policy-making.* Urbana, Ill.: University of Illinois, 1960. Pp. 1-21.

30. Morrison, D. G., and S. V. Martorana, *Criteria for the Establishment of Two-year Colleges.* Washington, D.C.: USGPO, 1960.

31. _____, *State Formulas for the Support of Public Two-year Colleges*. Washington, D.C.: USGPO, 1962.

32. Pollard, John A., *Fund-raising for Higher Education*. New York: Harper & Row, Publishers, 1958.

33. *Principles of Legislative Action for Community Junior Colleges*. Washington, D.C.: American Association of Junior Colleges, 1962.

34. Raub, M. A., *College and University Trusteeship*. Yellow Springs, Ohio: Antioch Press, 1959.

35. Russell, James R., "Realities of Policy-making for Education at State and Federal Levels of Government," in W. P. McLure and Van Miller (eds.), *Government of Public Education for Adequate Policy-making*. Urbana, Ill.: University of Illinois, 1960. Pp. 77–89.

36. Struthers, F. R., *The Development of Community Junior College Legislation in the United States to 1961*. Unpublished doctoral dissertation presented at the University of Texas, Austin, Texas, 1963.

37. *This We Believe*. Washington, D.C.: American Association of School Administrators and the National School Boards Associations, 1963.

38. Timmins, Richard H., "Fund-raising in Junior Colleges," *Junior College Journal*, XXXIII (September 1962), 306.

Knowledge about students in the two-year college is quite sparse, except in relation to their academic abilities and achievements before and after transfer to four-year colleges. There are many studies of the test scores, average grades, and academic successes or failures of students, but this information does not provide a picture of the student as a person. Fortunately, this deficiency has been recognized by some students of the junior college. There are now a number of studies under way in universities and two-year colleges which promise factual and comprehensive information about students and their attitudes, aspirations, values, and reactions to experiences in the freshman and sophomore years. [15:84]

Lack of evidence on student characteristics has been one of the major problems in the development of educational programs realistically geared to student needs. There has been a tendency to make the traditional assumptions about students—assumptions based upon preconceived ideas which are of questionable validity today. The dearth of objective evidence concerning the multitude of social, intellectual, and psychological factors which impinge upon the student in his relationships with the college and his total environment may be traced to two factors:

5

students
and the two-year college

(1)   Lack of interest by educators in the individual student except as an "academic man"

(2)   The extreme complexity of developing and applying research methods to basic but elusive sociological and psychological problems

The concept of the "academic man" has attracted scholars since Western education began in Greece over two thousand years ago. The Platonic ideal of the educated elite has not been lost on American society and is particularly strong among those involved in higher education. Fortunately, the student comes to the campus as a complete individual—with an individual's abilities, disabilities, aptitudes, motivations, and personal idiosyncrasies. "Fortunately," because the idealized concept of the intellectual, whose sole motivation is the search for knowledge, would make for a very unbalanced world indeed. American students, whether they be in two- or four-year colleges, reflect in their behavior their varied backgrounds, experiences, and personal psychological needs. The college must deal with these realities if there is to be constructive learning on the campus.

In spite of the lack of extensive and reliable evidence about students, it is possible to understand their perceptions and expectations of the two-year college by examining their experiences in their families and communities. From this information it is possible to generalize with regard to the relationships between the college and the student and the meanings of these relationships in the educational experiences of the individual. As the characteristics of the student are examined in the light of his expectations and perceptions, a clearer picture of the educational consequences of the historically expanding two-year college will emerge.

General Characteristics of Students

Two-year colleges serve two distinct populations. The first is in the seventeen–twenty-one age group, loosely classified as *college-age youth*. These are high school graduates who have entered college, immediately or shortly after high school graduation, to continue their education on a full- or part-time basis.

Although it is common procedure in discussing two-year college students to stress their unique characteristics, their obvious similarities with others in their age group should be considered. Like all individuals, they have certain social needs that demand satisfaction. It is during these years that many students find themselves as individuals and select marriage partners. The emotional problems arising out of attempts to meet these needs as well as the requirements for accurate reliable information place a heavy responsibility on the two-year college.

There are also a large number of students who are not of college age. These students make up a large portion of the "unclassified" and "part-time" students who constitute approximately 50 per cent of the total number of two-year college students in the United States. [14:27] These students range in age from the twenties to the sixties and seventies, and their perceptions and needs in relation to education often vary markedly from those in the younger-age categories. Adult students are substantially more mature than the youthful full-time students, and this maturity is reflected in their seriousness of purpose and specificity of behavior, both personal and academic. They view the college as a stepping-stone to the realization of their long-range personal and vocational goals. Generally, they have little or no interest in extracurricular activities, athletics, and other nonclassroom activities. Their interests are focused upon the completion of college courses required for graduation or to achieve a specific vocational goal.

A married student is commonly accepted on college campuses today. Medsker found that 23 per cent of the students in six colleges were married. Although no national statistics are available, it is probably true that approximately one quarter of all the students in two-year colleges are married. This group presents special problems for guidance services and for academic counseling by faculty members. Their economic needs are such that college studies can claim only a portion of their attention, for they must continue working to sustain themselves and their families.

In the fall of 1962, there were 367,136 men and 225,192 women enrolled in public and private two-year colleges in the United States. [18:23] This is a ratio of approximately three men to every two women. The ratio was much the same in 1961 when there were approximately 200,000 women enrolled, as compared with 321,000 men.

The study by D'Amico and Raines found that 57 per cent of the students studied had part-time jobs. Sixty-three per cent of the men and 47 per cent of the women worked on jobs which consumed a median of 22 and 16.8 hours per week, respectively. The authors raised the question as to whether the majority of these students needed to work in order to pay their personal and college expenses. [8:193–95] Approximately half of those with outside employment stated they did not need to work to stay in college. It is apparent that junior college students do not, in general, withdraw from the larger community during the years they are pursuing college work. They are, for the most part, intimately related to the vocational activities of the community and they continue to absorb its conventional attitudes toward occupations and its concepts of the value of a college education. Working and associating with an employer and other employees who stress the importance of educational and skill qualifications in relation to occupational advancement and increased personal income has a significant impact on the student and his perceptions of the benefits of a college degree.

An analysis of the outside employment of adult students provided additional information about current occupations and their relationships to college work. [26]

TABLE 5-1. Occupational Classification of 539 Evening-division Students (Flint Community Junior College)

Classification	Men	Women	Total
Occupation			
Clerical and sales	19%	36%	25%
Service	14	14	14
Unskilled	17		12
Professional and managerial		12	12
Skilled	16		11
Unemployed			7
Housewife		19	7
Semiskilled			5
Agricultural			less than 1
No response			6
Current employment			
Very satisfactory			57
Satisfactory			30
Unsatisfactory	17	8	13
Attending college to obtain better job	88	77	85
Contributions of college work to current job			
Very much			34
Some			43
Very little			33

The occupational classification of evening college students showed the largest group—25 per cent—in clerical and sales positions; 14 per cent in service occupations; 12 per cent in professional, managerial, and unskilled occupations; 11 per cent in skilled jobs; 7 per cent housewives and unemployed; 5 per cent in semiskilled jobs; and less than 1 per cent in agriculture. There figures support the thesis that adult students are motivated by the prospect of vertical mobility on the socioeconomic scale. It may well be that the large proportion of clerical and sales personnel represent individuals who did not or could not take advantage of post-high school educational opportunities immediately after graduation from secondary school. Once employed, they recognized the necessity for further education and those possessing adequate intellectual capacities embarked upon an educational program designed to lift themselves into the professional and managerial group. If housewives are included,

55 per cent of these students come from the upper occupational classifications, while 45 per cent are unemployed, unskilled, semiskilled, and service workers.

Sixty-seven per cent of these individuals saw a strong or average relationship between college course work and their current jobs, while 33 per cent felt there was little relationship between the two. From this it can be inferred that two thirds were using the combination of course work and work experience for further development of occupational competence, while approximately a third were using their current jobs as an economic mainstay to achieve their educational goals.

Educational background

Contrary to the impression sometimes created by the literature, individuals entering institutions of higher education have gone through a rigorous weeding-out process during their twelve years of public schooling. Although the number of high school graduates has increased consistently throughout the century, in 1961–62 almost one third of the population seventeen years of age did not graduate from high school. [8:41] Not only is there substantial attrition in education, but students are subjected to varying curricula and other influences in both the elementary and secondary schools (see Fig. 5-1).

Figure 5-1 demonstrates the existence of a common core of high school programs, consisting of English, social studies, mathematics, science, and foreign languages. It also illustrates the marked differences among the percentages of students (compared on the basis of ability) taking these subjects. Those in the upper 25 per cent take more foreign languages, science, and mathematics than those in either of the other two divisions. All groups take the same amount of English, but there is an expansion of the number of social science studies courses taken by those in the lower 75 per cent. Courses in business, home economics, industrial arts, and other fields take a larger proportion of the time of students in the lower 75 per cent, but are relatively unimportant for those in the upper 25 per cent.

Sexton's study demonstrated clearly how the measurement of students, the school environment, and the educational curriculum are dominated by middle- and upper-class mores. The effect of these conditions is to place at a disadvantage those individuals who come from families in the lower socioeconomic brackets. She pointed out, for example, that students from the low-income groups were heavily enrolled in health education, home economics, music, art, business education, and similar subjects, while individuals from high-income groups concentrated on foreign languages, mathematics, and science. [25:172–73] Not only are high school students segregated along intellectual lines, but there are substantial social differences in extracurricular activities. Durham and Cole found that, although students from the upper class constituted 7.9 per cent of the student body, they made up 21.2 per cent of the club memberships and 21.7 per cent of the student councils. [10]

It is extremely important for junior college personnel to recognize and understand the social and academic conditioning which takes place among students of various socioeconomic levels from their entrance into first grade until their graduation from high school. The abilities and attitudes which students bring to the college campus have their genesis in previous experiences and, if the college is to perform its educational functions effectively, it must understand these experiences. As will be

FIG. 5-1. Proportion of Public High School Programs Devoted to Certain Subject-matter Areas, by Pupil-ability Level, 1957-58* [29]

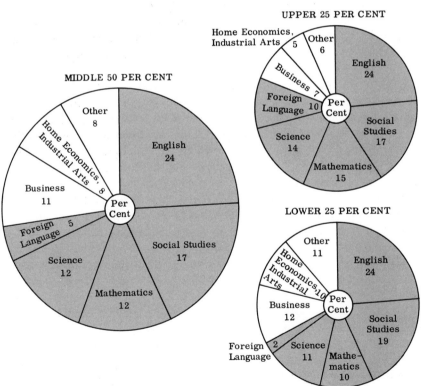

ABILITY LEVELS – ALL SCHOOLS

* NOTE: Data are for the United States excluding Alaska and Hawaii and the District of Columbia

seen, the heterogeneous character of the student body in community colleges has major significance in relation to student perceptions of themselves and of the college milieu.

Family influences largely determine whether or not an individual will succeed in academic work and continue his education beyond the high school (see Table 5-2).

The primary influences within the family are extremely important to academic success, particularly on the college level. Table 5-2 indicates the manner in which these values contribute to educational attainment from generation to generation.

The personality needs of parents and children are generally interrelated. Levels of aspiration and degrees of motivation in students reflect, in large measure, previous conditioning in the family unit. The satisfaction of personality needs is basic to the behavior patterns of students while they are a part of the college milieu. Thus, there is in many instances a wide divergence between the educational goals of students and the requirements imposed by the college. For example, the student may be seeking to meet the standards of achievement inculcated by his parents and, because of this motivation, selects an educational program quite unsuited to his abilities and interests. The opposite might also be true.

More important, many of the students who attend public community colleges do not enjoy the advantage of previous conditioning which encourages perception of education as a high-level value. This means that the two-year college has the additional problem and responsibility of developing this value, which serves as the foundation for successful academic achievement. The assumption is implicit in private junior colleges, university branches, and four-year institutions that the student's values are such that he has a strong achievement need and is thus motivated to meet institutional requirements. This assumption underlies admissions requirements, course content, and teaching techniques.

The close relationship between socioeconomic level (as shown by type of occupation) and higher education is further demonstrated in Fig. 5-2. According to this figure, in 1959, 68 per cent of the children from professional, technical, and managerial families planned to attend college. In contrast, only 37 per cent of the children of manual and service workers, and only 35 per cent of the children of farm workers definitely planned to continue their education after high school graduation. It should be noted also that these latter groups had the highest percentage of undecided students. It is more than probable that the two-year college receives the largest share of these students.

The academic abilities of junior college students, as measured by standardized tests, showed that freshmen were at about the twenty-fifth

Theoretical Determinants of Educational Attainments	*Indicators or Proxy Variables*
Motivation of parents and their values: Need-achievement of the parents.	A measure of need-achievement of the head * based on perception of the relative desirability of various occupations.
Attitude toward hard work and self-help as the means for attaining desired goals.	Expressed evaluation of hard work as the means for getting ahead.
Cultural norms stressing education, expressed in religious, community, and social groups with which parents are affiliated.	Religious affiliation and participation in religious activities by the head.
Achievements of parents that demonstrate the effectiveness of values held by the parents: Actual educational accomplishment of both parents.	Education of the head, and education of his wife, if he is married.
Educational achievement of the parents relative to the achievement of the grandparents.	Difference in the education of the head and his or her father.
Career paths demonstrating impact of education on earning power and advancement.	Occupation of the head.
Past mobility of the head which indicates attempts on the part of the parents to improve their situation.	Whether head moved off a farm. Whether head moved to the North.
Successful planning of finances and other activities of the family.	Age of the head at the birth of his first child.
Availability of education: Existence of local facilities.	Region. Urbanization. Color.
Economic ability to send children to college: a. Earning potential.	Peak income of the head in past years, his education, his occupation.
b. Demands on income and their timing.	Age of the head at the birth of his first child. Number of living children of the head.

Education achieved by children

* NOTE: The head of the spending unit is the husband in units containing a married couple; otherwise the head is the major earner in the spending unit.

113

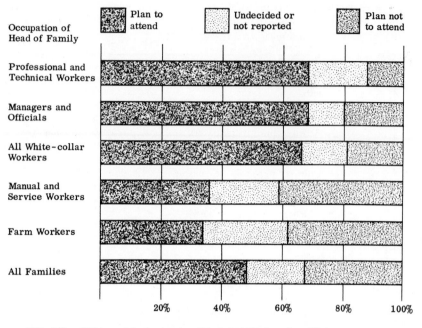

FIG. 5-2.   Children of Professional and Technical Workers Most Likely to
Attend College (Plans of High School Seniors, 1959) [6:20]

percentile in median score as compared with college freshman in four-year colleges; 24 per cent of the men and 20 per cent of the women in junior colleges scored higher than the medians achieved in four-year institutions. [24] In a study conducted by the Center for the Study of Higher Education, University of California (Berkeley), a similar overlap of scores was found—with a difference of one standard deviation between four-year and two-year college freshmen. [17:37] There is evidence from these comparisons to support the idea that junior college freshmen enter the institution with generally lower personal motivation and less academic ability as measured by standardized tests.

Socioeconomic background

Proportionally more two-year college students come from lower socioeconomic backgrounds than do their counterparts in four-year colleges and universities. The most comprehensive study of the socioeconomic origins of college students was made by Clark, who compared the occupations of students' fathers at Stanford University, the University of California (Berkeley), San Jose State College, and San Jose Junior College. [5:54] He found that 87 per cent of the Stanford University students studied were from upper-white-collar families, 7 per cent from lower-white-collar families, 6 per cent from upper-blue-collar families, and none from lower-blue-collar families. The University of California drew 69 per cent of the students studied from the upper-white-collar stratum, and only 6 per cent from the lowest socioeconomic group. San Jose State College had a more evenly balanced student population: 55 per cent from white-collar families and 45 per cent from blue-collar backgrounds. In contrast, San Jose Junior College had 38 per cent from the white-collar group and 62 per cent from families lower on the social scale. These families all resided in San Jose, so that the comparison of populations in the various colleges demonstrates the class variations among different types of institutions of higher education.

Clark's data were substantiated by a study of one hundred full-time male students at Henry Ford Community College. It was found that 11 per cent of the students' fathers were in the professional, technical, and managerial occupations, while 9 per cent were in clerical and sales positions and 67 per cent were classified as skilled, semiskilled, or unskilled. [12:313–21]

A follow-up study of 150 students completing junior college study and later graduating from Flint Community Junior College of The University of Michigan showed that 15 per cent of the students' fathers were professionals; 10 per cent, from the managerial level; 7 per cent, from clerical and sales; and 8 per cent, from service and farming occupations. Sixty per cent of the parents were classified as skilled, semiskilled, and unskilled. The parents of the students in this study had limited formal education: only 25 per cent had finished high school. [27]

The close relationship between socioeconomic level and college success needs to be emphasized here, because of the composition of the student bodies of two-year colleges. Wolfle showed that there was a marked relationship between the father's occupation and the student's success in college work. Table 5-3 shows that students from professional

TABLE 5-3. Relationship Between Father's Occupation and Student's Success in College

Father's Occupation	High School Graduates Who Enter College	College Entrants Who Graduate from College	High School Graduates Who Also Graduate from College
Professional and semiprofessional	67%	60%	40%
Managerial	50	55	28
White-collar (clerical, sales, service)	48	57	27
Farmer	24	44	11
Factory worker, craftsman, unskilled	26	58	15

and semiprofessional families have by far the best chance of graduating from college. The managerial group is second, and the white-collar (clerical, sales, service) group is third. Sons and daughters of factory workers, craftsmen, unskilled laborers, and farmers have the least chance of success in collegiate work. These facts have direct implications for college teaching, guidance services, and the totality of the relationships between students and the college. [30]

Anthony's study of 523 students in three public community colleges substantiates the consistency with which previous educational experience, family influences, and socioeconomic level affect the curricular and occupational choices of students. He found that students who had completed the high school academic program tended to enroll in college-transfer courses, while those with backgrounds in vocational education chose terminal courses. [1:156] Thus, 74.8 per cent of the college-transfer students came from college-preparation programs in high school, while only 25.2 per cent came from vocational programs.

TABLE 5-4. Relationship Between High School Background and Type of Program

College Program	General Academic		Vocational		Total	
Transfer	299	74.8%	101	25.2%	400	100%
Terminal	69	56.1	54	43.9	123	100
Total	368	70.4	155	29.6	523	100

He found, further, that students attributed a high degree of influence to their parents in the selection of curriculum or occupation. This influence, both direct and indirect, was demonstrated further by his conclusion that students who chose transfer programs came from homes of higher socioeconomic levels and showed significantly greater concern with the social status and prestige of the occupation for which they were being educated than did students in technical programs. He concluded:

> Enrollment of students from the upper and upper-middle classes in college-transfer programs appears to be a matter of course, since virtually all of these students come from homes in which at least one parent has a college education. Hence, for these students, a college degree may be regarded primarily as a means of retaining their current social status. In contrast, for students from the lower-middle and lower classes, pursuit of a college degree is indicative of a desire to rise on the social scale. [1:203]

Student Perceptions of Post-High School Education

The student's perception of the two-year college differs from that of all other individuals and groups related to the institution. Although not always aware of it, he is the object of the entire organization—the staff which activates its functions, and the community which supports it. Student perceptions of the college are as varied as the population of the college, thereby making generalization difficult.

Students represent two relatively distinct groups—college-age youths and adults. College-age youths arrive on the college campus from their recent high school experiences, little knowing what to expect, holding beliefs acquired from their peers, and hoping for the best in competition with others in their classes. They tend to enter the university-transfer programs with the assertion that they are pursuing work toward the baccalaureate degree. Many are unrealistic about their occupational goals, academic abilities, or obvious limitations. For some, it is a time for dreaming and unbridled ambition; their attitudes reflect that American myth which says any individual has the opportunity to achieve the highest office in the land, to enter a profession, or to achieve wealth through his personal dedication and hard work.

The students' lack of realism in occupational choice is pointed out in a study by Olsen. He ferreted out the reasons for the selection of career goals by 302 students, 80 per cent of whom were in the seventeen–nineteen age group. He found that 47 per cent selected their occupational goals in high school; 11 per cent, before entering high school; 11 per cent, while in college; and 17 per cent, while working full-time. Twelve per cent had either not made a selection, or were uncertain of their choice. The study made clear that students did not recognize the difference between liking an activity and actually performing it, nor the distinction between interest in an occupation and the ability to perform the duties it requires. Students also had little or no knowledge of the requirements of the occupation they had chosen: 28 per cent had made their choice on the basis of the rewards attributed to the occupation. [17]

Such students are likely to perceive the two-year college as a public institution supported by their parents and existing to provide them with the opportunity to acquire the material benefits of an affluent society. Individuals in this age group view educational opportunity as a "right" to which they are entitled. They are encouraged in this belief by their parents, the community, and the rapidly growing tradition that post-high school education is the key to personal success in the society. An application for a position above the unskilled level immediately brings to the fore the question of education. When students meet individuals for the first time, the conversational sparring invariably touches upon the college the youngsters are attending, or plan to attend, and their plans for a career. They are also subjected to strong pressures within their peer groups during high school, when other members of the groups with which they relate plan their admission to college and discuss, with obvious excitement and realistic or illusionary concepts of what the freshman year will be like.

Personal and peer-group identification

What does this type of student want from the two-year college? First, he wants visible personal identification as a college student. It is important—probably more so than teachers and parents realize—that he, too, be a college student along with others in his own age group. His appearance, language, and daily routine must mark him as a college student—one of the elite who will someday be business, professional, or governmental leaders. Such individual identification is particularly important during late adolescence. The symbols associated with late adolescence by parents and society, as well as by the adolescent's peer group, are powerful motivations amid the many uncertainties which are characteristic of this period.

Peer relationship and identification is a second powerful force in the life of college-age youth. The rapid increase in the number and percentage of high school graduates entering college each year has stimulated many young people, who in past decades would not have considered college work, to aspire to a post-high school experience, however brief. The strong group identification among high school students does not automatically end with graduation. Individuals in such groups are influenced strongly by in-group mores and attitudes, and as higher proportions of this group continue their schooling beyond the high school, all members will be increasingly encouraged to do the same.

Status and security

Third, the adolescent's need for status and security encourages him to seek identification with a status occupation or curriculum. Admissions officers see the process repeated with each freshman class as it passes through the routine of admission and enrollment. Time after time, students who have average or below-average academic records in high school and low admission test scores indicate their desire to embark upon preprofessional programs. Their stated educational and occupational goals include medicine, dentistry, law, business administration, architecture, science, and similar professions. When the admissions counselor attempts to help them relate their prior academic achievement and test scores to the requirements for such curricula, he encounters disbelief and resistance. The students insist they will do better if given a chance; after all, they were never really forced to study while in high school and now that they are in college a new leaf will be turned over. Despite their conviction that their motives are realistic and attainable, they are demonstrating the need for identification with important status objects acclaimed as wholesome and good by society. Students, then, see the two-year college as an opportunity school which offers them the same royal road to personal and material success as does the four-year college.

Unrealistic identification with status occupations leads many students to college-transfer programs when, in terms of their abilities and demonstrated achievement, they ought to be in technical or vocational courses. This is demonstrated by the comparatively small percentage who actually continue their education after graduation from the two-year college. Medsker found that a median of 32 per cent of junior college entrants fulfill graduation requirements. [16:95] At Everett Junior College, approximately 80 per cent of the entering students consistently chose transfer programs, but only 47.3 per cent of them actually transferred. In a study in the state of Washington, 56 per cent of all students expressed their intention to complete the requirements for a baccalaureate degree. [3:20]

Assertion of maturity and independence

Fourth, junior college students have the same motivation toward emancipation from home and parents that is so apparent among students in four-year institutions. Even though most junior college students live at home, they seek ways to assert their independence and maturity. Their class and study schedules make it necessary for them to deviate from the family pattern. If possible, they eat meals in the college cafeteria, go to meetings in the evening, attend social affairs on weekends, and become involved in activities which are identified as distinctly collegiate. They may also find part-time jobs which may or may not be essential to monetary needs. Thus the process of disassociation from the family, which began in high school, continues at an accelerated rate in college.

Fifth, the student sees the junior college as a milieu in which he can live and be treated as an adult. Although his own behavior may vacillate between maturity and immaturity, he will expect to establish and maintain typically adult relationships with instructors and other college personnel. Graduation from high school has become a line of demarcation between the boy and the man, the girl and the woman. Late adolescents are acutely sensitive to any behavior in others which implies that they are still children. Students at this age level, therefore, see the junior college as a major step in the liberating process which is their springboard into adulthood.

Occupational competence

Finally, the student comes to college in order to qualify himself for a vocation. Some of the student's motivations are direct outgrowths of his conditioning through the public schools, the home, and mass communication media. He hears repeatedly that the high school graduate will earn more than the nongraduate during his working life, and that the college graduate will earn far more than both. He finds it difficult to secure employment with only a high school diploma, no specialized technical skills, and no experience; at the same time, he notes that the beginning salaries offered to college graduates appear to be more than adequate for his needs.

The student's drive toward vocational training also springs from a deeper and more subtle motivation. The American society contains an underlying and tenuous thread of Calvinist puritanism which exalts devotion to work as a natural attribute of man. Those who are not productively engaged, preferably in a high-status occupation, are not conforming to middle-class standards and are, therefore, suspected of nonconformity. With their lower-middle- and upper-lower-class backgrounds, junior college students reflect the mores of their social origins. These attitudes are demonstrated by their preoccupation with part-time work while attending the junior college and by the curricular choices they make. The student comes to the campus with patterns of behavior and attitudes which are not radically altered by movement from one environment to another. Students attending resident colleges and universities leave parents, friends, and community when they depart for the distant campus. They become immersed in a student subculture unlike that of their home town. Because a minority of four-year college students must work part-time in order to pay a portion of their college expenses, the traditional patterns of the college campus relegate this aspect of their lives to a secondary level of importance and interest. The major emphasis of student life on the residential campus is upon peer-group activities and academic work. Such patterns of behavior and attitudes do not necessarily prevail among the majority of junior college students.

The junior college student usually remains at home, where the routines of living are not essentially altered by his involvement in higher education. He continues to associate with his former high school friends, and he may continue to work on the same part-time job, attend the same church, and date the same girl friend. The study by D'Amico and Prahl makes an interesting portrait of the continuity of interests and activities of junior college students. It surveyed four entering classes for the years 1951–54, whose members, indicated one or more of the following reasons for attending a community college. [7:474–77]

Reasons	Student Responses
Cheaper than going away	70%
The only way I could go to college	43
Wanted to live at home	32
Wanted to continue work in home town	20
Other reasons (not specified)	19
Wanted to see if I could do college work	16
Wanted a two-year college course	12
Wanted to be with my friends	12
Could not get into school of first choice	2

The reason most often given for attending the junior college was lack of financial resources, but it should be noted that a substantial percentage of the replies demonstrated the individuals' desires to continue their patterns of life in the home and community while attending college. This attitude is reflected by 32 per cent who wanted to live at home, 20 per cent who wanted to continue work in the community, and 12 per cent who wanted to remain with their friends. Thus, a significant number of individuals wanted a post-high school education, but they were also desirous of continuing their life patterns within the confines of previous experience.

The population of each college is unique. This is not a matter of chance, but the result of a process of natural selection. The college has a public image that appeals to one kind of student rather than to another. The spirit of the faculty, the kind of teaching, and the tradition of the institution help to determine whether or not the student will find the setting satisfactory. [28:311–15]

The aspirations of students in the two-year college are largely limited to college transfer. Two thirds of the students who enter two-year colleges do not go beyond the sophomore year. They need technical, vocational, cultural, and remedial courses rather than courses designed to prepare them for transfer to the four-year college.

Influence of personality on perception

Students in the two-year college perceive these years of educational experience as the time when they must make far-reaching decisions about occupational choice, marriage, and personal development. They bring with them their personality characteristics, their potential as individuals growing in a psychological sense, and the disabilities they have accrued during their previous life experiences. Their perceptions of the college are colored by their psychological needs. Peck made a comprehensive study of the distribution of personality types on a college campus. He divided them, on the basis of their mental health, into three groups: low, middle, and high: Those students having the poorest mental health had the following characteristics:

[Low]

(1) Many intense, primitively self-centered desires.

(2) Strongly conflicting feelings about major aspects of life. The specific nature of the emotions vary from person to person.

(3) Relatively poor forethought and self-discipline. In one way or another, these young people show a short-sighted grasping for satisfaction. . . .

(4) Destructive interpersonal behavior. Whether obviously or subtly, openly or covertly, students such as these flee from, antagonize, or alienate many of the people of their own age.

[Middle]

(1) They are dependent social conformists. Their life experiences have unavoidably left them with little practical skill in thinking for themselves, and not much impressive self-assurance or faith to motivate them to try.

(2) They get along ineptly, on a rather thin diet of human happiness and healthy pride. . . . While the more maladjusted of them can be described in conventional clinical terms of *neurosis* or even *psychosis,* most of this half of the college population seem less to suffer from distorted development of their personalities, than from insufficient training and example.

(3) Most of them show a pervasive anxiety, of a tolerable but uncomfortable kind. A great deal of this anxiety seems not to stem from guilt over specific transgressions, or fears of desertion by family, as happens in the case of neurotic disorders. Much of the anxiety seems, rather, to stem from a quite accurate perception that their lives lack shape and purpose.

(4) They have the desire and courage to keep going. Whatever the defects of human support or training they have experienced, whatever their deficiencies of skill or will to shape their own lives meaningfully, these young people do achieve occasional visions of what a fully realized life could be. They wish deeply that there were more success and happiness in their lives, but they do not give up on that account. They find some pleasures, some causes for just pride. Perhaps, above all, they have a hope that the future will somehow be better. However wishful this may be, however ill-buttressed by effective efforts of their own, this hope gives them a downright stubborn persistence in going ahead.

[High]

(1) They are strongly motivated to build self-realizing lives. They seem to be happiest and most successful precisely when they are most vigorously living out one or another of their diverse capacities.

(2) They have diversified personalities, well developed on many sides. Their personal relationships are as deeply important to them as is their intellectual grasp of life. They are effectively active in social affairs of one kind or another; at the same time, they show a great deal of self-insight and take time to become well acquainted with their inner thought, feelings, and needs. They savor the physical pleasures of life

with unashamed enjoyment, and yet they are basically disciplined in their behavior, rarely giving vent to a selfish impulse in an unthinking way. Thus, they have developed over a long period of years their physical responsiveness to life, their intellectual inquiry into its meaning, their emotional relationships with other people, and their exploration of their own spirits.

(3) They experience powerful emotions gladly, and find life deeper and richer for it. It part, this is probably because most of their feelings are of a happy or positive kind; but even intense negative feelings, when they occur, do not teach them distrust of the emotional side of life.

(4) They think clearly and far-sightedly.

(5) They are integrated people. Complex and differentiated though they are, they feel, think, and act in a self-disciplined way that unites thought, feeling, and purpose.

(6) They are genuinely ethical in their motives and in their behavior. It is not nearly as much of an effort or a strain for them to treat other people thoughtfully and decently, as it often is for the less-adjusted people.

(7) They like other people, and others seek their company. They are effective in their human relationships, in a mutually satisfying way. They may or may not be highly active in a variety of social groups; the important thing is the high quality of their relationships in the groups to which they do belong.

(8) These young people, too, have problems. Their lives have in no case been without disappointment or frustrations. Thus, they illustrate that good mental health is not "adjustment" in some sense of static contentment, requiring no effort. On the contrary, "good mental health" is simply a way of talking about a vigorous, continual process of coping effectively with each day's new problems. [19:183–89]

The two-year college has among its students representatives of all three groups described above. The fact that students are struggling with the development of a self-concept while attempting to meet academic requirements makes for a complicated and difficult relationship between the college and the individual. There is little question that psychological maladjustment is an impediment to learning. Consequently, if the two-year college is to meet its objectives, it must face this fact squarely and provide guidance counselors and administrators who are capable of helping the student develop personal confidence and self-reliance.

Adult students

Up to this point the discussion has been limited to the characteristics and perceptions of college-age youths. As has been pointed out, however, approximately 50 per cent of the students in two-year colleges can be classified as adults. The majority of these students are engaged in full-time jobs, have families, and are involved in extensive vocational and leisure-time activities which bear little or no relation to the college. They choose courses with care, using them as building blocks to lift them toward their goals. If the rules and regulations of the college are not too detailed and odious, adult students will accept its requirements and procedures and faithfully fulfill the demands of college and teachers.

Adult students perceive the college as a means to an end. They want to use its resources in ways which will contribute directly to their goals. They expect reasonable standards of achievement in courses, but they reject capricious or immature behavior by instructors and bureaucratic procedures and requirements by the administration. In this regard, these students often make it clear to the college that some of the procedures and requirements appropriate for college-age students are unnecessary and irrelevant for adults. The junior college must analyze these questions in the light of institutional and individual needs and modify its procedures in terms of a realistic adjustment to the adult student. [26]

TABLE 5-5. Characteristics and Interests of 539 Evening-division Students

Characteristics and Interests	Men	Women	Combined
Educational objectives:			
Preprofessional	68%	32%	56%
Vocational-technical	7	9	8
Teaching	5	24	11
Liberal arts	3	3	3
Undecided	17	32	22
Completed admissions test	61	59	60
Indicated need for educational advisement	30	25	29
Expressed interest in vocational guidance clinic	44	37	42
Desired separate student government for evening students	17	17	17
Would run for office in student government for evening students	15	12	14
Participation in college social, educational, cultural, and recreational activities:			
Extensive			5
Some			22
Little or none			73
Types of activities of interest to students:			
Dances			36
Educational moving pictures			34
Lectures			26
Recreational activities			23
Outings and picnics			21
Musical programs			16
Intramurals and clubs			15
Student newspaper			11
Tutorial service			7

These students represented an age range from seventeen to sixty-eight, with a median age of 24.5 years. The group achieved a 2.47, or a C+ academic average in their course work during the semester in which the survey was completed. Male students earned a median grade point average of 2.27; female students, a median of 2.79. Five per cent of the men and 11 per cent of the women earned a 4.0 grade point average—straight A's.

Members of this group worked a median of forty-three hours per week while attending college. The median hours worked by men were slightly higher than those for women. Fifteen per cent worked fewer than thirty-five hours per week, and 21 per cent worked forty-five or more hours per week.

Some indication of adult students' image of the junior college emerges from these data. A strong vocational orientation is evident: 75 per cent stated their objectives to be professional or vocational, and 85 per cent indicated that they were attending college in order to obtain a better job. In addition, 43 per cent implied dissatisfaction with their current employment. The 3 per cent who were enrolled in the liberal arts curriculum contrast strongly with the proportions of younger groups attracted to this program. The fact that 22 per cent did not have clearly defined educational objectives demonstrates the prevailing concept of the junior college as an opportunity school in which post-high school education can be sampled without irreversible commitment to a specific college degree program or an immediate vocational goal.

These students conformed reasonably well to the admission procedures of the college. They were required to complete the usual student-personnel forms and to submit high school transcripts, but were not required to take the standardized admission examinations. Sixty per cent of the group accepted the invitation of the college to take the admission tests, although not required to do so. The stability of the educational objectives of these students is open to question: 29 per cent of the group indicated a need for educational advisement and 42 per cent expressed interest in a vocational guidance clinic.

There was relatively little interest in extracurricular activities and college-sponsored cultural events. Only 17 per cent thought there was a need for an organized student government for evening students, and only 14 per cent indicated that they would run for office if such an organization were set up. The group did not indicate strong interest in social, educational, cultural, and recreational activities: 73 per cent participated in few or none of these activities; 22 per cent participated in some; and only 5 per cent participated extensively.

There is marked similarity between the amount of participation of college-age students and adult students in large metropolitan community colleges. In either age group, a small minority of students account for most of the participation in student activities. Students in these institutions do not have their interests centered upon the campus, as do students at resident institutions, where the routines of living and study are encompassed by the campus environment. A majority of the students at metropolitan community colleges have part-time jobs; some have family responsibilities; and most are generally occupation-oriented. The small, resident two-year college, on the other hand, would provide an environment which more closely resembles that of the nonmetropolitan four-year college.

Sixty-seven percent of the students saw a significant relationship between their course work in the college and their current occupations; 33 per cent stated that they saw little relationship between these two factors.

Women students

Women constitute an important segment of the total number of students attending junior colleges. There were 225,192 women enrolled full-time in the junior colleges in the United States in 1962. [18:3] Female students come to the college with expectations somewhat different from those of male students. They can be categorized into three general groups: single college-age women, single adult women, and married women. The single college-age student sees the college, first, as preparation for a vocation, second, as the stepping-stone to a higher socioeconomic status, and, third, as an opportunity for selecting a mate. D'Amico and Prahl found that 50 per cent of the women chose the liberal arts; 23 per cent, teaching; 10 per cent, business; 10 per cent, science; and the rest, other subject-matter areas. [7:474–77] Added personal status in family and community is accepted as a natural concomitant of college attendance and graduation. Undoubtedly, the desire to be married, whether or not overtly recognized, is a powerful motivation for women of college age. A survey of women students in colleges throughout the country found that "all of these girls vividly anticipated marrying immediately upon finishing college—or before—and having several children." Thus, these students are seeking more than academic study and improvement of the mind while attending college. [15:28] In most respects, women in this age category have interests and needs paralleling those of men of comparable age and maturity.

The second group of women—those who are beyond college age and who are single, divorced, or widowed—have somewhat different expectations of the college experience. For the most part, these women have some kind of employment, or are looking forward to finding a position as soon as they obtain the necessary qualifications. They reflect a strong stimulus for economic independence through vocational competence, a stimulus created by the lack of continuing support from husband or family. The attitudes of this group toward the college are quite similar to those of male students.

The third group is made up of married women who have returned to the campus or are sampling college study after having had children and experienced the responsibilities of family living. These individuals constitute an increasingly important segment of the college population. What are their motivations and expectations? The lives of many women may be divided into several stages: the premarital years, the family-raising years, and the post-family period. This pattern has changed considerably during the last sixty years: women marry earlier, their child-bearing period is shorter and earlier, and their life span has been dramatically extended. The average American woman in the 1960's will have her last child at age twenty-six and will live to be seventy-five; thus, she will have a potential working life of forty-six years beyond the birth of her last child. [15:28–29]

Married women attend college for a variety of reasons. Some of them are stimulated toward further study by economic reasons. They may want to supplement the family income in order to raise the material level of living, or they may find themselves facing the necessity of having to bolster their husbands' restricted incomes. Concern for the future education of their children is sometimes the motive for desiring education and training and, with it, increased economic security. Some realize that they face a bleak future devoid of stimulation after the children have left the home. Others recognize their need for broader intellectual, cultural, and personal interests and experiences if they are to continue to think and live in effective partnership with their husbands.

All three groups of women in the junior college see the institution as an avenue to vocational preparation, intellectual stimulation, and cultural improvement. There is, however, a marked difference in degree of expectation held by representatives of each group of the college in relation to these three areas. The college-age woman comes to the campus seeking social activities with her peers and some vocational preparation for the immediate postcollege or early married years, although many are committed to thorough professional qualification. The postcollege-age single women are interested in some social activities with men and women of the same age, but their major expectation is that the college will provide meaningful training to insure increased economic power and greater personal security. Married women see the college as an opportunity to escape the monotony of family living with its inherent limitations during the late and post-child-caring period.

It has been amply demonstrated that the academic achievement of women beyond the age of twenty-five is comparable to that of college-age youth and that, because of their stronger motivation and dedication to college requirements, they are often the academic leaders on the campus. [12:106–15]

The two-year college as an opportunity school

It is clear that the majority of students seek the two-year college as an opportunity for upward social and economic mobility. Hagemuier's study found that 86 per cent of the one hundred male students surveyed had exceeded the formal educational level of their parents. [11] The University of Michigan's study showed that only 25 per cent of the parents of the students considered had completed high school, while 90 per cent of their sons and daughters were moving into the professions—teaching (50 per cent), graduate school (17 per cent), business management (14 per cent), accounting (5 per cent), and other professional positions (5 per cent. Thus, these individuals moved—in a single generation—from a predominantly lower-middle-class background to an upper-middle-class level. [27]

Students are not immune to the changes taking place in our society. They recognize and perhaps overreact to the fact that we are moving into an exceedingly complex scientific and technological age in which success will depend upon educational achievement and occupational performance. Odious though it may be to educational administrators and faculty members, many students use the junior college as a sort of educational filling station in which they take courses to satisfy immediate and limited objectives which may or may not fit into their over-all life plans or complete educational programs.

A study of 217 students who entered Diablo Valley College in the fall of 1956 provides some evidence of the mobility of students in a particular junior college. [20:21]

TABLE 5-6.   Status at the Beginning of Each Semester

Status	Fall 1956	Spring 1956	Fall 1957	Spring 1957
Continuing in good standing		60.4%	57.1%	43.8%
Continued on probation		16.6	0.9	0.9
Didn't enroll		23.0	32.3	45.6
Dismissed (low grades)			9.7	0.9
Reinstated on probation				8.8
Total enrolled	100.0%	77.0	58.0	52.5

Shifts in the status of students took place rapidly after admission to the college. Almost one quarter of the group did not re-enroll during the second semester (42 per cent did not enroll or had been dismissed from the college because of lack of academic achievement). At the beginning of the fourth semester, 43.8 per cent continued in good standing, presumably making normal progress toward graduation. The total attrition rate, by the beginning of the fourth semester, was 46.5 per cent with 9.7 per cent of the group continuing on probation.

There is also marked mobility within curricula and courses. A study of class dropouts over a six-year period at Flint Junior College showed that 5–20 per cent of the students enrolled in courses in a given subject-matter area during a particular semester dropped one or more classes. The study included a total of 98,664 enrollments in applied sciences, art, business, home economics, English, foreign languages, music, nursing, physical education, psychology, education, retailing, sciences, mathematics, social sciences, speech, and journalism. A total of 8042 courses, or 8 per cent of the total, were dropped during the twelve semesters studied. Courses in business, sciences, and psychology suffered the highest attrition rate, while nursing and music had the lowest loss of students. [23]

The large number of part-time students in junior colleges (over 50 per cent) indicates clearly that students use the college as an aid to specific and limited objectives. The young man or woman who has previously failed in another college may try his wings again in one or two courses in the two-year college. A man who has a family and a full-time job might use the college to obtain specific technical information and training directly related to his job. A housewife who has not had previous college work might quietly sample a course or two in order to determine whether she might eventually enroll as a full-time student or begin a sequence of courses in a subject-matter area of particular interest. Students enrolled in summer sessions substantiate the "filling station" concept in that they come from other colleges and universities, live in the community, or are regularly enrolled junior college students. They may be taking additional courses in order to graduate sooner, to make up deficiencies or courses previously failed, or just because they cannot find satisfactory summer employment.

Conflicts Among Perceptions of Post-High School Education

Each of the four major groups associated with the college views it somewhat differently. Government officials—local, state, and national—and parents see the college as a social and economic necessity, as demonstrated by this statement:

(1) Education increases the productive capacity of the individual.
(2) Education is essential to consumption because it enlarges the area of

human desires so necessary in consuming the increased goods and services produced in our expanding economy.

(3) Education produces investment capital because it enables individuals to earn a surplus income above that necessary to supply basic needs.

(4) Education is essential to our national defense. [2:26]

Parents add the dimension of the desire that their children not only be economically self-sufficient but also enjoy fulfillment in life.

Students, faculty members, and administrators view the college in various ways. Rice's study showed that faculty members ranked the more abstract and intellectual college aims higher than did either students or administrators. Faculty members also rated visionary aims as the highest and practical aims as the lowest. On the other hand, administrators rated all aims of the college highly, but considered the practical aims to be most essential. Students, on the other hand, tended to rate the more abstract aims as least essential and the more practical aims as most essential. Students also ranked all types of guidance as more essential than did either administrators or teachers. They tended to reject interference by the institution with their value systems. Rightly or wrongly, students do bring to the campus their experiences, attitudes, and perceptions. These can be utilized in a positive way to achieve acceptable educational goals or they can exert a dilatory influence upon learning and individual self-realization. [22:165–73]

There are a number of practical indices that students' perceptions of the two-year college do not necessarily correspond to those of the faculty, the community, the administrators, or educational authorities. First, students are pragmatic about the reasons for which they are attending college. By their behavior, they demonstrate that they have practical occupational goals in mind. Their choices of occupations may be unrealistic, but this condition is also characteristic of students in four-year colleges. Their primary concerns are with achieving academic success and acquiring the necessary preparation for entry into an occupation.

They are also interested in peer-group relationships, the development of self-realization and understanding, and the fulfillment of needs growing out of problems of personal development, group acceptance, and occupational competence. This does not mean that students are essentially anti-intellectual; it simply means that student behavior encompasses a larger environment that that usually defined by the traditional academician. One of the primary responsibilities of the college is to provide intellectual experiences which stimulate the complete development of the individual, both in terms of his immediate personal preoccupations and in terms of a deeper and more significant understanding of the milieu within which he lives.

Students tend to come from socioeconomic groups whose values are not congruent with those of middle- and upper-middle-class faculty members, administrators, and board members. This condition has both positive and negative effects upon the relationships between students and faculty in the teaching-learning situation. The expectations of students about the requirements of collegiate study are all too often unrealistic, and their lack of conventional middle-class attitudes makes their adjustment to college more difficult. The attitudes of faculty members, trained in university graduate programs and holding middle-class mores and attitudes, induce expectations of students which are also unrealistic and tend to stimulate a higher rate of student attrition. A positive aspect of this divergence is that the questioning of attitudes and preconceptions by the faculty forces the students to find more realistic and logical bases for their beliefs. Thus, the conflict of attitudes and expectations between students and faculty can and does serve a beneficial function in the total educational experience.

The primary problem faced by the comprehensive community college is the challenging of students to grow to the limits of their abilities. At the same time, the college must avoid developing educational policies which will exclude students, discourage them from attempting college work, or ruthlessly eliminate those who cannot immediately meet the traditional patterns of baccalaureate programs. There is a fine balance between lowering the quality of education and encouraging students with low levels of motivation and previous academic achievement to attempt post-high school studies suited to their dispositions and talents. The problem of the public two-year college is to strike this balance.

Bibliography

1. Anthony, Donald M., "The Relationship of Certain Socioeconomic and Academic Factors to Student Choice of Occupation and Program in the Public Junior College." Unpublished doctoral dissertation presented at the University of Texas, Austin, Texas, 1964.

2. Bailey, Thomas D., "Social and Economic Necessity of Community Junior Colleges," in *Community Colleges in the South*. Southern State Work Conference, sponsored by State Departments of Education and State Education Associations, 1962. Pp. 122–28.

3. Berg, Rodney K., "A Follow-up Study of Students Leaving the Everett Washington Junior College Between 1948 and 1958." Unpublished doctoral dissertation presented at the University of Washington, Seattle, Washington, 1958.

4. Brazer, Harvey E., and Martin David, "Social and Economic Determinants of the Demand for Education," in S. J. Mushkin, *Economics of Higher Education*. Washington, D.C.: USGPO, 1962. Pp. 21–43.

5. Clark, Burton R., *The Open Door College: A Case Study*. New York: McGraw-Hill Book Company, 1960.

6. "College Attendance and Youth," *NEA Research Bulletin*, XL (February 1962), 18–21.

7. D'Amico, Louis A., and Marie R. Prahl, "A Follow-up of Educational, Vocational, and Activity Pursuits of Students Graduated from Flint Junior College, 1953–56," *Junior College Journal*, XXIX (April 1959), 474–77.

8. ————, and Max R. Raines, "Employment Characteristics of Flint Junior College Students," *Junior College Journal*, XXVIII (December 1957), 193–95.

9. *Digest of Educational Statistics*. Washington, D.C.: USGPO, 1963.

10. Durham, R., and E. S. Cole, "Social Class Structure in Emporia Senior High School," *Midwest Sociologist*, XIX (May 1957). Pp. 104–8.

11. Hagemuier, Richard H., "Socioeconomic Background of Full-time Male Students at Henry Ford Community College," *Junior College Journal*, XXIX (February 1959), 313–21.

12. Halfter, Irma T., "The Comparative Academic Achievement of Women," *Adult Education*, XII (Winter 1962), 106–15.

13. *Junior College Directory*. Washington, D.C.: American Association of Junior Colleges, 1963.

14. Knoell, Dorothy M., "Significant Current Research on Community Junior College Students," in *Community Colleges in the South*, Southern States Work Conference, sponsored by State Departments of Education and State Education Associations, 1962. Pp. 84–97.

15. Lloyd-Jones, Esther, "Education for Re-entry into the Labor Force," *Work in the Lives of Married Women*. New York: Columbia University Press, 1958. Pp. 27–40.

16. Medsker, L. L., *The Junior College*. New York: McGraw-Hill Book Company, 1960.

17. Olsen, L. R., "Junior College Student's Reasons for Occupational Choice," *Junior College Journal*, XXX (March 1960), 396–99.

18. *Opening (Fall) Enrollment in Higher Education, 1962: Institutional Data*. Washington, D.C.: USGPO, 1962.

19. Peck, Robert F., "Student Mental Health: The Range of Personality Patterns in a College Population," in *Personality Factors on the College Campus*. Austin, Tex.: The Hogg Foundation for Mental Health, 1962. Pp. 161–99.

20. *Pilot Study*. Concord, Calif.: Diablo Valley College, 1956.

21. *Report from Office of the State Superintendent of Public Instruction on Community College Enrollments for the Fall Quarter, 1962*. Olympia, Washington, 1962.

22. Rice, Joseph P., Jr., "Differing Views of Institutional Aims Among College

Students, Teachers, and Administrators," *California Journal of Educational Research*, XII (September 1961), 165–72.

23. School-Community *Development* Study Monograph, Flint College, University of Michigan, 1955–61.

24. Seashore, Harold, "Academic Abilities of Junior College Students," *Junior College Journal*, XXIX (October 1958), 74–80.

25. Sexton, Patricia C., *Education and Income: Inequities of Opportunity in Our Public Schools.* New York: The Viking Press, Inc., 1961.

26. Unpublished Study of Adult Students, Flint College, University of Michigan, 1959.

27. Unpublished Survey, Flint College, University of Michigan, 1961.

28. Wack, Dunstan J., "A Program for Student Selection at the College Level," *Journal of Higher Education*, XXXIII (June 1962), 311–15.

29. *What High School Pupils Study.* Washington, D.C.: USGPO, 1962.

30. Wolfle, Dael (ed.), *America's Resources of Specialized Talent.* New York: Harper & Row, Publishers, 1954.

There is a clear-cut distinction between the liberal and conservative approaches in respect to the faculty of the two-year college. Probably no other problem is causing more delay in the rapid development of the two-year college than the confusion as to the type of faculty member that is needed, the best methods of training and selecting these faculty members, and a clear delineation of faculty roles in regard to the functions of the two-year college.

If one were to consider the two-year college faculty from a conservative point of view, he would need only look at the current faculty relationships on many junior college campuses, where the image of the faculty is clearly that of the four-year liberal arts faculty. In such schools, the faculty is interested only in those students in the upper quartile in ability: those who can successfully pursue a baccalaureate program. Some of these faculty members are actually people who would prefer to teach in a four-year college but have not completed the requirements for the doctorate or have faltered in their search for the frontiers of knowledge and have found a haven in the junior college. Many of these faculty mem-

6

faculty-college relationships

bers are very devoted and excellent teachers of academic subjects, but they would limit the function of the junior college to serving the academic student.

The liberal approach, on the other hand, emphasizes the selection of faculty members devoted to the specific functions of the two-year college and able to define their own image without leaning on academic tradition. The liberal position is represented by faculty members who are challenged by the median or below-median student and whose thinking is not restricted to a curriculum handed down by the four-year college. They are willing to innovate; they are willing to do additional research to find those programs that will challenge a much larger group of students than the four-year college has ever attempted to educate. Much of the problem has not been a lack of courage on the part of faculty members but the lack of clarity in the definition of roles that would make it possible to challenge new faculty people with new areas of responsibility.

In summary, the conservative faculty members wish to grow gradually, following the patterns that have been established over a long period of time. They believe that tradition must not be discarded. They feel that the past provides a good model and they would rather not change it. They favor a very high level of scholarship in all program offerings. They will not accept some of the functions of the two-year college. If they had their way, the only move toward liberality would be for the junior college to take over all freshman and sophomore work and to turn four-year institutions into graduate schools. They feel that adult education does not belong in the two-year college because that field is generously covered by other community activities.

The liberal faculty members, on the other hand, are not afraid of introducing occupational training designed to meet the area's needs. They are eager to develop technical and occupational programs at the college level. They are able to think in terms of cooperation with the community in programs of adult education. They recognize the need for higher development of diagnostic skills in analyzing a student's abilities before his admission to various programs. And, finally, they are able to adapt to the student and to community needs. They want student success at all levels of ability and will constantly search for new methods to achieve this success.

The two-year college may still be regarded in some circles as a questionable quantity in American education, but there can be little question that, as an institution, it has "arrived." A characteristic of any new movement, however, is a sensitivity to criticism, an unwillingness to admit that present philosophies do not necessarily represent eternal verities. This point of view prevails among some of the leaders of the two-year college who fostered and supported the institution in its less affluent days.

With the rapid expansion of the junior college came large numbers of able persons from the secondary schools and from the universities and colleges. The influx of new ideas has provided a challenge to the traditionalists: they must examine their positions, defend them when facts permit, and alter those practices which are no longer applicable.

Conflict between the defenders of an established order and those who see a need for new approaches to meet new problems inevitably results in change. When the two-year college was still struggling for existence, little time was available for healthy controversy within the ranks of the faithful; all effort was required to sustain the fledgling institution. No one today, however, can claim that the existence of the two-year college as an important segment of American education is in serious peril. The time has come to raise issues and to challenge relationships.

There is yet another reason for questioning certain beliefs regarding the role and organization of the two-year college. Many hold to these beliefs with the emotional fervor of religious zealots. Such fervor is necessary during the early period of an organization's existence; with age comes maturity: emotional fervor gives way to reasoned hypotheses and research and a willingness to examine a variety of points of view regardless of how heretical some may seem.

Society and education

The writers of this volume have undertaken two major tasks. The first is to focus the viewpoint of the reader upon the relationships between the two-year college and the society which created and supports it. The second is to analyze the college as an organization having unique characteristics and internal problems. Too frequently the temptation is to study the college as a reality in and of itself, without stressing the essential relationships that exist between the institution and its environment and the effect this relationship has on its evolution and change. It would be much simpler if institutions could be studied as chemicals are: in isolation from contaminating external factors. But such an approach is neither feasible nor realistic for the study of such a dynamic element of society. This study will stress relationships between society and education in an effort to chart the present location and future course of the two-year college.

Every attempt has been made to inject controversial issues into the treatment of the various aspects of the two-year college. The writers, conceding a pragmatic outlook, are reluctant to espouse existing practices as absolutes. The continuum of events leading to the present moment may make certain of these approaches the best and truest practice at this time but, in a rapidly changing society, these practices will not be true for all time. New approaches must be evolved. Through ordered change the increasing responsibilities assigned by society to the two-year college can be met with vigor and dispatch.

The faculty constitutes the professional core of the community college. It translates the philosophy, purposes, objectives, and functions of the institution into meaningful action through teaching, educational guidance, and quasi-administrative work on committees. Instructors, both individually and in concert, determine the effectiveness of the institution through their contacts with students. It would seem fitting, therefore, to examine in some detail the background, attitudes, and expectations of this group as they relate to and influence the destinies of the community college.

Medsker found that 64.6 per cent of the faculty members in junior colleges studied had master's degrees, 9.6 per cent had doctorates, and 17 per cent had completed bachelor's degrees, while 8.8 per cent had no degree or were unclassifiable. Twenty-seven per cent had once attended a junior college. Over half the group had family origins in the middle or upper-middle class; 20 per cent came from families in which the fathers were engaged in farming, skilled, semiskilled and service occupations. [25:171–73]

A study by Eckert and Stecklein concluded that junior college teachers enter college teaching more by accident than by intention: they begin their educational service as high school teachers, take graduate work on a part-time basis, and later move to community college teaching posts. The study also showed that junior college faculties have greater upward mobility (fewer parents in managerial and professional work and more parents who did not finish high school; less than 40 per cent finished high school and less than 12 per cent finished college). [12:88–89]

A study of fourteen public community colleges in the South and Southwest added some more information on faculty characteristics. In the colleges studied, 9.7 per cent of the faculty had doctorates, 78 per cent had the master's degree, and 12.3 per cent had bachelor's degrees. In this group of 570 instructors, men outnumbered women by three to two; over 90 per cent were married, and the median age was forty-one years. The group had a median of fourteen years of teaching experience encompassing: (1) six years in Grades 1–12; (2) seven years in two-year colleges; and (3) one year in four-year colleges. The median period of service in the colleges studied was five years. Teachers of the humanities (English, speech, and foreign languages) had the largest number of years of experience in Grades 1–12 and in four-year colleges. Teachers of the humanities also had the longest service in the colleges studied. Mathematics and science teachers tended to be younger than English teachers and to have less experience in either Grades 1–12 or four-year colleges. Those in the social sciences had experience almost equally divided between the secondary schools and the two-year colleges, with little experience in four-year colleges.

Thus the typical junior college faculty member is an individual who has adequate-to-superior preparation and personal perceptions typical of the middle and upper-lower class. Given this individual, it would seem profitable to examine the influences which have shaped him as a person and which will influence his behavior and attitudes toward himself, his students, the college, and the community of which he is a part.

Faculty Attitudes

Junior college teachers are the products of rather standardized undergraduate and graduate programs in subject-matter fields. During their years of study, they also absorb and react to the mores and traditions of the institution itself. Universities, particularly those with outstanding graduate schools, have strong traditions of faculty control and limited direct administrative intervention in the work of the teaching faculty. Dodds describes colleges and universities as follows: "... the university displays a sort of split personality. It stems from a constant internal tug of war between the demands of conformity and of nonconformity, between the need for order and the university's mission to cultivate individuality in self expression." [11:13] It is apparent to graduate students that the professional future of university professors depends upon the senior members of the department, individual proficiency in subject matter, and the production of writing and research rather than upon broad institutional loyalties.

Reece McGee points out that professorial perceptions of the university make possible the "owning" of courses, the assessment of personnel in terms of subject-matter competence, and a closed "guild" aspect in some disciplines. He points out further that there is a conflict between the "disciplinary orientation" and the "institutional orientation," concluding:

> It is a little-recognized fact that universities are relatively lawless organizations in some respects. The professor may object to this characterization and protest that trivialities of procedure are a source of constant harassment, but such regulation is conspicuously absent in one area of great significance in the university: personnel policy and relationships and in particular the authority structure of the university as it is related to these. [24:108–109]

Factors affecting attitude

The community college teacher is not immune to the influences of his professors in graduate school. Far more than factual matter is conveyed in the classroom; the former graduate student comes to the community college with beliefs and attitudes about what a college should be.

The university also presents different perceptions of the community college from the standpoint of presidents and other university administrators. The president of a midwestern university made his opposition to community colleges clear when he pointed out to a national association of collegiate personnel that the establishment of such colleges posed a threat to both public and private institutions already in existence. He claimed that additional colleges, especially public community colleges, would unnecessarily dilute taxpayer financial support without significantly improving or expanding higher education. Another administrator in an eastern state cautioned the public that public community colleges would be a serious threat to the quality of higher education in his state.

On the other hand, community colleges have received strong support from university officials in some states. Robert Gordon Sproul, former president of the University of California, maintains:

> Without the excellent junior colleges that have developed [the University of California] would hardly have been able to establish and maintain its present high standards of admission and graduation, as would also have been true had there been no state colleges. [31:101]

Another problem which clouds the status of the community college in the eyes of faculty is the institution's general lack of the trappings so important to status in our society. For example, four-year college and university presidents, deans, and other major administrative officers are automatically listed in *Who's Who in America*. The chief executive officers of community colleges are not listed as a matter of course in spite of the fact that many such administrators are responsible for more students, more faculty members, larger budgets, and generally greater educational service than presidents of smaller colleges. Society's lack of acceptance is also apparent in the community college's lack of recognition by honorary scholastic fraternities, its restricted membership in some professional organizations, and the low status accorded the Associate of Arts degree.

Although there are many positive reactions by university professors to the work of community colleges, there are also significant negative attitudes held. These attitudes, in some cases, may be more nearly revelations of the lack of understanding of the community college than they are valid criticisms. In a survey of all the colleges in Oklahoma [28], community college faculties were criticized by university professors

(1)   For not engaging in research
(2)   For not writing sufficient articles, books, and monographs
(3)   For not having enough training in their field
(4)   For not having practical experience in those fields in which they
      instruct
(5)   For not belonging to or participating in professional societies
(6)   For not having the proper background in college teaching
(7)   For not having the depth of experience in college teaching necessary
      to do an effective job
(8)   For not maintaining high standards
(9)   For not continuing their professional growth

Examination of these criticisms reveals that the university personnel represented in the study equated the roles of the community college
faculty with their own roles in the four-year schools. Yet many of the
roles of the community college are different from those of the university. The community college is willing to deal with the average population—those who will comprise the lower-middle class, who will be neither
great successes nor failures.

The conditioning of two-year college faculty members is more pervasive than is apparent to the casual observer. A study by Kimball of fourteen public community colleges in Michigan revealed some significant
contrasts in the attitudes of administrators and faculty members toward
the community college and its purposes. [19] Eighty-two per cent of all
individuals indicated that they thought the college-transfer program was
of far greater importance than any other aspect of the college curriculum.
They were quite critical of the guidance program, 62 per cent stating that
it was the weakest segment of the college program and, although quite
important, was not functioning near the level of expectation. Most important, many faculty members did not believe that admissions standards
were high enough, that there was sufficient emphasis upon the traditional
liberal arts courses, or that the college should be closely wedded to the
community. The majority of faculty members thought the college should
be transformed into a four-year institution should the opportunity arise.

These faculty attitudes conform to their personal need for status
and recognition as members of the academic community, but such a
point of view does not contribute solutions to the problems of educating
larger and larger numbers of students. There is no question that gifted
individuals should be given appropriate opportunities for higher education but, at the same time, the needs of those students who represent the
large middle group of high school graduates should be met. The true
genius of the community college lies in its freedom from the inflexible
tradition of higher education.

According to Dean Harold G. Shane of Indiana University:

> The opportunity to develop competence must be available to all children, not just the elite. We err tragically if we try to ration educational opportunity. Ability and talent must be cultivated but we must never forget the hundreds of thousands of youngsters who inevitably must fall below the median. [30]

The faculty must take students as they are and be willing to experiment in new teaching techniques without trying to blame other schools for student deficiencies or relying on experts, for, according to Thornton, there are no experts in teaching community college students. [32]

Harris has stressed that occupational education at the semiprofessional and technical levels is definitely an obligation of higher education and that the community college is the logical unit of higher education to assume this obligation. At least three changes will have to be made:

(1) The idea of the comprehensive community college will have to grow from an idealized concept into a practical reality. Lay leaders, boards of trustees, and faculty will have to organize and administer these institutions for the benefit of all youth, not just for the 25 per cent who will go on to a four-year college.

(2) Junior college presidents will have to identify themselves personally with the occupational education program and boast about it down at the Rotary Club just as enthusiastically as they brag about the transfer program.

(3) The greatest changes of all will have to occur in the attitudes of faculty members themselves. The most significant actions are the ones they personally take. The individual day-to-day involvement of the faculty in the total educational program of the college will determine the success or failure of the enterprise. [16]

Community colleges must have a faculty of well-qualified teachers who understand the place and functions of community colleges and who are dedicated to this type of education.

Faculty Activities

A search for the image of the community college inevitably leads to a comparison of the job responsibilities and personal and professional roles of university and community college faculty members. If there are meaningful differences in the educational purposes of the two institutions, there should be discernible differences in the work of the two groups. These differences are clearly demonstrated when the professional responsibilities of the two groups are compared.

Teaching

University teaching assignments may include undergraduate, graduate, and conference or short courses. The spread of such courses in the particular subject-matter area is generally quite narrow, the courses being taught having a close relationship to the specialty of the professor. Thus, a faculty member in English may teach perhaps four different courses during the academic year—undergraduate English literature, Victorian poetry, and two graduate courses in nineteenth-century English literature. The professor of management might be teaching two or three courses in his specialty and directing the work of a number of doctoral candidates.

In contrast, the community college instructor of English might have a teaching assignment which includes five sections of English composition or three sections of composition and two of literature. The faculty member in business administration would probably be teaching three or four different courses ranging from "Introduction to Business" to "Typing."

These descriptions illustrate an essential difference between the work of the college faculty and the community college faculty: the college teacher tends to become wedded to a specific subject-matter field while the community college teacher is a generalist, teaching a cluster of courses which are a part of a broad area of study. [24:108–9]

TABLE 6-1.   Comparison of Job Responsibilities

Area	University	Community College
Instruction	Lower division	Lower division
	Upper division	Technical courses
	Graduate courses	Vocational courses
	Direction of research	Short courses
	Short courses	(credit and noncredit)
	(credit and noncredit)	
Research		
Specialized and theoretical	Extensive	Limited
Institutional	Limited	Extensive
Consultation with business		
and industry	Extensive	Limited
Government service	Extensive	Limited
Relationships with students		
Disciplinary	Limited	Limited
Academic advisement	Limited	Extensive
Counseling	Limited	Extensive
Supervision of student activities	Limited	Extensive

Research, Writing, and Consulting

A second important difference between the expectations of these two groups is related to research. University personnel are generally employed to teach and to contribute to knowledge through research. Many universities have tempered the official emphasis upon research and extended some recognition for outstanding teaching in the classroom.

Yet there continues to be strong influence bearing upon the professor to become involved in research and to produce scholarly materials largely for consumption by his colleagues. The professor is stimulated to produce not only by the desire for professional advancement, but also by the economic advantages accruing from royalties and the status he will achieve as a consultant. Consulting is a major industry in the educational world, such personnel being used extensively by schools and colleges, business, industry, and government. Consulting not only contributes to the improvement of the organizations which make use of the college professor in this role, but it constitutes an important source of income for the professor himself.

Faculty members in community colleges are, in general, not required to produce specialized and theoretical research; rather, the focus of their assignments is in the classroom. A review of faculty handbooks shows that most instructors are assigned from twelve to fifteen lecture hours and from fifteen to twenty laboratory hours per week. The responsibilities of instructors at Los Angeles City College indicate a clear delineation between pure research and applied research related to the teaching function. These instructors participate in research studies related to teaching materials, student achievement, course structure, and student follow-up studies. The purpose of these inquiries is to measure the effectiveness of teaching and learning in the college. [21:15] Institutional research of this type is carried on rather extensively in community colleges. The direction of the research rests with the academic dean and the division or department chairmen; instructors may or may not participate directly in the development of such projects. [18]

Rainey polled fifty-eight junior college presidents and deans and found that 41.4 per cent use professional writing as a criterion in hiring or promoting teachers, while 58.6 per cent do not consider it. Only 20.7 per cent reported that professional writing had a positive effect on salary. [29]

A community college instructor may do consulting but if so, it is usually limited to the surrounding geographic area and nearby industries. In some cases, such involvement is encouraged by the college administration but, by and large, it is carefully limited to prevent interference with instructional duties on the campus:

> Full-time instructors are required to give full time to the service of the college. They shall not accept outside employment except on approval of the President. Outside employment which interferes with regular duties assigned to the instructor will not be permitted. [28:13]

The third area in which there is a marked contrast in the job responsibilities of university and community college personnel centers about faculty-student relationships. Counseling, discipline, and supervision of students have grown into a specialized and highly organized activity on university campuses. University teachers are responsible for students while in the classroom, for evaluation of the students' academic progress, and for academic guidance. Community college faculty members, on the other hand, are assigned specific responsibilities in relation to students, particularly in academic advisement, counseling, and supervision of student activities.

The university vs. the community college

There are many common elements in the responsibilities of university and community college faculties. However, there are substantial differences in the frames of reference within which they, as individuals, function, the kinds of responsibilities which are assigned to them, and the amount of administrative direction they receive in their daily activities. Comparison of the defined roles of university personnel with those of two-year college faculty members demonstrates these differences. In general, universities define the roles of faculty members as including teaching, research, publication, and general contributions to society as specialists and as responsible citizens. In actual fact, the primary criterion for promotion of university personnel is research and publication despite the somewhat pious policy statements to the contrary by university administrators. The axiom "publish or perish" is the central reality on the university campus.

In contrast, community college criteria cluster around scholarship and professional growth, teaching effectiveness as evaluated by colleagues, supervisors, and administrators, and contributions to the college, department, student, and community welfare as demonstrated in a variety of leadership roles. These descriptive criteria demonstrate again the broad nature of the expectations which must be met by community college faculty members. [15]

An understanding of the roles of the community college faculty can be further enhanced by an examination of the degree of self-direction in relation to faculty functions in the college as compared with that found in the university. Such a subjective analysis cannot, of course, be used casually to evaluate the relationships of faculty to institution in individual situations; however, it can give a generalized picture of some of the more apparent differences between the roles of the faculty of a university and those of community college personnel.

The Role of the Faculty in Institutional Policy-making

The involvement of faculty members in the affairs of the community college and in those of the university can be divided into two categories: (1) general institutional policies, and (2) curricular changes.

In the university

In the university, a large measure of self-direction is vested in the various subdivisions of the organization. Faculty influence upon the general development of the university is exerted through faculty committees, the faculty senate, individual college faculties, and subject-matter departments. In many institutions, faculties have a voice in the selection of administrative personnel: e.g., department chairmen, deans, and even presidents. Their influence is felt, sometimes very strongly, in personnel policies governing appointments, evaluations, promotions, and terminations. For example, at the University of California all promotions must be approved by a committee of the faculty senate before they can be considered by the administration. This ad hoc committee is made up of faculty members appointed by a portion of the faculty senate, and the names of the committee members are known only to a very small number of faculty.

University faculties are generally insulated from external influences generated by pressure groups, state governments, or local governmental agencies. They are, however, sensitive to the attitudes of their professional colleagues. Status with their colleagues is their most important criterion of success.

In the community college

In contrast, the influence of the faculty in a community college is limited by the administrative organization of the college. The formal organization of most such colleges originally grew out of the public school pattern in which the college administrator was classified as a school principal. Direction from the board of control through the superintendent and the college dean has characterized community colleges for many years. The formal organization of the college has been set up in a traditional, well-knit, line-staff pattern.

As a result of this background, the community college faculty, until very recently, has had little impact upon the development of general institutional policies. The over-all educational objectives have been developed and enunciated by the board of control and the chief executive

TABLE 6-2. Comparison of Self-direction of Faculty Roles

Role	University Institutional Direction	University Self-direction	Community College Institutional Direction	Community College Self-direction
Influence upon institutional changes				
Curriculum	†	†	†	*
Techniques of instruction	*	†	†	†
Administrative organization				
Department	*	†	†	*
Division				
College	†	†	†	*
University	†	*		
Appointment of administrative personnel	†	†	†	*
Finance				
Department	*	†	†	*
Division			†	*
College	†	†	†	*
University	†	*		
Personnel policies				
Appointments	*	†	†	*
Evaluation	*	†	†	*
Terminations	*	†	†	*
Salaries	†	†	†	*
Promotions	*	†	†	*
Policy development	†	†	†	*
External influences, general				
Local community	*	†	†	†
State	*	†	†	†
National	*	†	*	*
External influences, professional				
Local community	*	†	†	†
State	*	†	†	*
National	*	†	†	*
Administrative direction				
Office hours	*	†	†	*
Attendance at meetings called by administration	*	†	†	*
Course outlines required	*	†	†	*
Texts and other materials used in teaching	*	†	†	*

* NOTE: † = strong
       * = limited

officer. The formal organization of the institution has been set up by administrators rather than by faculty members; appointment of administrative personnel is a board or presidential responsibility; and faculty members have little or nothing to say about college finance. Appointments and promotions are centralized in the administration. Furthermore, the administration and faculty are both more sensitive and responsive to external influences from both local and state governments.

Indeed, considering the antecedents of two-year colleges, it is understandable that the structure and influence of the faculty more nearly approximates that of secondary school teachers. The amount of direct administrative direction of faculty is revealed in community and junior college handbooks. [20] Directions for the work of faculty include a specification of office hours, an outline of duties in and out of the classroom, the encouragement of participation in community activities, and in general a multitude of other specifics customary in public school systems.

In recent years there appears to be a trend toward the strengthening of faculty influence upon policy-making. This change is the result of at least two factors: a generally more aggressive teaching profession, and the shift of community colleges from a subordinate position in public schools to independent status. The drive of professional education groups toward self-determination in recent years has been constant and vigorous. The emancipation of community colleges from public school control has been less apparent but equally important.

The two-year college may be said to resemble an organizational pyramid, while the university is a cluster of semiautonomous and self-directing units. The differences are illustrated in Fig. 6-1.

FIG. 6-1. A Comparison of the Organizational Structures of the University
and the Two-year College

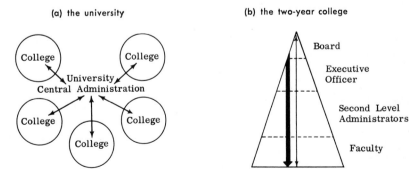

(a) the university

(b) the two-year college

The Role of the Faculty in Curriculum Change

As has been pointed out, there is a greater degree of self-direction of both an individual and a group nature in the university. Consider, for example, the evolution of the curriculum. The university has historically developed its curriculum through the evolutionary fragmentation of existing disciplines. Thus, business administration evolved from economics, and medicine grew out of the biological sciences. These changes took place when the members of the faculty, and perhaps a forceful administrator, recognized the need for further specialization. Such changes are the result of faculty interaction, usually through permanent or ad hoc committees.

Long-range revision results from social and economic pressures, the expansion of knowledge, and the availability of funds to support new educational programs. Faculty reactions to these forces, however, determine how such changes are implemented.

External forces

The community college, on the other hand, builds its curriculum in response to external influences, although these influences may be modified by the administration and the faculty. The two strongest influences on the development of the community college curriculum are university curriculum requirements and state legislation. [8] The college-transfer program, for instance, is directly controlled and limited by the colleges and universities to which transfer students apply. In some states, there are specific legal requirements and limitations upon the types of courses which can be offered by the community college.

In Texas, state financial aid is extended only to those community college courses which also appear in the offerings of four-year colleges in the state. Most state legislation also limits the community college transfer curriculum to courses normally a part of the freshman and sophomore years of four-year colleges. The community college curriculum is also the outgrowth of more specific and direct community needs as expressed by the leadership of the community. The effect of such influence can be seen in the development of the two-year nursing program. There is a critical need for more professional nurses, but the most important factor in the development of such programs has been the interest and support of local leaders, university personnel, and educational foundations.

Faculty members also recognize other external forces which have an impact upon their participation in curricular change. In a study of fourteen two-year colleges, the 349 faculty members were asked to indicate the most important influences upon curricular change. The influences, in order of importance, were:

(1)   The administration
(2)   The faculty
(3)   The students
(4)   State and regional accrediting agencies
(5)   Four-year colleges and universities
(6)   State department of education
(7)   The board of control
(8)   Other two-year college faculties
(9)   State government and agencies
(10)   Lay advisory committees

This list illustrates again the pre-eminence of college administration in the determination of curriculum but, more important, it demonstrates the faculty's awareness of the importance of groups outside the college. The faculty considers itself important in curricular matters, but there is a significantly larger distribution of influence among other groups than is characteristic of the university.

The administration

An important factor in attracting community college faculty is an administrative organization that involves the whole staff in policy decisions. If the whole staff participates in policy formation, everyone will know the policies and the reasons for their adoption whether he agrees with them or not. Although faculty control of policy-making with reference to the broad aspects of the college has allegedly eroded during the past thirty years, faculty members continue to exert strong influences upon the curriculum: what is taught and how it is taught.

It is apparent that decisions are, in Dill's words, "a series of choices and commitments that have been made in sequence." [10] It should be pointed out that decision-making may involve positive or "negative" action (i.e., no action at all). Thus, in the academic setting, lack of action is actually a decision, and the curriculum may well be controlled as much by the lack of definitive action as it is by clear-cut decisions.

Blocker and McCabe analyzed the comparative involvement of administrators and faculty members with the curriculum in an effort to define and clarify the roles of faculty members in this essential area. The study included 303 faculty and staff members in six colleges. The involvement was analyzed in three dimensions: communication, influence, and reliance. [3]

Communication refers to the transference of thought or feeling from one person to another through gesture, posture, facial expression, vocal tone and quality, as well as by speech in a face-to-face situation. *Influence* is the potentiality for inducing other persons to act in a certain manner or change in a given direction. *Reliance* refers to the willingness of members to depend upon other members within the system.

This study showed that faculty members have significant influence upon the development and implementation of the curriculum. This influence is apparent when the formal line-staff organization of a public college which offers a comprehensive group of educational programs is compared with the informal organization. While the formal organization traditionally reflects a four-level hierarchy (see Fig. 6-2), the informal

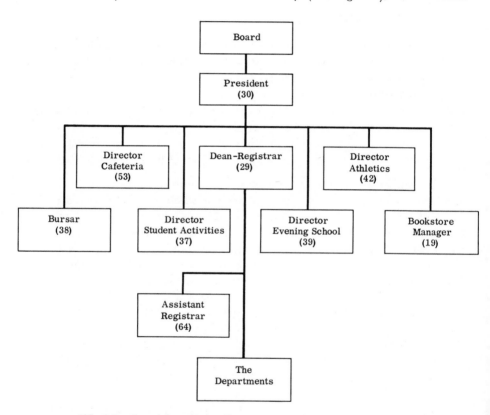

FIG. 6-2. Formal Organization Chart

organization reveals the actual individual interactions affecting the curriculum (see Fig. 6-3). Figure 6-2 (formal organization) indicates that the board of control assigned specific responsibility for the development and supervision of the curriculum to the president, who then delegated this responsibility to the dean-registrar.

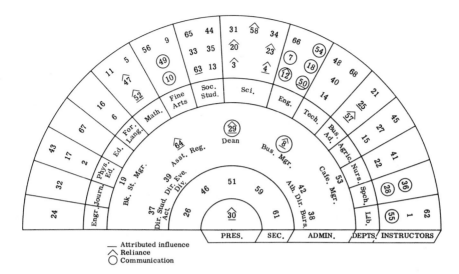

FIG. 6-3. Informal Organization Staff

Figure 6-3 (informal organization), however, reveals that there are a number of influentials who contribute to curriculum development and change. The business manager, although he has no formal assignment on educational policy-making, occupies an important place in the informal organization. The assistant registrar is also in an influential position, second only to that of the dean-registrar and the business manager.

There are influentials in the departments of mathematics, fine arts, social sciences, science, English, business administration, speech, and the library. The two most important departments are English and social science; these have the most individuals with high influence, communication, and reliance. Rank order, in the three dimensions, of the top ten individuals in the college was as follows: [3:23–30]

Communication	Reliance	Influence
Dean-Registrar (29)*	Dean-Registrar (29)	Dean-Registrar (29)
Instructor—English (18)	Instructor—Business (57)	Business Manager (8)
Librarian (55)	Instructor—Science (23)	President (30)
Instructor—English (12)	Instructor—Mathematics (52)	Assistant Registrar (64)
Instructor—Music (10)	President (30)	Instructor—English (50)
Business Manager (8)	Instructor—Science (3)	Instructor—Business (57)
Instructor—Speech (36)	Instructor—Science (58)	Instructor—Science (4)
Instructor—English (7)	Assistant Registrar (64)	Instructor—Business (25)
Instructor—English (50)	Instructor—English (12)	Instructor—Mathematics (52)
Instructor—English (54)	Business Manager (8)	Instructor—Social Science (63)

---

* The numbers identify individuals in the college.

This study showed that the faculty was a major force in decisions related to the curriculum. The college president was not the most powerful individual in this sphere; rather, the dean was the central figure, with the registrar second, the president third, and the business manager fourth in importance among administrators. Department chairmen were influential in about half the colleges, and in those instances they consistently had a number of influential faculty members in their departments. The departments with the most influence were English, social science, and science. In no case was a technical or vocational department dominant in curriculum matters.

These data, however limited, indicate that there are important changes taking place in the relationship of the faculty to educational policy-making. There seems to be a trend toward the diffusion of decision-making on curriculum matters, a trend that is of major significance to the further development of the two-year college and the services it will provide in the future.

Faculty Rank Systems

One of the undecided issues in community colleges is the awarding of academic rank to faculty members. According to the American Association of University Professors, more than one hundred community colleges have academic rank systems. [2:89-93] Surveys by the National Education Association showed that, of the reporting colleges, 59 had academic rank systems in 1962, and 106 had them in 1964. [22:21]

The surveys mentioned above were used by Blocker and Wolfe in a study to determine: (1) which colleges had academic rank systems, (2) when the systems were adopted, and (3) details of the policies governing the systems. [5] The results showed that 88 colleges (53 public and 35

TABLE 6-3. Adoption of Academic Rank Systems

| | Number of Colleges | |
Year	Public	Private
No date given	2	6
1920–57	15	12
1958	6	4
1959	3	3
1960	3	2
1961	8	2
1962	8	3
1963	6	3
Effective 1964	2	0
Total	53	35

private) had faculty rank systems. The systems were adopted by the various colleges over a thirty-four-year period, with most adoptions taking place in the late 1950's and 1960's. Table 6-3 shows that the increase in the number of colleges establishing rank systems has noticeably accelerated in recent years.

Introduction

Who was responsible for the introduction of academic rank as a personnel policy? The primary responsibility seems to lie with the college administrators. In seventeen public colleges, the major impetus for adopting rank came from administrators; in ten instances, from a combination of administrators and faculty members; and in three cases from a combination of administrators and board members. Boards of control, state or local, participated in the development of the system in a total of seventeen colleges, and in ten cases the board took the initiative for establishing the policy (see Fig. 6-4).

The majority of private colleges—twenty—reported that the administration initiated the academic rank system. In six colleges the faculty requested that the system be adopted. In four, adoption resulted from the combined efforts of faculty members and administrators; in five, the governing board implemented the policy.

The reasons given by administrators for the adoption of academic rank systems in two-year colleges indicate a desire for the status symbols

FIG. 6-4. Venn Diagram of Sources of Impetus for Adopting Faculty Rank System

(a) public community colleges   (b) private junior colleges

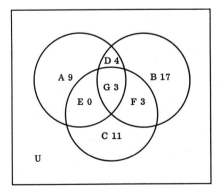 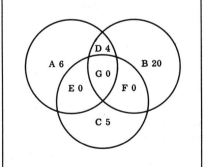

A = Faculty
B = Administration
C = Governing board
D = Combined faculty and
 administration
E = Combined faculty and
 governing board

F = Combined administration
 and governing board
G = Combined faculty,
 administration, and
 governing board
U = Universe

characteristic of higher education. The reason most often given was the desire to conform to the university system; the second, to link salary and teaching proficiency; the third, to increase the status and morale of the faculty. Other reasons were: to recognize and reward service, to motivate graduate study by the faculty, and to attract better faculty members.

TABLE 6-4. Reasons for Adopting Faculty Rank Systems *

| | *Number of Schools* | |
Reason	Public	Private
To conform with practices of universities	24	4
To link salary with teaching proficiency	8	15
To increase status and morale of faculty	15	7
To motivate graduate study by faculty	3	4
To recognize and reward service	4	4
To attract better faculty	5	3
To provide line of responsibility		3
To aid in accreditation and evaluation		2
To encourage scholarly publication	2	
To conform to state employment system	5	
To improve opportunity for grants and fellowships for faculty	1	
To aid students make transition from high school to college	2	
To establish salary scale separate from that of public schools	1	
Unknown		2

* NOTE: Respondents gave one or more reasons.

The private college emphasized the relationship between teaching proficiency and salary twice as much as public colleges. This is not surprising: most public colleges have detailed salary schedules which include annual increments for the teaching faculty. The reactions of both public and private colleges show a tendency to use faculty rank as a mark of professional status and membership in the academic fraternity.

Policies

A majority of the reporting colleges had developed policies for the promotion of faculty members. The criteria used differed from those traditionally used in four-year colleges and universities—i.e., research, teaching, and professional service; there was more emphasis upon professional growth, teaching performance, experience and length of service, and contributions to the development of the college. There are good reasons for these differences. Salary schedules in public two-year colleges are based upon education and service; private colleges have a similar, but more flexible, policy. Furthermore, teachers in two-year colleges do not generally hold doctorates; thus, they can continue to take courses in their fields which will help them become better classroom leaders.

TABLE 6-5.   Criteria for Promotion of Faculty Members *

Criteria	Number of Schools	
	Public	Private
Academic preparation and continuing education (professional growth)	42	25
Teaching performance and effectiveness	37	20
Experience and length of service	24	20
Contributions to development of the college	26	9
Scholarly research and publications	17	6
Community service	16	4
Attitude toward the profession	13	3
Rapport with students, faculty, and administration	6	3
Miscellaneous	4	2

* NOTE: Respondents listed one or more criteria.

Criticisms

There are two opposing points of view regarding the appropriateness of faculty rank systems in two-year colleges. Differences between four-year and two-year faculties are pointed out by Eckert and Stecklein. Community college teachers give a higher percentage of their working time to teaching (74 per cent, as compared with 63 per cent for four-year college teachers) and to other student services such as counseling and work with various clubs and sports. They devote less time to research, which is not surprising in view of their median credit hours (13.6 hours) and class contact hours (17.3 hours, five more than reported by faculty in four-year colleges). Most junior college faculty members (59 per cent, as compared with 41 per cent for the four-year college teachers) said they would like to spend still more time on teaching, counseling, and other student services if they were able to reduce their working hours. This contrasts sharply with the stress faculty members in four-year colleges place on research (specified by only half as many junior college as four-year college people).

Furthermore, 31 per cent of those teaching in junior colleges and 50 per cent of those teaching in four-year colleges said they were "very satisfied" with their career choice. Faculty in both types of college identified low salaries as the greatest single cause for dissatisfaction. Heavy teaching loads constituted the second major complaint of junior college faculty. Other faculty members commented on the lack of a collegiate atmosphere (when two-year colleges are housed in the same building as high schools), the similarity in regulations and pay scales with those for high schools, the difficulty in obtaining leaves for further study, and the necessity for members to pay their own expenses at professional meetings and functions. [12]

Certain advantages are enjoyed by community college teachers:

(1) They are a part of a highly dynamic movement.
(2) They have an opportunity to experiment in teaching.
(3) They occupy excellent positions for which no doctorate is required.
(4) They have status in the community: they are recognized as college teachers.
(5) They have less supervision and control than teachers in K–12.
(6) They have opportunities for promotion.
(7) They can develop stimulating relationships with students because the emphasis is upon teaching rather than on research.
(8) They receive good pay.
(9) They can go on to university teaching and other educational agencies.
(10) They can finish work on their doctorates while teaching.
(11) They have the opportunity to shape an image of the new or rapidly expanding community college and thus to make a creative contribution to higher education.

Tillery has admonished junior college personnel to consider the unity of purpose for which two-year colleges were established:

> The status of research and scholarship, the dictum of "publish or perish," and the emphasis on academic standards and curriculum are increasingly characteristic of the university and four-year college models. However appropriate these demands and values may be for senior and graduate education, they are in conflict with the teaching, guidance, and service functions of the junior college. [33]

Hendrix also questioned the wisdom of establishing such procedures:

> Academic rank policies and procedures are associated with some desirable characteristics, but are also uniquely related to sufficient undesirable characteristics to cast suspicion on the advisability of such policies for the public junior college. [17:30]

Those who think professorial rank is imperative include Freiberger and Crawford:

> For or against is no longer the consideration regarding the established standard of academic rank and title. The big question lies in how to arrange, organize, and balance this distinction in the hundreds of junior colleges all over the country. [14:89]

The two-year college faces a difficult dilemma in connection with the faculty rank system. The advantages of having such a system are important in that they shift the image of the college from that of a secondary school to that of an institution of higher education and can, if properly administered, improve faculty recognition and morale. The identification of the college as a part of higher education is important in its relations with high schools, colleges and universities, the community, students, and local and state governing bodies which supply financial support. More important, the distinguishing symbol of professional status and acceptance can attract and hold teachers with excellent academic and teaching qualifications. Furthermore, the morale of the teaching staff can be enhanced through promotion. As has been pointed out, one of the significant weaknesses of the two-year college, as seen by faculty members, is the lack of opportunity for professional advancement.

If the granting of professorial rank would contribute to more favorable self-perception and professional status for faculty members, it might well be worth the disadvantages claimed by some authors.

There are more explicit questions which cast doubt upon the wisdom of establishing academic rank in two-year colleges. Some of these are immediate and practical, and others involve long-range considerations as to the future of this type of institution. There should be thoughtful deliberation of the following questions:

(1) Will the introduction of faculty rank improve instruction in the college?

(2) Who should be given faculty rank—only teachers of traditional subjects, or all members of the faculty? Should teachers of technical and vocational programs be given professorial rank?

(3) Is the establishment of faculty rank an indication of a drift toward traditional personnel policies and internal organizational structure which will inhibit the further development of the two-year college as a unique institution of higher education?

(4) Will faculty rank shift the emphasis of the two-year college from broad educational service for unselected students to a narrower concept of education based upon the university model?

(5) Will faculty rank policies encourage rigidity of personnel policies and educational programs to the detriment of the objectives of the two-year college?

The question as to whether community and junior colleges should have faculty rank is currently an open issue. If present trends continue, there is little doubt that most colleges will have some such policy in the future. The patterns which are adopted and the reactions of administrators and faculty members to them will determine, to a large measure, the future development of two-year colleges.

Faculty Morale

With the exception of Medsker's study, there is a dearth of substantive information about the attitudes and morale of instructors in two-year colleges. Medsker found that 78.9 per cent of the individuals polled were either completely satisfied or well satisfied with their present positions, 8.2 per cent were neutral, and 11.4 were dissatisfied. [25:174] A study by Blocker and Richardson examined the morale of faculty members in six public colleges. [4] The analysis was based upon a morale inventory which included twelve categories:

(1)   Communication
(2)   Confidence in administration
(3)   Relations with immediate supervisor
(4)   Relations with fellow employees
(5)   Relations with students
(6)   Status and recognition
(7)   Identification with institution
(8)   Opportunities for professional advancement
(9)   Adequacy of salary
(10) Adequacy of fringe benefits
(11) Work environment
(12) Work load

There was wide variation among the colleges studied; but, more important, morale in several categories was consistently low in all the institutions.

The most serious problem appears to lie in the belief that there is little opportunity for professional advancement. If possibilities for advancement are limited, the professionally mobile instructor may come to view the two-year college as a stepping-stone to a four-year college. The result might be a constant flow of the better teachers from the junior college to the four-year college.

Other areas which should be of concern to college administrators are: dissatisfaction with salaries, work load, work environment, and relations with students. Faculty members apparently have expectations which are not satisfied by their opportunities for professional advancement and work conditions. Low salaries are a perennial problem which, in many instances, is beyond the scope of administrative action, but work load and work environment can be adjusted to conform more closely to the patterns generally associated with institutions of higher education.

Perhaps the most significant implication of these data is the amount of faculty dissatisfaction with students. Some representative statements revealing attitudes of faculty toward their students were:

(1)   "The students in this college are not interested in learning."
(2)   "Many of the students are very immature and tend to be narrow in their interests."
(3)   "Students here show little concern for the feelings of other people."

TABLE 6-6. Comparison of Faculty Morale
in Six Public Junior Colleges * [4:19]

Score	1	2	3	4	5	6	7	8	9	10	11	12
100												
90												
							C					
							B					
80							DEF					
				D								
										D	D	
			E	B		B						
			B			E						
70	B	E		E		C						E
		B										
										B		
				E			A				E	
				F								
			D								B	D
60	E	D	C			D				F		
						F						
	D				A				D			
			F			A						B
		F	A									
50				C						AC		
	F											
		C										
	C											
				B								F
40											F	
				D								
								A				
								B				
	A							F			C	
								C				C
30				A								
					F				E			
								E				
					C							
								C				
20		A						B				
								F				
												A
10										E	A	
								A				
0								D				

* NOTE: The six colleges are identified by letter designations.

As we have seen in Chapters 2 and 5, there is little reason to expect students in the two-year college to conform to the traditional expectations of college-age youth. The "open door" admission policy and the relatively low socioeconomic origins of students are quite different from policies and origins in the selective four-year colleges. Lack of faculty understanding of and rapport with students indicates, at least to a limited degree, that a substantial proportion of two-year college faculty members do not clearly understand or accept the primary function of the public community college. There is a tendency for faculty members to disparage student capabilities and seek methods of upgrading admission standards. The purposes of the colleges would be better served if faculty members bent their energies toward the development of basically important reforms in instruction and guidance which would assist students to master college requirements and to achieve personal and intellectual competence.

Faculty perception of personal identification with the college, status and recognition, relations with fellow employes, relations with immediate supervisors, and fringe benefits were generally positive. Thus, it would seem that interpersonal relationships in these colleges were generally good. Perhaps these factors account for the relative stability of faculty members in spite of the many opportunities for movement to other educational institutions.

Academic Freedom

Academic freedom has been a persistent problem in American education since the 1600's. The two-year college has not escaped from the problems of controversial issues related to the subject matter being studied and taught. The relationship between academic freedom and education has been pointed out by Brode:

> The scholar has, in fact, no rights or immunities that other citizens do not possess, but he does have a substantially greater responsibility for the full exercise of these rights. It will be possible to develop an intelligent and creative society only if the scholars in our educational system plant and keep alive the freedoms of thought and speech. . . .
> A teacher cannot properly present his subject if he is restrained in the expression of his own thoughts and beliefs. A student also must be free to express his opinions and beliefs. . . . The freedom to think includes not only the right of the individual to think and to believe; it also includes his freedom to communicate these thoughts to others. [6:90-91]

During the past two decades, there has been increasing conflict between the academic community and nonacademic groups and individuals, growing out of ideological differences, both domestic and inter-

national. The emphasis upon national security and the emergence of
what amounts almost to national dogma has generated pressures in society for the restriction of free discussion of controversial subjects in the
classroom. In several instances, individual teachers have been attacked
and particular colleges have been subjected to threats of retaliation (i.e.,
the withdrawal of financial support) because of disagreements as to the
meaning of academic freedom.

Expectations and perceptions

This policy, however applied, is probably of greater importance to
the faculty than any other aspect of their relationship with the college
and the community. Being professionals, they expect maximum freedom
in teaching, and external interference can result in a general debilitation
of the quality of teaching and of the morale of the faculty. Perhaps more
important is the impression made upon students, who quickly realize that
they are being denied the opportunity to consider and debate essential
questions and to form their own opinions concerning these areas.

Consistent with the growing maturity of the two-year college is the
shift from provincial to cosmopolitan attitudes toward academic freedom. Rather than tailoring classroom discussion and course content to
avoid conflicts with the views of a few individuals in the community
power structure, most colleges are adopting the position of the American
Association of University Professors on academic freedom:

> The teacher is entitled to full freedom in research and in the publication
> of the results, subject to the adequate performance of his other academic
> duties; but research for pecuniary return should be based upon an under-
> standing with the authorities of the institution.
>
> The teacher is entitled to freedom in the classroom in discussing his
> subject, but he should be careful not to introduce into his teaching contro-
> versial matter which has no relation to his subject. Limitations of academic
> freedom because of religious or other aims of the institution should be
> clearly stated in writing at the time of the appointment.
>
> The college or university teacher is a citizen, a member of a learned
> profession, and an officer of an educational institution. When he speaks
> or writes as a citizen, he should be free from institutional censorship or
> discipline, but his special position in the community imposes special
> obligations. As a man of learning and an educational officer, he should
> remember that the public may judge his profession and his institution by
> his utterances. Hence he should at all times be accurate, should exercise
> appropriate restraint, should show respect for the opinions of others, and
> should make every effort to indicate that he is not an institutional spokes-
> man. [1:192–93]

There are marked regional and institutional differences in perceptions of academic freedom. Two-year colleges which are branches of

public colleges and universities enjoy the same degree of freedom characteristic of the parent institution; community colleges located in urban
areas tend to have more permissive policies than small colleges in rural
or semirural areas. In some states (Texas, for example) legislation has
been passed to insure the freedom of teachers to participate in political
activities. In contrast, church-related private colleges impose restrictions
upon faculty members consistent with the tenets of the supporting denomination. Such limitations are reasonable if they are made clear at
the time the appointment is made.

The public two-year college continues to have problems in the
matter of academic freedom. First, the college functions as a part of the
local community. Its faculty members are also friends and neighbors of
the parents of students, board members, and influential citizens. There
is continual interaction between the college faculty and the citizens, so
that any deviation from the traditions and mores of the community
is immediately apparent to all. This close relationship exerts a subtle but
pervasive influence toward conformity by the faculty.

Second, local communities tend to be conservative on issues which
have a direct bearing upon the status quo. If the social or economic balance of the community is threatened by the faculty, there may well be a
strong negative reaction. Such is not the case when the college serves a
large area or a large population and interaction is more tenuous and of
less immediate importance to the values and self-interest of the adult
population.

Third, students in two-year colleges tend to be more conservative
and less sophisticated than those in other collegiate institutions. They
are generally less tolerant of new ideas and resist those which challenge
their preconceptions. Although this condition may be altered through
further educational experiences, it can have important implications for
academic freedom. The transmission of new and different ideas from the
college to the home through the student can lead to incidents and misunderstandings as to the content of courses and the concepts being considered in the classroom. If the community has conservative or reactionary
tendencies, there can be serious limitations imposed upon the free discussion of controversial material in college classes.

The balance between responsible teaching and learning and externally imposed restraints by conservative groups has not been successfully maintained in some two-year colleges. In some communities there
have been vigorous attacks upon the patriotism and honesty of teachers,
with the result that there is a constant gnawing fear that inhibits free
and open discussion of issues of importance to the immediate area and
to the country as a whole.

Attracting Able Faculty Members

Charles and Summerer identify the following characteristics as criteria for competence in faculty members: [7]

(1)   His credentials should give clear evidence that he can be effective with students in the classroom and individual relationships. He should not have the attitude that all responsibility for learning rests with the student.

(2)   He should have at least a master's degree in his subject-matter field. He should also demonstrate continuing interest in his field through reading, further graduate study, travel, and related research.

(3)   He should have positive attitudes toward extracurricular activities and an understanding of the importance of such activities for the social maturity of students.

(4)   He should have some courses in education which will help him be a better teacher and help him have a better concept of the educational mission of the two-year college.

(5)   He should have a well-adjusted personality which will aid him in establishing effective personal relationships with others in the community.

(6)   He should be willing to become a part of the activities of the community.

Contrary to the first impression one might get from this list, Charles and Summerer are not saying that the college instructor should be a strict conformist. They point out, "Part of the experience students should receive in attending college is contact with instructors who possess different philosophies, characteristics, and backgrounds." In order to insure variations in faculty members the administration of the college should employ faculty members from a number of different universities, from different regions of the country, and from various socioeconomic backgrounds.

If the college faculty can shake off the research image and emphasize the contribution that teachers can make *as teachers* to the community college concept, progress will be made toward developing real community college teachers. Those who cannot recognize the function of this type of college should not be encouraged to vegetate at the community college with a continuous salary schedule; they should be encouraged to seek reward elsewhere.

Alvin Eurich says that enough good faculty members can be attracted by:

(1) Higher salaries and flexible salary scales with merit properly re-
     warded (across-the-board salary scales, with the sole criterion for
     advancement being the number of years of service, attract across-
     the-board mediocrity)
(2) Prestige of the community college through some noticeable distinc-
     tion—administration, faculty, community, or experimentation
(3) A close relationship with a university through internships, exchange
     of teachers, or the use of university teachers on a part-time basis
(4) A nationwide effort to prepare college teachers
(5) Establishment of cooperative arrangements between groups of
     junior colleges
(6) Use of retired people
(7) Employment of part-time people such as married women with
     master's degrees and professional people in industry

Eurich feels that staff members will also have to be used more effectively. He suggests television instruction, team teaching to include
students, the use of long-distance telephone lectures by outstanding lec-
turers, and a variety of opportunities for individual study, such as language laboratories, programed learning, independent study, and honors
programs. [13]

Faculty Perceptions

It is apparent that there is no consistency between the perceptions
of faculty members and the stated objectives of two-year colleges. Absolute congruence is not necessarily desirable, for it could lead to complete
stultification, but there must be a stronger link between the values, attitudes, and motivations of individual staff members and the objectives of
the college if the educational program is to be a success. General institutional purposes are translated into action and behavior patterns by
faculty members, and these patterns are subsequently transmitted to students. At this point, a synthesis of institutional and individual objectives takes place. If there is a high level of conflict between individual
and institutional objectives, the educational program is endangered.

There appears to be a continuing struggle between the conservative
position and the liberal concepts. The conflict also involves a persistent
tug-of-war between faculty desire for strong professional identification
and the college's need for equally strong institutional identification. The
conflict is pointed up by the attitudes of the faculty toward selective
admission policies and academic rank systems, their preference for college-parallel programs, and the ineffectual position of technical personnel
in the informal organization. On the other hand, the public community

college feels the pressures of society for meaningful adaptations of its educational services to the changing needs growing out of a complex technical economic order.

Consider the relationship of professional-institutional identification. One of the fundamental motivations of all professionals is personal identification as a member of a clearly defined and socially acceptable professional group. Teachers at all levels of education regard participation in professional organizations as a mark of status. Academic status is also accorded the individual who writes in learned journals and whose name is well-known to those in his field of study. These status symbols are important to the individual who aspires to reach the top of his professional group. They also reflect credit upon the college with which he is associated. On the other hand, the two-year college needs individuals who have status in their professional groups, but who are also deeply committed to service to the college itself. Two-year colleges, if they are to achieve their stated objectives, cannot afford to have a faculty which is so "profession-oriented" that services to students and community become a secondary consideration. Ideally, there should be a balance between these two extremes, so that individual and college status can be achieved in a mutually beneficial relationship.

Faculty relationships with the college in the context of the liberal-conservative continuum encounter the same problem. The two-year college must find some middle ground to develop its own unique role, while also providing acceptable transfer programs. There must be a successful balance between traditionalism and experimentation. Faculty members and administrators must carefully re-examine accepted concepts of quality and purpose in higher education in light of the needs of society. The easy way is to accept traditional assumptions and drift toward highly selective, university-oriented two-year colleges, thus sidestepping the critical issues facing higher education today. But the two-year college and its faculty members are viable enough to develop new patterns of education relevant to the multivariant demands of a rapidly changing society.

Bibliography

1. "Academic Freedom and Tenure, 1940 Statement of Principles," *AAUP Bulletin,* XLIX (June 1963), 192–93.

2. American Association of University Professors, "Two-year Institutions with Systems of Rank," Bulletin No. 189-2-61, 1961.

3. Blocker, Clyde E., and Robert H. McCabe, *Relationships Between the Informal Organization and the Curriculum in Six Junior Colleges.* Austin, Tex.: University of Texas, 1964.

4. _____, and Richard C. Richardson, Jr., "Human Relations Are Important," *Junior College Journal*, XXXIV (April 1964), 19–22.

5. _____, and Wendell Wolfe, "Academic Rank in Two-year Colleges," *Junior College Journal*, XXXV (December 1964), 21–25.

6. Brode, Robert B., "The Responsibilities and Freedoms of the Scholar," in Charles Frankel (ed.), *Issues in University Education*. New York: Harper & Row, Publishers, 1959. Pp. 80–97.

7. Charles, Searle F., and Kenneth H. Summerer, "Building a Junior College Faculty," *Junior College Journal*, XXIX (March 1959), 421–23.

8. Colvert, C. C., "A Study of Official External Influences in the Curriculum of Public Colleges," *Junior College Journal*, XXXI (December 1960), 210–13.

9. Crawford, William H., and Henry M. Reitan, "The Junior College Challenge of the Sixties," *Junior College Journal*, XXXI (December 1960), 183–89.

10. Dill, William R., "Administrative Decision-making," in S. Mallick and E. H. Van Ness (eds.), *Concepts and Issues in Administrative Behavior*. Englewood Cliffs, N.J.: Prentice-Hall, Inc., 1962. Pp. 29–48.

11. Dodds, Harold W., *The Academic President—Educator or Caretaker?* New York: McGraw-Hill Book Company, 1962.

12. Eckert, Ruth E., and John E. Stecklein, "Career Motivation and Satisfactions of Junior College Teachers," *Junior College Journal*, XXX (October 1959), 83–89.

13. Eurich, Alvin C., "Staffing Junior Colleges," *Junior College Journal*, III (March 1963), 8–12.

14. Freiberger, Helenes T., and W. H. Crawford, "Junior College Academic Rank and Title," *Junior College Journal*, XXXIII (October 1962), 89–92.

15. *Guidelines: Criteria for Appointment, Reappointment, Tenure, and Promotion*. New York: Bronx Community College, 1962.

16. Harris, Norman C., Speech at the Institute of College and University Administration at the University of Michigan, Ann Arbor, Michigan, June 27, 1963.

17. Hendrix, Vernon L., "Academic Rank: Mostly Peril?" *Junior College Journal*, XXXIV (December 1963), 28–30.

18. Johnson, B. Lamar, "Institutional Research in Western Junior Colleges," *Junior College Journal*, XXXII (March 1962), 370–79.

19. Kimball, John R., "Analysis of Institutional Objectives in Michigan Community Colleges." Unpublished doctoral dissertation presented at Michigan State University, East Lansing, Michigan, 1960.

20. Kintzer, Frederick C., *Faculty Handbooks in California Junior Colleges*. Los Angeles: School of Education, University of California, 1961.

21. *Los Angeles City College Faculty Handbook*. Los Angeles: Los Angeles City College, 1960.

22. Maul, Ray O., "Are Junior College Salaries Competitive?" *Junior College Journal*, XXXIV (March 1964), 20–23.

23. McCleary, Lloyd E., "A Study of Interpersonal Influence Within a School Staff." Unpublished doctoral dissertation presented at the University of Illinois, Urbana, Illinois, 1957.

24. McGee, Reece, *Social Disorganization in America.* San Francisco: Chandler Publishing Company, 1962.

25. Medsker, Leland L., *The Junior College: Progress and Prospect.* New York: McGraw-Hill Book Company, 1960.

26. Miller, James G., Summer Session Lecture at University of Michigan, Ann Arbor, Michigan, June 22, 1963.

27. *Odessa College Faculty Guide.* Odessa, Tex.: Odessa College, 1960.

28. Rainey, William G., "Analysis of Criticisms of Junior College Teachers by University and Senior College Staffs," *Junior College Journal,* XXX (December 1959), 208–12.

29. _____, "Philosophies Related to Research and Publication by Faculty Members," *Junior College Journal,* XXXII (October 1961), 86–90.

30. Shane, Harold G., Speech at the 34th Annual University of Michigan Summer Conference, Ann Arbor, Michigan, July 15, 1963.

31. Sproul, Robert Gordon, "Many Millions More," *The Educational Record,* XXXIX (April 1958), 101.

32. Thornton, James W., Jr., "Who Are the Students in the Junior College?" *Junior College Journal,* XXIX (October 1958), 89–96.

33. Tillery, Dale H., "Academic Rank: Promise or Peril?" *Junior College Journal,* XXXIII (February 1963), 6–9.

34. Williamson, E. G., "An Outsider's View of Junior College Guidance Programs," *Junior College Journal,* XXX (May 1960), 489–501.

Organizational Models

Basic to the analysis of the structure and functioning of any organization is the rationale within which the examination is carried out. The theoretical position adopted will set the general framework and will. to a large extent, determine the conclusions. The two-year college will be analyzed as an organization within the context of two variant points of view: one essentially mechanistic and traditional, the other based upon recent developments in sociology and psychology. Both positions can be useful in acquiring a better understanding of the structure and functioning of the college.

Gouldner outlined the two points of view under the classifications of *the rational model of organizational analysis* and *the natural-system model of organizational analysis.*

> In the rational model, the organization is conceived as an "instrument"—that is, as a rationally conceived means to the realization of these group purposes. Organizational behavior is thus viewed as consciously and rationally administered, and changes in organizational patterns are viewed as planned devices to improve the level of efficiency. The rational model assumes that decisions are made on the basis of a rational survey of the situation, utilizing certified knowledge with a deliberate orientation to an

7

administrative structure and functions

expressly codified legal apparatus. The focus is, therefore, on the legally prescribed structures—i.e., the formally "blueprinted" patterns—since these are more largely subject to deliberate inspection and rational manipulation.

This model takes account of departures from rationality but often tends to assume that these departures derive from random mistakes, due to ignorance or error in calculation. Fundamentally, the rational model implies a "mechanical" model, in that it views the organization as a structure of manipulable parts, each of which is separately modifiable with a view to enhancing the efficiency of the whole. Individual organizational elements are seen as subject to successful and planned modification, enactable by deliberate decision. The long-range development of the organization as a whole is also regarded as subject to planned control and as capable of being brought into increasing conformity with explicitly held plans and goals. . . .

The natural-system model regards the organization as a "natural whole," or system. The realization of the goals of the system as a whole is but one of several important needs to which the organization is oriented. Its component structures are seen as emergent institutions, which can be understood only in relation to the diverse needs of the total system. The organization, according to this model, strives to survive and to maintain its equilibrium, and this striving may persist even after its explicitly held goals have been successfully attained. This strain toward survival may even on occasion lead to the neglect or distortion of the organization's goals. Whatever the plans of their creators, organizations, say the natural-system theorists, become ends in themselves and possess their own distinctive needs which have to be satisfied. Once established, organizations tend to generate new ends which constrain subsequent decisions and limit the manner in which the nominal group goals can be pursued.

Organizational structures are viewed as spontaneously and homeostatically maintained. Changes in organizational patterns are considered the results of cumulative, unplanned, adaptive responses to threats to the equilibrium of the system as a whole. Responses to problems are thought of as taking the form of crescively developed defense mechanisms and as being importantly shaped by shared values which are deeply internalized in the members. The empirical focus is thus directed to the spontaneously emergent and normatively sanctioned structures in the organization.

The focus is not on deviations from rationality but, rather, on disruptions of organizational equilibrium, and particularly on the mechanisms by which equilibrium is homeostatically maintained. When deviations from planned purposes are considered, they are viewed not so much as due to ignorance or error but as arising from constraints imposed by the existent social structure. In given situations, the ignorance of certain participants may not be considered injurious but functional to the maintenance of the system's equilibrium.

The natural-system model is typically based upon an underlying "organismic" model which stresses the interdependence of the component parts. Planned changes are therefore expected to have ramifying consequences for the whole organizational system. When, as frequently happens, these consequences are unanticipated, they are usually seen as divergent from, and as not supportive of, the planner's intentions. Natural-system theorists tend to regard the organization as a whole as organically "growing," with a "natural history" of its own which is planfully modifiable only at great peril, if at all. Long-range organizational development is then regarded as an evolution, conforming to "natural laws" rather than to the planner's designs. [17:404–7]

Neither of these models, in its pure, undiluted form, is adequate for the analysis of the college as an organization; however, both positions are useful in that each contributes to better understanding of institutional form and functions. More important, perhaps, is the relationship between one or the other of the models and the beliefs of individuals, both inside and outside the colleges, as to the appropriateness of one position or the other. The rational model conforms more closely to the conservative attitudes and perceptions described in Chapter 1, while the natural systems concept incorporates more permissive and liberal attitudes. The primary difference between the two positions is the stress, or lack of stress, upon rationality or individual and group interaction as the primary foundation of organizational life. The administrative style of responsible officers in the organization, and the institutional climate itself, will depend heavily upon which of the two positions is given greatest value.

Both models must be employed if the administration of the two-year college is to be understood. Every organization must have a quantum of the rational in order to meet minimal levels of efficiency, and, at the same time, psychosocial interactions, both rational and irrational, must be considered an important dimension of the organization. The analysis of administration of the two-year college will use both points of view as they are appropriate to the structure and functioning of the organization. Thus, the formal structure of the college will be examined as background for the analysis of the functional aspects of administration in this particular setting.

Getzels has developed a model which concisely outlines the essential elements of any organization. This scheme includes two principal dimensions—nomothetic-sociological and idiographic-psychological. [15] In the case of the two-year college, the nomothetic dimension includes the college as a functioning entity, its educational roles, and the expectations for its task performance. The individual staff member and the student bring to the organization the idiographic dimension which continually interacts within the social context, with observed behavior as the end product.

A Concept of Administration

Administration is simply the direction and coordination of these two components of the organization. Or, as Knezevich puts it:

School administration is defined as a process concerned with creating, maintaining, stimulating, and unifying the energies within an educational institution toward realization of the predetermined objectives. [27:12–13]

It should be noted that this definition considers administration as a process, not as a static entity existing for purposes contained within itself. The distinction is of major importance: too often administrative structure becomes the end rather than the means to the achievement of institutional objectives. Parkinson's Law, the geometric expansion of administrative bureaucracy within organizations, is a phenomenon not unknown in community colleges. The human personality being what it is, the overexpansion of structure for reasons other than service to students can be a serious impediment to effective administration. Administration is creative. That is, it provides both the structure and the functions necessary for the systematic operation of an organization. Furthermore, it maintains equilibrium and stability within the organization, hopefully without stultifying the creativity of individuals and the necessary trend toward gradual change and improvement.

Administration should be effervescent enough to stimulate organizational change and modification and adaptation to changing needs. Finally, administration provides within its structure and various functions that unifying force which makes it possible for individuals of varying backgrounds, interests, attitudes, and goals to work together toward the achievement of institutional objectives.

Knezevich also describes the administrator:

The administrator fulfills such demands by executing policies related to organizing, allocating, and coordinating human and material resources (the basic sources of energy) within the organization, being ever mindful of the purposes of education. It is through administration that the often contradictory social energies within an organization are adroitly synchronized to produce a unity of operations. [27:13]

This definition of the administrator's role again stresses the dynamic quality of the administrative process and the material and human resources that sustain the organization.

The thesis of this volume has been that the organization functions within the larger framework of society which, in general, represents a conservative or liberal position toward social questions, including education. Individual values and attitudes are seldom, if ever, purely conservative or liberal although most individuals tend to be consistent in thought and action. Inconsistency of attitudes does exist, and this fact is important to the college staff member and particularly to the administrator.

The frame of reference

The frame of reference will be a modification of the tridimensional concept developed by Funk and Livingston and elaborated by Ramseyer. [14; 32] This model shows the major dimensions of the social milieu within which the college functions and the specific influences which impinge upon decision-making on all levels within the organization. The influences, as shown in Fig. 7-1, include:

(1)   Social setting
(2)   Institutional setting
(3)   Administrators and faculty
(4)   Objectives
(5)   Controls
(6)   Processes

The administrator-faculty team must deal with all the factors intrinsic to the college as well as with the external factors which impinge upon it. Every decision—whether it be made by the president, another administrator, a faculty member, or a combination of these individuals in a committee—is based upon individual perceptions of the problem and the factors which relate to it. These decisions are made in terms of sociological and psychological factors in a particular juxtaposition in time.

The college may be regarded as an integrated social system. The social system exists in any group which functions in relation to goals meaningful to its members. An institution is the more formal structure within which the routines of the social system are carried out. The roles are assigned within the social system and imply certain expectations for performance. The roles are actuated by individuals who bring to the situation personality characteristics and personal needs which color their behavior patterns.

Two types of roles function simultaneously in all situations: organizational and individual. Both types of roles are defined as a pattern of behavior or action consistent with a defined position of the general culture or social system. The various roles assigned two-year colleges have been reasonably set forth by society, but the realization of those goals depends, in large measure, upon the leadership exerted—not only by formally appointed administrators, but by all members of the professional staff.

Selznick identified four concepts of leadership which must be understood by college administrators if the organization is to function effectively:

(1) There must be a clear definition of institutional mission and role.
(2) There must be a clear embodiment of institutional purpose.
(3) There must be effective defense of institutional integrity.
(4) There must be effective ordering of internal conflict. [34:62–63]

Selznick sees each of these concepts as fundamental to the development and continuance of the effective life of all organizations. The neglect of any of these tasks by the administrator, whatever his level in the formal organization, will lead to dysfunction detrimental to the achievement of the objectives of the organization. These statements im-

FIG. 7-1.   Dimensions of College Administration

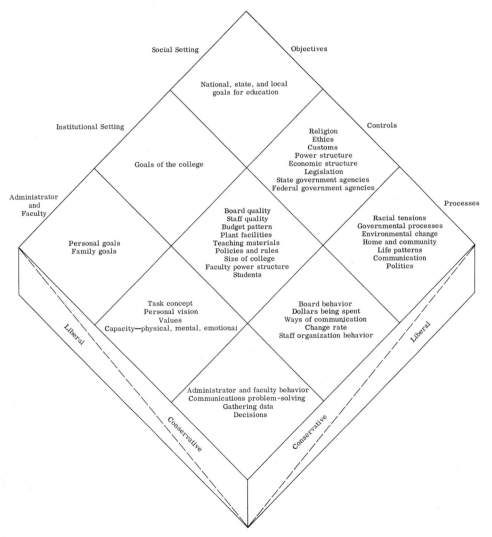

ply additional facets of the administrator's role as mediator, agent for change, power figure, and decision-maker. These activities grow out of the four concepts outlined, and they effectively embody the college administrator's leadership roles.

The leadership process can be illustrated by the development of an admission policy for the college. The evolution of this policy and its final form will depend upon the college's mission and role as defined by legislation, the governing board, the administrators, and the faculty. The educational purposes of the college will also be an important consideration when the pattern of student admissions is formed. There may be, and many times are, external and internal pressures upon the college to modify admission requirements. This very important policy must, therefore, be developed by all those concerned with the problem under the leadership of the college administrator. His function is to make certain that the policy is consistent with the mission of the college.

Interaction in administration is further illustrated by Guba in his model of administrative relationships (see Fig. 7-2).

The conflicts which might become active during the discussion of the admission policy grow out of the differences in concepts and values of administrators and faculty members. An unselective admission policy, as has been pointed out in Chapter 6, may be the antithesis of the values

FIG. 7-2. Model of Internal Administrative Relationships [19:124]

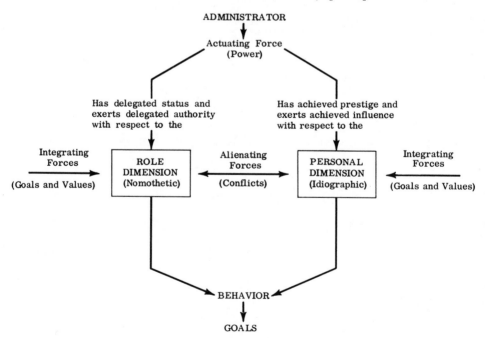

of some or all of the members of the faculty. On the other hand, the administrator, under the influence of the board of control, may see that nonselective admissions are essential to an effective relationship between the college and the community. It is in this kind of setting that the administrator must exert his own influence in order to find common ground on which an acceptable policy can be built.

The Formal Organization

The formal organization is any organization which has been set up to accomplish stated objectives requiring collective effort on the part of many individuals. [6:2] The objectives of the college are achieved through a formal organization based on the laws and regulations governing post-high school education and the principles of administration and group interaction. Despite criticisms of the formal structure of organizations and the problems which grow out of the necessity to have complex administrative structures, it is apparent that any enterprise, however small, must have clearly defined lines of authority and responsibility and specialized personnel whose duty it is to support the educational process through administrative tasks. Weiner puts it this way:

> The purpose of all organizations is to deal with a set of externally imposed conditions which the individual is incapable of handling by himself and which require integration of his activities with the activities of others. If the organization is to succeed, the individual must replace his independence and autonomy of function with cooperative actions in dealing with external conditions. [39]

The formal organization assumes substantive form through the board of control policy manual, the faculty handbook, the student handbook, the college catalog, and the organization chart. Public institutions are required by law to keep complete records of the official actions of the board of control. This is also the custom in private institutions. In addition, however, many college boards also publish manuals which include comprehensive policy statements accumulated over the years that are used to guide and govern the institution. Such manuals outline the organization and responsibility of the board itself and describe the responsibilities of administrative officers and faculty members, personnel policies, educational policies, financial policies and procedures, and policies governing student activities and behavior. [25]

Faculty handbooks enjoy widespread use in two-year colleges. In general they describe the philosophy and objectives of the institution, the responsibilities of the board of control, the responsibilities of administrative officers and faculty, student personnel services, routine procedures, college regulations, and faculty personnel policies. [26] Examination of 63 faculty handbooks from all sections of the country indicates wide variations in style and comprehensiveness. A significant overlap of policies and administrative and procedural materials was also noted.

Student handbooks are provided for the purpose of interpreting the formal organization and the programs provided by the college. Again, there is wide variation in their comprehensiveness and content. In general, however, they include information regarding the purposes and objectives of the institution, its administrative organization, rules and regulations, and general information concerning services to students, curriculum, student government, the library, and student activities. Much of the information in student handbooks duplicates that contained in the college catalog, but it is presented in a less formal way and, in most cases, with an attempt to project the best possible image of the college.

College catalogs not only describe the institution in detail but they actually constitute the official definition of the relationship of students to the institution. Although they mention the formal organization, the major stress of such documents is upon courses of instruction and other information particularly pertinent to the academic programs.

Line-staff charts

The formal organization is also illustrated by the line-staff chart showing the positions in the hierarchy and the specific structure of the organization:

> A chart can show (a) the span of control at various levels within the administrative hierarchy; (b) responsibility of officers to other officers; (c) responsibility of certain personnel to other personnel; (d) various coordinate (staff) assignments which are set up in relationship to administrative positions; (e) routes of communication; and (f) suggestions of commensurate authority which should accompany assigned responsibility. [3:2]

Figure 7-3 shows a typical line-staff organization. The responsibilities of each of the individuals on the five levels would typically be outlined in the faculty handbook and in the policy manual of the board of control. In theory, at least, the academic dean, the dean of student personnel, and the business manager are responsible for three discrete areas or functions. In practice, however, the success of the organization depends as much upon horizontal coordination and cooperation as it does upon vertical implementation of authority and responsibility. The primary functions of the college are implemented by the academic dean and the dean of student personnel; that is, the services provided by these divisions of the college have a direct educational impact upon students.

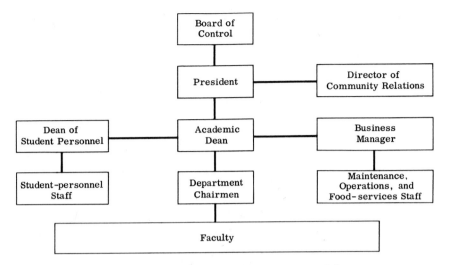

FIG. 7-3.   Conventional Line-staff Organization of a Two-year College

All other segments of the formal organization are subordinate to these divisions in the organizational plan and should function to support the academic and personnel programs.

The administration of the college would be improved if the conventional line-staff organization plan were modified to place more direct emphasis upon the educational and personnel functions of the college and to assign personnel and administrative responsibilities for supporting services in a more meaningful relationship with the other segments of the institution. The suggestions are illustrated in Fig. 7-4, which shows that the director of community relations and the business manager would occupy a staff relationship with the administrative line officers of the college rather than be classified as line officers themselves. These two functions are not central to the basic educational services of the colleges; rather, they are supporting services necessary for the effective implementation of the educational programs of the college.

It is axiomatic that control of college finances means control of the educational program. In all too many instances fiscal officers have exerted undue influence upon the program through their control of the funds necessary for its development and implementation. It should not be the responsibility of the business manager to allocate funds in specific amounts to particular activities of the college; unfortunately, there are far too many situations in which the business manager does just this. Requests for funds are channeled through the business office, and the decision regarding such requests too often is made by the business manager or by members of his staff. Such staff members are the custodians

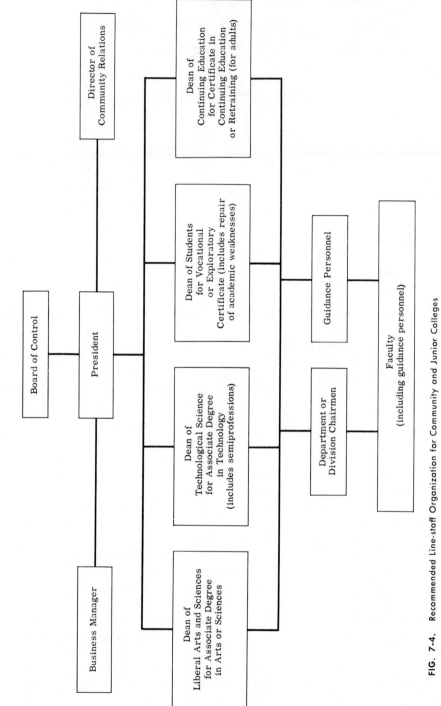

FIG. 7-4. Recommended Line-staff Organization for Community and Junior Colleges

of college funds; their responsibility is to safeguard monies and to perform services—e.g., accounting, purchasing, contracting—designed to support and implement the educational programs of the college.

Another problem is the domination of budget development by the business manager. Budgets should originate with the departments and should be reviewed by the president and the deans of the various divisions. After the allocations of monies for various purposes have been agreed upon by these administrative officers, it is the responsibility of the business manager to implement the decisions. The business manager should not be permitted to make decisions which would alter or nullify the meaning and purposes of the original budget.

The line-staff chart in Fig. 7-4 also has the advantage of placing the four major educational administrators on the same level. In all too many colleges the academic dean is placed above officers responsible for equally important aspects of the college program. Student affairs, technical and vocational sciences, and community services are as important as the college-parallel program; if these segments of the comprehensive educational program of the college are to prosper, they must have status equal to that of the transfer program.

Administrative Structure

The administrative structure of the college should be designed to achieve the educational purposes of the institution. If the college purports to offer a comprehensive spectrum of curricula, it must be organized so that each of the different areas will receive equal attention and direction. The assignment of clear-cut responsibility for the development and implementation of each of the four primary educational functions of the college must, therefore, be assigned to individuals of equal status within the college. Each individual, along with his staff, should feel the same degree of responsibility and each should have equal access to the president when the available resources of the college are distributed. As long as guidance programs, technical and vocational sciences, and community services are subordinated to the college-transfer program, the chances of these segments of the college achieving maximum potential are limited.

This type of administrative organization is demonstrably significant in the organization of curriculum and instruction for the achievement of the institution's educational goals. The recommended patterns for curriculum and instruction set forth in Chapter 8 can be attained most expeditiously through an administrative structure of this type. Of course, the pattern should be modified on the basis of the size and resources of the individual college; however, the pattern can be applied in most situations.

The administrative structure suggested in Fig. 7-4 is based upon a concept of functional organization in which there is close and effective cooperation among administrators, faculty members, and supporting personnel for the purpose of providing students with an integrated educational experience. It is apparent that such an organization does violence to some of the current shibboleths of educational administration. It is equally apparent that if higher education is to improve educational services to students, the administrative structure of colleges must be organized for service rather than for neatness and convenience. Students in any one of these four divisions of the college will probably take courses in another division which is under the control of another second-line administrator. There should, therefore, be planning and coordination by these administrators and faculty members for the purpose of meaningful and logical educational programs for students.

This type of structure envisions effective interaction among department or division chairmen, guidance personnel, and faculty. Furthermore, all guidance personnel, except the dean of students, would have some classroom responsibilities. The assignment of both guidance and teaching responsibilities to all members of the faculty should encourage more effective instruction in the classroom and more meaningful individual guidance of students.

The functional aspects of the formal organization can be illustrated best in terms of levels of authority and responsibility. Figure 7-5 defines the various levels of responsibility and functions within the college.

FIG. 7-5.   Functional Levels of Administration in Two-year Colleges

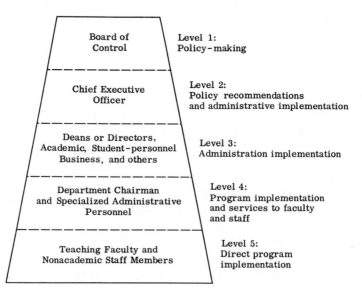

Here the role of the board is confined to policy-making and, very importantly, it does not include matters of administration. The recommendation and implementation of policy, after its approval by the board, is the responsibility of the president, while administrators on Level 3 are responsible for the implementation and coordination of policies and procedures. Level 4 includes those individuals who direct and coordinate the work of the faculty and staff and supply supporting services which are required for quality teaching and learning in the classroom.

The board of control

The board of control is the body legally responsible for the affairs of the college. It may be a local board elected by the voters within the district; a state board appointed by the governor or elected; the board of control of the college or university of which the two-year college is a part; or a self-perpetuating group representing a denominational or private group. The board is the bridge between the college and the community. Its primary function is to translate the needs of society into policies which will meet these needs and to insure the integrity of the college in the face of external demands.

(1) The major task of the board of control is the selection and appointment of the chief executive officer of the board. You see this point made repeatedly in the literature on college administration. The selection and appointment of the chief executive officer of the board is stressed as perhaps the biggest single decision of the board. It is so emphasized because of the importance of the leadership of an educational institution in setting the character and tone as well as efficiency of its operations. Since community colleges are unique, a president should be chosen who understands their special functions.

(2) Another function of an institutional governing board is the definition of institutional purpose, again within the framework of the legislation establishing community colleges and statewide policies such as have already been described. Within these limits the definition of institutional purposes becomes a large and important job of the local board of trustees.

(3) Another related function is the approving of programs of instruction, community services, and related offerings by the college. This matter of having policies which encourage, stimulate, and give a soundness to the development of programs of services is a responsibility of the local board.

(4) The development of policies pertaining to recruitment, appointment, working conditions, and remuneration of staff is also a function of the local board.

(5) So is the acquiring, maintenance, and protection of needed physical facilities and equipment because a college needs these resources if it is to fulfill its full scope of academic services. A good board works hard to be sure that this need is met.

(6) Program requirements, staffing, and physical facilities depend for their full accomplishment on the proper budgeting and financing of the institution. The board has definite obligations in this area of operation. The acquisition and safeguarding of funds controlled by the institution is a matter over which the board of control typically keeps a very close watch. This, again, is a function that is stressed repeatedly in writings about membership on college boards and the duties of these boards. Board members should be interested in the process of budgetary development and have clear-cut policies related to this process. Policies should be clear on the groups in the institution who are to be involved in the process and the timetable by which the process should be carried out. Safeguarding funds and assets of the institution is, of course, a legal obligation of the board that it cannot delegate to others.

(7) Local boards also have a proper function in interpreting to the public the unique role and place of community colleges in the total educational structure of the locality and the region. . . .

(8) An all-encompassing duty of a college board of trustees is the evaluation of the results achieved by the institution's operation and its program of educational services. [28:24–36]

There is no practical way to draw a clear line between the functions of the board of control and the administrative responsibilities of the president. Where does policy-making end and administration begin? This is one of the most perplexing problems in all college administration. When members of the board of control have close personal relationships with the citizens of the community, they often become involved in matters which are in fact the responsibility of the president. Questions regarding the admission of students, the selection of faculty members, and the content of courses are all too often the burden of board discussions, with resultant decisions wrongfully being made by the board rather than by the administration in cooperation with the faculty.

At the other extreme may be found the board of control of the university with two-year branches. This group is so remote from the realities of the branches that it has little knowledge or understanding of their specific problems and needs. Information is thoroughly filtered by the various administrative levels in the university before it reaches the members of the board. Their major attention is focused upon the main campus, which is the center for the status personnel of the university.

The socioeconomic level of members of the boards of control of public junior colleges tells an interesting story and has some implications of importance to these colleges. A study by Barnett showed that most board members come from professional and business occupations. [4:9–20] He found that, of 487 board members in twenty states, 255 (or 52.4 per cent) were in business; 83 (or 17.0 per cent) were professional; 36 (or 7.4 per cent) were in agriculture; 37 (or 7.6 per cent) were housewives; and 44 (or 9.0 per cent) were in other occupations.

TABLE 7-1. Formal Education of Junior College Board Members

| Education | Board Members | | Total Population |
	Number	Per Cent	in U.S. (Per Cent)
Elementary school	14	2.9	39.6
High school	67	13.8	52.7
College (no degree)	110	22.6	
Bachelor's degree	148	30.4	7.7
Graduate degree	104	21.4	
No report	44	9.0	
Median years completed		16	10.6

The educational level of board members was higher than that of the general population. [4:14; 36:120] The general population showed only 7.7 per cent having one or more college degrees, while 51.8 per cent of the board members had one or more degrees. The educational level of board members is consistent with their occupational levels and with the positions of leadership they enjoy in their communities.

Board members also had annual personal incomes markedly higher than those of the general population: 391 individuals reported incomes ranging from $1000 to $300,000, with a median of $8525. The median family income in the United States at that time was $4200 per year. Thus, the median income for board members was approximately twice as high as that of the average family.

The two-year college president

The presidents of two-year colleges are as diverse in education and experience as the colleges they head. Schultz and Roberts studied the backgrounds of 333 college presidents. [33] They found that 46.2 per cent had doctorates; 51.4 per cent, master's degrees; and 2.4 per cent, baccalaureate degrees. The degree specialization was primarily in education.

TABLE 7-2. Area of Specialization for Highest Degree of Public Junior College Presidents [33:9]

Area	Number	Per Cent
Education (without designation)	212	63.7
Higher education	28	8.4
Humanities and social sciences	59	17.7
Science	30	9.0
Business	4	1.2
Total	333	100.0

Further analysis showed that college presidents held a total 611 degrees of which 50 per cent were in subject-matter areas other than education. These degrees were in the social sciences, English, the behavioral sciences, and the physical and biological sciences.

This study showed that the majority, 70.8 per cent, of the 333 college presidents came to their current positions either from administrative positions in other two-year colleges or from administrative positions in elementary or secondary schools. The trend in recent years, however, has been for a larger number of presidents to be chosen from four-year colleges and universities and two-year colleges. [33:12]

TABLE 7-3. Type of Institution from Which
Incumbent Public Junior College Presidents Were Recruited
in Relation to Period of Employment (N=333)

| | *Period of Employment* | | | |
| | *Before 1941* | *1941–51* | *1952–53* | *1959–63* |
Type of Institution	*Per Cent of 12*	*Per Cent of 56*	*Per Cent of 122*	*Per Cent of 143*
Senior college or university	8.3 (1)*	10.7 (6)	13.1 (16)	21.0 (30)
Same institution	25.0 (3)	30.4 (17)	25.4 (31)	21.6 (31)
Another junior college	33.3 (4)	14.3 (8)	27.0 (33)	28.7 (41)
Elementary or secondary school	33.3 (4)	30.4 (17)	28.7 (35)	22.4 (32)
State department of education	0	5.3 (3)	4.1 (5)	2.8 (4)
Other (including graduate school)	0	8.9 (5)	1.6 (2)	3.5 (5)

* NOTE: Figures in parentheses indicate number of individuals.

It is clear in Table 7-3 that the percentage of junior college presidents who were formerly affiliated with the public schools has consistently declined since 1941. At the same time, the number formerly affiliated with the university and the two-year college has increased consistently during the same period. It would appear that as two-year colleges mature, boards of control insist that they have collegiate personnel to direct the institutions.

The previous experience and educational backgrounds of two-year college presidents bears out Stokes' statement:

> If I were to make a general observation about the qualifications of college presidents, it would be this: in recent years the factor of educational distinction has declined while factors of personality, management skills, and successful experience in business administration have increased in importance. This fact reflects the gradual transformation of the college president from an intellectual leader into a manager, skilled in administration, a broker in personal and public relations. [37:15]

The responsibilities of two-year college presidents have increased and become more complex as the two-year college has assumed a larger and larger share of post-high school education during the last twenty years. These changes are the results of increasing size and complexity, which will continue to expand the functions and problems of the college president in the future. Henderson defines the problem of role definition as follows:

> The concept of the community junior college has changed radically during the half-century of its existence, and with this change has come the need of more imaginative and versatile leadership. What formerly was a job as the principal of a preparatory program has become a role as educational leader, as community leader, and as the executive of a complex enterprise with many facets of management relating to personnel, program, plant, finance, and public relations. It has become highly important that this educational leadership shall be exercised with the social vision and the professional understanding needed to implement the new concept. [23:2]

The president is the central link between the college and the community, as well as the director and coordinator of the organization's activities. The activities of the president vary with the personality characteristics of the individual as well as the situational factors bearing upon the college at a particular time. The activities of the president of a public college differ from those of the president of a private college because the needs of the two colleges differ. A comparison of the ways in which the two presidents spend their time reveals some significant differences (see Table 7-4).

TABLE 7-4. Percentage Distribution of the Time Spent by Two Two-year College Presidents

Activity	Public	Private
General administration: Decision-making, meetings with administrative staff and faculty members, buildings and grounds, library, correspondence and office routines	37.5	36.4
State and national educational organizations	8.0	6.5
Meetings with members of board of control (individually and as a group)	15.1	5.3
Coordination with other educational programs and institutions (public schools, colleges and universities, hospitals, and so on)	13.5	1.4
Public relations: Speeches, civic meetings, radio and television, newspapers, campus visitors, publications	10.0	14.6
Recruiting and selecting faculty	4.0	1.4
Coordination with other community programs and organizations (art, music, and other cultural groups; religious groups)	3.5	6.5
Fund-raising: For building construction, equipment, scholarships, and other purposes	2.0	21.9
Relations with state legislature and agencies	5.0	.5
Student-personnel program and problems	1.4	5.5

Both individuals spend the same proportion of their time on general administration and activities related to state and national educational associations and organizations. The president of the public college, however, spends substantially more time with the board of control, in coordination with other educational institutions, in faculty recruiting and selection, and with the state legislature and state agencies. In contrast, the president of the private college is more deeply concerned with public relations, coordination with community groups, fund-raising, student personnel programs, and student problems.

The differences shown here demonstrate the pervasiveness of situational factors in shaping the activities of the chief executive. Nevertheless, it is interesting to note that both presidents have delegated much of their administrative authority and responsibility for the internal operation of the college to other officers, spending only about a third of their time on general administration.

The activities of all college personnel can be divided into categories of responsibility—e.g., supervision, management, special services, and teaching. Overriding all these is general administration, which is the force binding these functions into a coordinated unit. [21:8] Each of the five levels of administration shown in Fig. 7-6 have a greater or

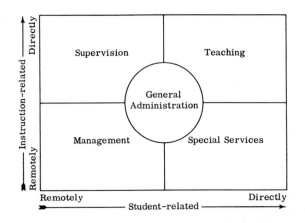

FIG. 7-6. Major Functions of the College Operation [21:8]

smaller share in general administration: the board, in the sphere of policy; the president, in policy recommendation and decision-making; and the other members of the college staff, in more restricted and specialized spheres. The administrative officers found in the line-staff chart have responsibilities for general administration in their interactions with the president, the faculty, and their subordinates in their divisions of the college.

The dean of academic affairs would find his major activities in the areas of teaching and supervision, with relatively little emphasis upon management problems. The same general pattern would apply to the dean of technical and vocational sciences. The dean of student affairs would be heavily involved in special services, some management, and supervision, while the dean of community services would be only lightly involved in management functions. The business manager would have primary management responsibilities designed to support the educational program. The director of community relations would be primarily externally oriented and would have little effect upon any of these functions except as he interprets them to the community.

Administrative skills

Descriptions of the activities of administrators tell only a part of the story of successful college administration. In addition to being a part of a formal organization and possessing technical knowledge, administrators on all levels must possess personal understanding and skills which enable them to reach the objectives of the organization through other members of the staff. These abilities would include:

(1) The ability to determine which logistic approach or technique is appropriate to securing maximum productivity in any given administrative situation (presupposes a broad subject-content background on the part of the administrator)

(2) The ability to coordinate many different functions so that a well-ordered organization results

(3) The ability, even while maintaining a well-ordered organization, to "disturb" its stationary character in order to effect change toward improvement

(4) A constant awareness of the roles performed by faculty and staff members in order to appraise the abilities, strengths, and weaknesses of each

(5) The willingness to delegate responsibility (and the necessary amount of corresponding authority) to faculty and staff members according to their abilities, strengths, and weaknesses

(6) A knowledge of who should participate, when, and to what extent, in each of the administrator's decision-making situations

(7) The ability to get to the real heart of a situation; i.e., to recognize which pre-existing conditions cannot possibly be changed and which can; to identify many of the ancillary connections implied, and to evaluate which, if any, of the outcomes will be crucial

(8) The skill of leading discussions, eliciting responses, and synthesizing and summarizing points

(9) An awareness of the power structure of the environment, which includes both the community and the faculty

(10) The ability to establish and maintain efficient and accurate communications

(11) Not only the willingness, but also the desire to join with others in an appraisal of the quality of one's own leadership

(12) A tendency toward continuous self-analysis in order to determine the effects of one's self-image, status, ambitions, and power upon one's actions

(13) The ability to maintain relative consistency in one's personal role while dealing with faculty and staff

(14) The ability to predict probable faculty, staff, student, and community reactions to proposed leadership

(15) Sensitivity to the organizational structure: social, formal, and informal

Faculty participation

Public community colleges and private junior colleges are currently becoming the testing grounds in the competition between the rational model and the natural-systems model. This conflict has become increasingly severe as public community colleges have received more attention from legal bodies on the state and national levels, as the institution began to shed the hallmarks of the secondary schools, and as the competition for qualified faculty members increased. Although there seems, at least at present, less agitation for greater power in the faculties of private colleges, there are also indications of some unrest in this sector of higher education.

These opposing points of view clashed head-on in an emotionally charged exchange between Bartky and two college instructors, Taylor and Dick, in 1957. [5; 38] Bartky took the position that the administrative pattern universally accepted for universities is not appropriate for two-year colleges. His thesis was that the power centered in the faculty and "nondirective powerless leadership by those designated administrative responsibility" is inappropriate in the two-year college. He states further:

> Mature organizations become the reflexes and the established and acceptable habits of a democratic society. Society employs them to care for its necessary routines and to provide for its basic needs. Society does not suggest to these organizations that they devote any great effort to an examination and reconsideration of their purposes. It insists that they accept its delegated leadership. Hence, mature democratic organizations are not miniatures of democratic society and might because of this fact be labeled autocratic by those who do not consider their birthright. Taylor and Dick take the opposite position: that is, the two-year college should and must have internal organization and faculty participation similar to that [which] characterize[s] the university in order to achieve quality of educa-

tional services and to permit faculty members to realize their roles as professionals. They would attribute little power and influence to administrators in the development and implementation of educational policies and procedures. Rather, administrators should be responsible for the details of the day-to-day operation of the college leaving the determination of educational policies and essential procedures to the faculty. [5:4]

These two points of view essentially represent the rational and natural-systems concepts of organizations, and neither of them can be accepted as representative of the ideal of administrator-faculty relationships in the two-year college. Administrators perform functions which cannot be carried out by faculty members. The size and complexity of the educational enterprise is such that the making of policy and its implementation requires the full-time attention of highly specialized individuals with experience relevant to the tasks being performed. Competence in a subject does not necessarily insure competence in a specialized administrative role. In addition to this requirement, both public and private colleges find themselves more closely related to and dependent upon external groups and individuals for financial support and public understanding. These relationships are essential to the continuing health of the organization, and effective individuals with clear responsibility for such matters must constantly provide a bridge between the college and the communities it serves.

The continuing trend toward more intensive specialization is another factor limiting faculty participation in college administration. This trend tends to create two conditions inimical to faculty control of the college. The primary interest of faculties in two-year colleges is competence in the academic disciplines being taught in the classroom. Merely keeping abreast of changes and additions in knowledge and, at the same time, meeting teaching and guidance responsibilities in the college is as much as the faculty member can comfortably do, and the addition of major, time-consuming administrative responsibilities can detract from needed concentration upon these other, more important responsibilities. Furthermore, the college needs individuals relatively detached from specialized academic interests to coordinate the diverse functions of the college and insure balanced emphases of educational programs relevant to community needs.

There are some even more pervasive reasons to question strong faculty control of the two-year college. If one accepts the thesis that the two-year college is a unique institution devoted to the changing needs of society, he must face the fact that faculties tend to be conservative and resistant to innovations. If the college was created by society "to care for its necessary routines and to provide for its basic needs," faculty resistance to necessary changes might well endanger the status of the institution and society might find it necessary to create another parallel institution to perform the functions needed for a rapidly changing social and economic order. Other problems identified by Corson were:

(1) Only a few institutions accumulate and have regularly available analytical data about the capacity of applicants for admission and about class size, course proliferation, and faculty work load to facilitate decision-making.

(2) A minority among the members of most faculties have thought deeply and analytically about educational programs (e.g., curriculum make-up), or teaching methods (e.g., size of class), or factors influencing instructional costs (e.g., course proliferation and size of class). Most faculty members are subject-matter specialists; few are educators in a comprehensive sense. [13:104]

He goes on to point out that too much of the policy formulation proceeds in piecemeal fashion without comprehensive consideration of the educational program. Furthermore, faculty control of policy-making encourages inefficiency, instability, and time-lag, which undermines the over-all educational effort of the institution.

The other side of the coin shows that faculty participation in educational policy-making encourages the recruitment and retention of highly qualified faculty members. Teachers with a strong professional dedication believe in their ability and right to participate in such matters, and they are generally intolerant of overly centralized college administration. The retention of these individuals insures the preservation of the traditions and character of the college and tends to restrain the overambitious administrator who might attempt to introduce unrealistic innovations inappropriate to the college or the community.

It must also be pointed out that there are many individual faculty members who are interested and active in educational innovations, and who develop—with or without encouragement from the administration— new concepts and procedures which improve and enrich the educational processes in their classrooms. Although these efforts may not be apparent to any other than those intimately related to the college, the significance of such work should not be underestimated. The impact of these finite changes might, in the long run, stimulate major educational policy changes affecting the entire college.

Committee Structure

Organization and functions

Typically, the administration of two-year colleges has included some sort of committee structure, either permanent or ad hoc, in the over-all pattern of relationships of the institution. The purposes of committees include the development of effective communication, broad participation in college affairs, and the utilization of all the human resources within the college and the community. Another function, perhaps not generally recognized, is the provision of a forum in which latent and overt conflicts among the members of the college community can be resolved. Conflict is an inherent quality in all organizations, and it can be an important stimulus for change and improvement. If conflict is to be translated into constructive change, however, there must be well-defined avenues of communication for the development of consensus and group action. Committees can serve this function well if they are organized with some basic principles in mind:

(1) Purposes and problems should be clearly defined and understood by the committee members.
(2) The committee should know when and to whom it will report.
(3) The committee will produce effectively if they know that their recommendations will receive serious consideration.
(4) There must be follow-up, in communications and action, of the committee's recommendations.
(5) The administration of the college should consider committee reports carefully, insisting that reports be completed on time and that the findings be based upon the best knowledge and judgments of the committee members.
(6) There should be specific organizational and administrative regulations concerning committees.
(7) There should be a clear understanding that the chief administrative officer has the authority to override a committee report based upon specific reasons for doing so. [2:40–42]

Advisory committees

Advisory committees have been a part of two-year colleges for many years. They were first organized for assistance in the original founding of the college or for the development and implementation of new educational programs in existing colleges. [24:2] Such committees provide the following services:

(1) They serve as public relations avenues from the college to the community.
(2) They provide knowledge and experience not accessible to the college from other sources.
(3) They stimulate community, state, and national support for the educational policies of the college.
(4) They provide an opportunity for members of the community to be heard before policies or programs are implemented by the college.
(5) They tend to reflect and protect the public interests.
(6) They provide advisement for placement of graduates.

Advisory committees may be organized for any purpose which supports the educational programs of the college, but they are most widely used in connection with technical and vocational programs. Some colleges have general advisory committees or councils which meet with the college administration regularly to discuss problems pertinent to the community and the college and to make recommendations to the board of control and the president for the improvement or revision of the educational services. Such general advisory committees can perform an important service both to the college and to the community through their evaluation of the results of the programs being provided for students. In some instances, Florida being the best example, an advisory committee is required by regulation for each public community college in the state.

Advisory committees for technical and vocational programs have specific responsibilities related to the occupational group they represent. Their advice may be sought on such matters as:

(1)   Standards for the selection of students
(2)   Recommendations regarding the content of courses
(3)   Placement of graduates
(4)   Recommendations for physical facilities and equipment necessary for the program
(5)   Aiding the college in obtaining competent instructors
(6)   Development of informational programs about the curricula
(7)   Securing of more effective cooperation with management and labor in the industry
(8)   Trends in educational requirements and employment opportunities in the industry

Colleges may have no advisory committees, these responsibilities being retained by the board of control, or they might have as many as fifty. If the college is responsible for apprentice training, it will have an advisory committee for each trade or craft. In addition, it might have committees related to any number of technical programs. A short list of the committees associated with two-year colleges will illustrate the wide range of occupations which might be related to the college through such groups.

(1)   Professional nursing
(2)   Vocational nursing
(3)   Electronics
(4)   Business education
(5)   Insurance training
(6)   Aircraft tool design

(7) Machinist apprenticeship
(8) Merchandising
(9) Cosmetology
(10) Apparel design

The membership of advisory committees consists of from two to fifteen members, usually selected by the president of the college with the advice of the board of control and, in the case of technical advisory committees, the suggestions of individuals in the field. Careful selection of members on the basis of their interest in the college and their willingness to work is, of course, essential to the successful functioning of these groups.

There are, to be sure, some dangers resulting from the organization and use of advisory committees. The general rules which apply to faculty committees apply to advisory committees as well. General advisory committees, made up of community leaders, can easily become administrative or policy-making, and conflicts with the board of control may result. The same problem may develop with occupational advisory committees unless their roles and limitations are clearly spelled out at the time they are organized. Furthermore, there should be members of the college administrative or teaching staff on each committee so that an effective relationship between the college and the committee is maintained. If there is adequate planning and direction of the work of advisory committees, they can be an indispensable adjunct to the administrative structure of the college.

Because staff members serve on both faculty and advisory committees, it becomes obvious that there are many opportunities for fourth- and fifth-level personnel to exercise influence on the administrative process of decision-making. A chief administrative officer who consistently ignores the advice of such formally constituted groups does so at his own peril.

The Informal Organization

Yet another avenue exists through which faculty members influence the administration of the college: the informal organization may be a stronger force in the institution than any of its formalized counterparts, depending upon the degree of congruence which exists between the prescribed way of doing things and the way that things actually get done.

The formal organization of the two-year college defines and limits the responsibilities of the positions within the organization, thereby creating a structure of sanctioned power and authority as well as the communication which affords stability and unity of functioning and purpose. It represents the normative dimension in the social system. The informal organization is an outgrowth of the personal dimension, based upon the individual personalities, and need disposition of those within the organization. [16] Thus, the informal organization is defined as "interpersonal relations in the organization that affect decisions within it but either are omitted from the formal scheme or are not consistent with that scheme." [30:148]

To understand the dynamics of the administration of two-year colleges, one must be aware of the interactions which take place within the institution as it seeks to adapt itself both to external and to internal demands. In order to do so, there must be some consideration of the concept of roles, these being the substance of psychological interaction within the organization.

Although Griffiths has maintained that the greater the congruency of the formal and informal organization, the closer the organization will approach maximum achievement, there have been few studies which have supplied empirical data to sustain or refute his contention. [18:90] In order to determine the degree of faculty involvement in general college administration and the configuration of the informal organization in two-year colleges, three studies of eleven colleges were completed in 1963 and 1964. [10; 12; 31] The dimensions of analysis are described in Chapter 6.

In all the institutions analyzed, it was found that the communications dimension had the least congruence with the formal organization. In other words, while there was some relationship between the position of the individual in the organization and his interaction with others, such interaction did not generally follow the formal organization. There were consistently large amounts of communication among faculty and administration without significant delineation on the basis of subject-matter specialization or formal work assignment within the college.

On the other hand, there was consistent congruence between the formal and the informal organizations in both the reliance and the influence dimensions. In all the colleges studied, the administrative officers were perceived by faculty members as the most influential members of the organization. This would indicate that the roles of these members of the college staff were clearly perceived by the faculty, and that the college administrators were the most important arbiters of college policies. There were, of course, some faculty members who were perceived as influential in administrative matters, these being a few instructors in the liberal arts areas who had long service with the institution. Thus, there was faculty participation in college administration, but it was subordinated to the direction of administrators having defined positions of authority.

Types of Organization and Control

Implicit in the preceding discussion of organization and administration of the two-year college has been the assumption that these colleges are controlled by independent state or local boards whose sole charge is the policy direction of such colleges. This, of course, is not true. Two-year colleges are organized in three general patterns: under an independent local board, as branches of universities, and under local boards of education (K–14). Each of these types of organization has some advantages, but there is little doubt that the college which has its own board and taxing power is the strongest of the three types. Branches are weak, administratively, because they are satellites of the main campus. Two studies show some of the problems and limitations inherent in this type of organization.

Morton found little serious effort to define the responsibilities of extension and campus personnel to encourage a maximum contribution to the expansion and improvement of their programs. He also found little effective adaptation of education programs to the needs of mature adults, a lack of long-range planning, and administrative confusion as to the control of branches. [30]

Further disadvantages of the branch organization were identified in a study by Blocker and Campbell. [7] The most important of these were:

(1) Little campus life for students
(2) Distance of branches from the campus, impeding communication
(3) Lack of financial support
(4) Cumbersome administrative organization
(5) Limited physical facilities
(6) Lack of permanent instructional staff
(7) Inadequate library

Two-year colleges which are an integral part of the public school system also have some serious weaknesses. Hall has commented that the junior college cannot achieve full stature until it becomes independent of the local board of education. [20] He adds that states are amending their laws to remove colleges from K–12 systems. Such laws have been passed in California, Minnesota, and Wyoming. Several states which recently initiated junior college systems have separated the junior college from other segments of public education—e.g., New York, Ohio, and Massachusetts.

In a study comparing the advantages of public school control with autonomous control of community colleges, it was found that 78.5 per cent of the 130 administrators questioned preferred an autonomous board of control. Those favoring continuation of the college under the superintendent and public school board of control gave these reasons for their preference:

(1) The superintendent and board of education develop a better image of the college.
(2) Supporting services—i.e., purchasing, guidance, accounting—can be provided to the college by the existing public school organization.
(3) There is better articulation of educational programs between high school and college. [8:23]

On the other side of the coin, those who thought the college should be independent of the board of education gave these as the five most important reasons for an autonomous board:

(1) A separate organization makes for better administration.
(2) A separate board will be concerned with college problems only and can devote full time to them.
(3) Autonomy permits greater experimentation in planning and developing a program to meet community needs.
(4) The institution becomes a college rather than merely the thirteenth and fourteenth grades of a public school system.
(5) A larger tax base is available to support the college with no need to compete with K-12 for funds. [7:24]

The need to organize public community colleges under a separate board of control is supported by Medsker, Henderson, and Bogue. [11; 22; 29] Bogue recognized the need for such a pattern of organization:

We strongly recommend that it be (a) locally controlled under the supervision of a designated state agency, (b) well-equipped with its own campus and facilities, (c) provided with its own faculty of well-qualified teachers who understand the place and functions of community colleges and who are dedicated to this type of education, (d) authorized and required to have its own financial budget and structure and its formula for the determination of costs, (e) authorized and required to use funds appropriated from the state and/or raised by local taxes, and/or paid in tuitions and fees, or from other sources for the community college only. . . . [11:10]

The problems of the board's understanding and consequent direction of the two-year college toward the goals ascribed to it grow from two sources: (1) the complexity of the organization being controlled, and (2) the filtration of information and ideas by administrators whose objectives and values are not closely related to the needs and functions of the college. Members of the board of control respond to the information they receive from the administrator; if there is a lack of information concerning the college, as is the case when it is a part of a larger organization, the college is less likely to attain its greatest possible potential. The two-year college must have close and effective communication with the board of control if it is to function efficiently, achieve its objectives, satisfy the needs of the faculty, and educate its students.

Trends in College Administration

There are a number of trends which promise to stimulate significant changes in the two-year college. First, the development of the W. K. Kellogg Junior College Leadership Programs in ten major universities has stimulated the professional education of larger numbers of individuals for administrative posts in two-year colleges. The impact of this foundation support will be felt within the next few years when these well-trained leaders begin to fill top administrative posts in colleges in the various states, universities, and state departments of education. Perhaps of equal importance is the encouragement of the scholarly study of two-year colleges by professors of educational administration and graduate students. The fruits of this research are beginning to appear in publications and, hopefully, will encourage innovations and improvements in college administrative practices.

There has been a slow but consistent trend toward the coordination of higher education in the various states, and this coordination and planning has included college and university branches, private junior colleges, and public community colleges. In other words, there has been a clearer perception of the various types of institutions of higher education and a better definition of their roles within the total state system. Such changes have not taken place without resistance from entrenched educational interests and without some pain on the part of traditionalists; however, it is clear that two-year institutions are going to play an increasingly important part in higher education in the future.

Internally, the two-year private and public colleges have not demonstrated outstanding leadership in the implementation of new concepts of administrative organization and functioning. College administrators have been slow to recognize that, as the roles of their colleges expand both in terms of programs and in number of students served, administrative organization and relationships must be adapted to new needs within their institutions. This may be, in part, the result of the conservative nature of boards of control, whose values and attitudes are not necessarily consistent with rapidly changing organizational and educational needs. On the other hand, it may reflect the basic conservatism of faculty and administration—the desire to build colleges which conform to traditional college and university patterns.

There is little doubt that the relationships among the board of control, the administration, and the faculty are undergoing changes which have significant long-range implications for the two-year college.

The roles of these three groups are going to shift from a hierarchical pattern to one in which there is constant and effective interaction—one in which the changing needs of the community and institutional integrity are more nearly balanced. This, of course, means that one of the increasingly important roles of college presidents will be the mediation of conservative and liberal streams of thought.

Finally, the organization will be faced with stronger and more persistent pressures from external sources—parents, business and industry, state and national agencies, and legislative bodies—to adapt more rapidly to changing social and economic needs. There will be suggestions that the college must accommodate all individuals who wish to enter and that educational programs must shift with the immediate and sometimes transitory problems in society. Such demands may be met if there is strong leadership in administrative and faculty personnel, but there must also be some checks and balances designed to avoid opportunistic responses which will endanger the quality of programs made available by the college. It will require foresight and statesmanship to avoid overexpansion and the dissipation of resources over too many programs of limited usefulness and of short-range value.

Bibliography

1. Adams, Brooks, *The Theory of Social Revolution.* New York: The Macmillan Company, 1913.

2. Ashmore, Henry L., "The Committee in Administration," *Junior College Journal,* XXIX (September 1958), 40–42.

3. Ayers, A. R., and John H. Russel, *Internal Structure: Organization and Administration of Institutions of Higher Education.* Washington, D.C.: USGPO, 1962.

4. Barnett, W. H., *Qualifications and Philosophy of Public Junior College Board Members.* Unpublished doctoral dissertation presented at the University of Texas, Austin, Texas, 1953.

5. Bartky, John, "The Nature of Junior College Administration," *Junior College Journal,* XXVIII (September 1957), 3–7.

6. Blau, Peter M., and W. Richard Scott, *Formal Organizations.* San Francisco, Calif.: Chandler Publishing Company, 1962.

7. Blocker, C. E., and H. A. Campbell, Jr., *Administrative Practices in University Extension Centers and Branch Colleges.* Austin, Tex.: University of Texas, 1963.

8. _____, and H. A. Campbell, Jr., *Attitudes of Administrators Toward the Administrative Organization of Public Junior Colleges in Seven States.* Austin, Tex.: University of Texas, 1962.

9. _____, and Robert H. McCabe, *Relationships Between the Informal Organization and the Curriculum in Six Junior Colleges.* Austin, Tex.: University of Texas, 1964.

10. _____, Robert H. McCabe, and A. J. Prendergast, *A Method for the Analysis of the Informal Organization Within Large Work Groups.* Austin, Tex.: University of Texas, 1964.

11. Bogue, Jesse P., *The Development of Community Colleges.* Washington, D.C.: American Association of Junior Colleges, 1957.

12. Campbell, Henry A., Jr., *An Analysis of Communications, Influences, and Reliance in Public Two-year Branches of State Universities and Independent Public Two-year Colleges.* Unpublished doctoral dissertation presented at the University of Texas, Austin, Texas, 1963.

13. Corson, John J., *Governance of Colleges and Universities.* New York: McGraw-Hill Book Company, 1960.

14. Funk, Howard V., and Robert T. Livingston, *A Tridimensional View of the Job of Educational Administration.* New York: CPEA-MAR, Teachers College, Columbia University, 1951. Mimeographed.

15. Getzels, J. W., "Theory and Practice in Educational Administration: An Old Question Revisited," in R. F. Campbell and J. M. Lipham (eds.), *Administrative Theory as a Guide to Action.* Chicago, Ill.: University of Chicago, 1960. Pp. 37-58.

16: Getzels, Jacob R., and E. G. Guba, "Social Behavior and the Administrative Process, *School Review,* LXV (Winter 1957), 423-41.

17. Gouldner, Alvin W., "Organizational Analysis," in Robert K. Merton, Leonard Broom, and Leonard S. Cottrell, Jr. (eds), *Sociology Today: Problems and Prospects.* New York: Basic Books, Inc., 1959. Pp. 400-428.

18. Griffiths, Daniel E., *Administrative Theory.* New York: Appleton-Century-Crofts, 1959.

19. Guba, Egon G., "Research in Internal Administration—What Do We Know?" in R. F. Campbell and J. M. Lipham (eds.), *Administrative Theory as a Guide to Action.* Danville, Ill.: Interstate Printers and Publishers, 1960. Pp. 113-30.

20. Hall, George L., "Confusion in the Control of the Junior College," *Junior College Journal,* XXXII (April 1962), 432-36.

21. Harris, Ben M., *Supervisory Behavior in Education.* Englewood Cliffs, N.J.: Prentice-Hall, Inc., 1963.

22. Henderson, Algo, *Policies and Practices in Higher Education.* New York: Harper & Row, Publishers, 1960.

23. _____, "How Shall We Get Top Leadership for Community-Junior Colleges?" Paper delivered before a meeting of the American Association of Junior Colleges, New York, February 1958.

24. King, Sam W., *Organization and Effective Use of Advisory Committees.* Washington, D.C.: USGPO, 1960.

25. Kintzer, F. C., *Board Policy Manuals in California Public Junior Colleges.* Los Angeles, Calif.: University of California, 1962.

26. _____, *Faculty Handbooks in California Public Junior Colleges.* Los Angeles, Calif.: University of California, 1961.

27. Knezevich, Stephen J., *Administration of Public Education.* New York: Harper & Row, Publishers, 1962.

28. Martorana, S. V., "Some Observations on Layman Educational Control of Higher Education and Its Emerging Patterns in the United States," in *Proceedings, Arizona Conference for Junior College Board Members and Administrators.* Scottsdale, Ariz.: Coordinating Committee, California Junior College Leadership Program, University of California, Berkeley and Los Angeles, and Stanford University, November 1963. Pp. 24–36.

29. Medsker, Leland L., "Patterns for the Control of Community Colleges," *Establishing Legal Bases for Community Colleges.* Washington, D.C.: American Association of Junior Colleges, 1962.

30. Morton, John R., *University Extension in the United States.* University, Ala.: University of Alabama Press, 1953.

31. Nicholson, Samuel N., *A Comparison of the Communication, Reliance, and Influence Networks in Two-year Colleges Operating Under the Independent District System and Under the Public School System.* Unpublished doctoral dissertation presented at the University of Texas, Austin, Texas, 1963.

32. Ramseyer, John A., *et al., Factors Affecting Educational Administration: Guideposts for Research and Action, School-Community Development Study Monograph,* No. 2. Columbus, Ohio: The Ohio State University Press, 1955.

33. Schultz, Raymond E., and Dayton Y. Roberts, *Presidents of Public Junior Colleges: An Analysis of Selected Background Factors.* Tallahassee, Fla.: Florida State University, 1964. Unpublished study.

34. Selznick, Philip, *Leadership in Administration: A Sociological Interpretation.* New York: Harper & Row, Publishers, 1957.

35. Simon, Herbert A., *Administrative Behavior.* New York: The Macmillan Company, 1957.

36. *Statistical Abstract of the United States.* Washington, D.C.: USGPO, 1963.

37. Stokes, Harold W., *The American College President.* New York: Harper & Row, Publishers, 1959.

38. Taylor, Morris F., and Herbert W. Dick, "More About 'The Nature of Junior College Administration,'" *Junior College Journal,* XXVIII (December 1957), 220–22.

39. Weiner, Milton G., "Observations on the Growth of Information-processing Centers," *Rand Paper P-529.* Los Angeles, Calif.: The Rand Corporation, May 1954.

The increasing numbers of students and the multiplicity of curricular needs have magnified the difficulties inherent in institutional attempts to develop multiple integrated curricula appropriate to students and to the culture. Sanford states:

> The crisis in higher education is chronic. The great problem today is not essentially different from what it has been for a long time. It is how to do better the things that the colleges are intended to do; how to realize more fully, despite pressures from without and divided counsels within, the aim of developing the potentialities of each student. [27:19]

The vehicle for developing these potentialities is the curriculum. Unfortunately, despite its critical importance to the college, curriculum has little, if any, literature based upon systematic investigation. If two-year colleges are to meet the challenges of the future, they must develop clear-cut concepts of both curriculum and instruction, and the impact of these functions of the college upon its students.

The authors will examine curriculum and instruction within the framework of three principles developed by Thomas:

(1) The educational principles which have been invoked in determining the content and aims of the programs

8

curriculum
and instruction

(2) The administrative structures designed to make the operation of the programs effective

(3) The pedagogical methods adopted for the better implementation of the programs [29:100]

There can be no clear-cut distinction between curriculum—"a group of courses and planned experiences which a student has under the guidance of the school or college"—and instruction, which is defined by the interaction between the student and the teacher, in which teaching and learning occur simultaneously. [13:149]

The writers take the position, developed by Katz and Sanford, that thinking and knowledge are inexorably intertwined with personality development. [27:418–35] It was pointed out in Chapter 5 that the basic student motivations for college attendance are need-fulfillment. These needs involve not only basic personality characteristics but externally applied motivations arising from the society in which the individual lives:

> It is our thesis that all the individual's knowledge is a part of his personality, and that all curricula either favor or hamper personality development, regardless of whether they were designed with such development in mind. . . . Our major concern is with the kind of learning in college that can bring about a developmental change in the personality structure [27:425]

Curriculum and instruction are the two major dimensions stimulating the learning process in students. The content of courses is not only relevant in terms of knowledge and cognitive processes, but there is also an essential relationship between content and the methods through which it is presented to the student. The object of all college functions is the student, and the purpose of both curriculum and instruction is to induce change, demonstrated in more mature behavior, intellectual development, and personal competence.

Determinants of the Curriculum

The curriculum represents the culture to be transmitted by the institution; however, there is and will continue to be disagreement as to the exact nature of this culture. These differences may be traced to a number of sources, not the least of which is the liberal or conservative perspective of the individual defining the culture. In addition to this central difference of perspective, a number of other curriculum determinants present themselves. In general, these may be subsumed under three main headings: extrainstitutional influences, intrainstitutional influences, and administrative or mediating influences.

Extrainstitutional factors

Extrainstitutional influences include all those external requirements which constantly impinge upon the curriculum. The transfer
program, for instance, is determined almost entirely by the four-year
colleges and universities to which students will transfer. Technical and
vocational offerings must meet the occupational requirements of the
fields in which training is offered. Local attitudes and traditions will
influence not only the scope of the curriculum, but also its depth. The
literature is replete with examples of how local peculiarities influence
the activities of instructors.

Curricular offerings are also influenced by changing social and
economic patterns. At present, the two-year college is caught between
contradictory pressures. Social pressures continue to place a high premium
on the liberal arts curriculum, while economic requirements stress the
expanded need for technicians. The result is increasing numbers of technical curricula to which it becomes ever more difficult to attract able
students. Of course, the type of student is, of itself, a curriculum determinant: an institution must define the requirements and level of difficulty for various curricula in terms which are realistic for the ability level
of the student attracted. Finally, state and national policies and regulations serve also to shape and mold the curricula. A required course in
state government means that much less time for other areas. Federal
requirements for assistance in various programs are powerful forces
which cannot be easily denied.

Intrainstitutional factors

Just as many variables outside the institution condition the curriculum, so do numerous factors within it.

Increasingly, accreditation teams are closely examining the philosophy and objectives of the two-year institution. Spelled out in specific
terms and viewed as evolving, dynamic principles, these concepts should
be a vital factor in shaping the curriculum.

Physical plant and equipment play their roles in a somewhat more
subtle fashion. In the technical area, particularly, a dominant criticism
of educational institutions has been the obsolescence of the teaching
aids. This aspect of the internal environment also helps to shape faculty
attitudes. A well-defined problem area exists in promoting healthy respect and good working relationships between technical and academic
faculty. The expense of equipment and the small numbers of students
may prompt acrid comments from heavily loaded academic faculty members, who often display a pronounced distaste for occupationally
weighted offerings.

The training of faculty members is an added curriculum determinant, for it frequently resolves the issue of whether a traditional or an experimental attitude is taken toward the role of the institution. The traditional viewpoint, with its conservative overtones, may inhibit change and operate to keep curricular offerings limited in scope. Not only do these concepts affect the offerings but they also dictate the methods to be utilized in presenting content. The attitudes of the staff also relate to the sensitivity with which societal needs are perceived. In contrast to the myopic, local viewpoint of the traditionalist, the experimentalist is more likely to perceive needs in terms of their over-all societal context.

Some way must be found to balance these influences. This function is assigned to the administrative structure of the organization. Through a series of decision-making situations, priorities are determined and responses initiated. Financial support determines the emphasis given to each of the perceived roles of the institution and also determines such major curricular factors as the quality of the faculty, plant, and equipment. The policies of the board of control provide direction and objectives and also help to determine the institutional climate. These policies provide a gauge of the importance ascribed by the board to each of the external influences exerted on the institution. They also suggest the board's concept of those roles proper to the college's mission. The institutional climate reflects the wisdom with which administrative officers are able to balance internal and external factors. Serious imbalance may destroy public confidence or ruin faculty morale. Figure 8-1 is a schematic summarization of the various determinants of curriculum.

It should be noted that the perceptions of curriculum determinants among two-year college staff members are not entirely consistent. In a study of 663 administrators and faculty members in five branch colleges and nine community colleges, the following influences were perceived to be most important in sources of change in curriculum:

(1) The administration
(2) The faculty
(3) The students
(4) Accrediting agencies (state and regional)
(5) Four-year colleges and universities and their faculties
(6) The state department of education
(7) The board of control
(8) Two-year colleges and their faculties
(9) State government and agencies
(10) Advisory boards and committees

Faculty members in the sciences, social sciences, languages and mathematics perceived the influence of four-year colleges as most important.

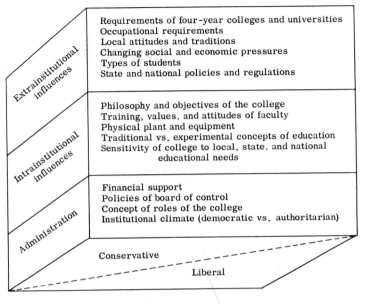

Nature of the Culture to Be Transmitted

Requirements of four-year colleges and universities
Occupational requirements
Local attitudes and traditions
Changing social and economic pressures
Types of students
State and national policies and regulations

Philosophy and objectives of the college
Training, values, and attitudes of faculty
Physical plant and equipment
Traditional vs. experimental concepts of education
Sensitivity of college to local, state, and national
       educational needs

Financial support
Policies of board of control
Concept of roles of the college
Institutional climate (democratic vs. authoritarian)

Extrainstitutional influences

Intrainstitutional influences

Administration

Conservative

Liberal

FIG. 8-1.   Determinants of the Curriculum

Administrators and teachers of business, technical subjects, fine arts, and physical education ranked the administration, the students, the faculty, and the state department of education as being of prime importance. All groups mentioned community organizations and individuals but ranked them substantially lower than the categories listed.

These findings are quite logical, when observed from the point of view of the faculty member. Those groups mentioning the influence of four-year colleges as most important are those which look to these institutions for acceptance of their efforts. In a very real sense, the transfer institution is both a beacon and a taskmaster. Administrators and non-transfer-oriented faculty are free to consider a somewhat wider range of determinants. The fact that all groups ranked community organizations and individuals well down on the list holds some interesting implications for the concept of the two-year college as a community-centered institution.

Organizing for Effective Instruction and Curriculum

The seven levels of competence appearing in Table 8-1 effectively define a structure within which the community college can serve the needs of the majority of citizens. If this objective is to be accomplished,

TABLE 8-1. Scale of General Educational Development [32:110–11]

State of development involving *capability* to function immediately in *one or more* of the following ways:

Level	Reasoning development	Mathematical development	Language development
7	Apply principles of logical or scientific thinking to a wide range of intellectual and practical problems. Deal with nonverbal symbolism (formulas, scientific equations, graphs, musical notes, etc.) in its most difficult phases. Deal with a variety of abstract and concrete variables. Apprehend the most abstruse classes of concepts.	Work with a wide variety of theoretical mathematical concepts and make original applications of mathematical procedures, as in empirical and differential equations.	Comprehension and expression of precise or highly connotative meanings, as in— *Journal of Educational Sociology. Scientific Monthly.* Works in logic and philosophy, such as those of Kant, Whitehead, Korzybski. Literary works, such as those of Stein, Eliot, Auden.
6	Apply principles of logical or scientific thinking to define problems, collect data, establish facts, and draw valid conclusions. Interpret an extensive variety of technical instructions in books, manuals, mathematical or diagrammatic form. Deal with several abstract and concrete variables.	Make standard applications of advanced mathematics, as differential and integral calculus.	Comprehension and expression as of— *Saturday Review, Harper's. Scientific American.* "Invitation to Learning" (radio program).
5	Apply principles of rational systems * to solve practical problems. Interpret a variety of instructions furnished in written, oral, diagrammatic, or schedule form. Deal with a variety of concrete variables.	Perform ordinary arithmetic, algebraic, and geometric procedures in standard, practical applications.	Comprehension and expression as of— *Popular Science.* "America's Town Meeting of the Air" (radio program).

206

TABLE 8-1. (Cont.)

Level	Reasoning development	Mathematical development	Language development
4	Apply commonsense understanding to carry out instructions furnished in written, oral, or diagrammatic form. Deal with problems involving several concrete variables.	Make arithmetic calculations involving fractions, decimals, and percentages.	Comprehension and expression as of— *Reader's Digest.* *American Magazine.* "Lowell Thomas" (radio program).
3	Apply commonsense understanding to carry out detailed but uninvolved written or oral instructions. Deal with problems involving a few concrete variables.	Use arithmetic to add, subtract, multiply, and divide whole numbers.	Comprehension and expression as of— Pulp detective magazines. Movie magazines. Dorothy Dix. Radio "soap operas."
2	Apply commonsense understanding to carry out spoken or written 1- or 2-step instructions. Deal with standardized situations with only 1 or 2, very occasional, variables entering.	Perform simple adding and subtracting.	Comprehension and expression of a level to— Sign name and understand what is being signed. Read simple materials, such as lists, addresses, and safety warnings. Keep very simple production records.
1	Apply commonsense understanding to carry out very simple instructions given orally or by demonstration. No variables.	None	No speaking, reading, or writing required.

* NOTE: Examples of "principles of rational systems" are: bookkeeping, internal combustion engines, electric wiring systems, house building, nursing, farm management, ship sailing.

however, community colleges must rigorously re-examine their internal organization and find an effective rationale between traditional college programs and the broader needs of individuals and society in general.

Definition of function

There is an urgent need to define the type of student with which the two-year college must be concerned. The concept is frequently advanced that "the opportunity for competence" must be available to all, not just the elite. [23] Although paying lip service to this truism, many community colleges serve, rather, to imitate the role of the four-year institutions. Those that do have so-called developmental programs have frequently organized them in haphazard fashion and have uniformly ignored the responsibility to evaluate their contributions honestly. If stated objectives are not fulfilled, then new objectives are found. Some institutions may require a student to take remedial English and yet permit this same person to enroll in college-level courses in economics and history, to his detriment and to the consternation of his instructors.

It is possible, given unlimited resources, that the two-year college might become all things to all people. The history of public and private education in this country, however, would more nearly support the thesis of limited resources. From this premise, it can be deduced that decisions will have to be made and priorities established. Furthermore, it will probably not be possible to serve all the strata of post-high school education needs, and it will certainly not be possible to serve them all equally well. A given institution, then, may have to choose between doing many things in a haphazard fashion, or doing a limited number of things well.

The developing institution (and all two-year colleges can be so classified at this point) must examine community needs and decide where its resources may be most effectively applied. Once the decision is made, the college must determine accurately the criteria for success in these programs and then disseminate this information as widely as possible to prospective students. This approach does not eliminate the need for constant self-analysis to determine at which points needs and resources can be combined for new programs, but it does eliminate the necessity of offering something to every college-age student, regardless of his ability.

The current organization for instruction leaves something to be desired in the effective implementation of these goals. Course offerings are loosely combined into several groupings which are termed *transfer, technical, terminal, community service,* and the like. Most frequently, supervision of the entire program is entrusted to the dean of instruction, who is selected for his strong academic background. Not surprisingly, a pecking order of class offerings frequently evolves, with the transfer curriculum at the top. The student is free to select whatever offerings strike his fancy. Counselors may advise and persuade but, except in a few selective programs (such as nursing), the student makes the final decision. Courses labeled *terminal* or *not for college credit* find few takers.

In order to maintain acceptable standards while fulfilling its societal role, the two-year college must make a clear-cut distinction among the four separate programs. What is needed is a restrictive admission policy for the more demanding programs and a more logical plan for the over-all organization of administration. In many junior colleges, the dean of instruction or a department chairman in the transfer division is also in charge of directing the remedial and community-service functions. In one college in a tight budget year, for example, an additional instructor for English composition was hired rather than adding a second instructor in remedial reading. The reading diagnostician, who had developed a fine remedial program, resigned because of the lack of staff to meet the needs of a large segment of the students in the college.

The tasks currently being carried out by the two-year college under the general heading of *instruction* might well be subsumed under four co-equal administrators, who would each report directly to the chief administrator of the college. As was noted in Chapter 7, the four areas of responsibility would be labeled *academic affairs, technical and vocational science, community services,* and *student affairs.* Currently, most institutions have someone who is responsible to the president for the first and fourth areas. The second and third most commonly have a supervisor who reports to the academic dean. The innovation suggested lies primarily in a redefinition of responsibilities and an upgrading of certain areas.

Academic division

The academic division would include all the work presently offered in the transfer curriculum. All courses would parallel those offered by four-year institutions, and those students successfully completing two years of work would receive the Associate of Arts or Associate of Science degree. Admission to this division would be selective, based on standards comparable to those of four-year institutions offering similar programs. The faculty members in this division would be selected for teaching proficiency and academic qualifications, and would be awarded professorial rank.

The academic division of the two-year college needs considerably less emphasis than it is currently receiving. The transfer program lowers the economic barrier to higher education because it is geographically accessible to students. The fact that it performs a function somewhat less expensively than other institutions engaged in the same type of work entitles the two-year college to no particular distinction. The emphasis upon teaching as opposed to research, the willingness to give students who have failed a second chance, and the flexibility provided by the wide range of nontransfer courses into which those not suited for baccalaureate work may be channeled are the chief justification of the two-year college's claim that it offers students special advantages that cannot be found elsewhere in higher education.

The technical and vocational science division

The technical and vocational science division would closely resemble the academic division in terms of admission practices and organization. Faculty members could qualify for professorial rank on the basis of a combination of educational qualifications, technical background, and teaching proficiency. The administrator of this division would report directly to the chief administrator. The technical program would be designed to meet the needs of college-age and adult students in or above the middle quintile of ability. The contribution the two-year college has made in the last decade in its professional nursing program is a convincing illustration of what should be done in a number of technical areas. Technical programs are costly, requiring subsidization from industrial sources, private foundations, technical associations, and state and federal sources. Teachers for such programs are difficult to find. The prestige of the technical program is yet to be built. One consideration for prestige is assurance by the technical profession of placement in good jobs for all who graduate. The program should not be started until the college has this assurance. It is equally important that faculty attitudes and the organization of course content break away from the four-year model. Technical faculty members are often more guilty than academic faculty members in seeking to preserve the academic model. They do not display the courage of their convictions when they seek college-transfer credit for each new course. The technical program must create its own proud model.

The vocational science programs constitute a somewhat controversial area of the junior college curriculum. Should this institution seek to serve students who are interested only in learning specific vocational skills? The most feasible answer would seem to lie in an emphasis upon the unique nature of the two-year college and its close relationship to the community. If there is a need for such training, and if available resources can be diverted to this area without limiting development in others, then there should be no hesitation in offering it. If, on the other hand, there are other agencies within the community seeking to provide comparable training, the junior college might very well assign the vocational area a low priority.

The service division

The service division would be administratively organized under the dean of student-personnel services. There would be unrestricted admission to this division. Instruction would not be organized in the traditional course pattern, nor would grades be given. Instead, periodic written evaluations would be made, sketching the progress of each student and containing recommendations for his future work. Progress from one level to another within the service division would be exclusively by recommendation of the instructor. Classes might or might not follow standard semester patterns. College academic credit might or might not be given for courses in the service division.

The organization of the service division within the student-personnel program stems from the recognition that academically oriented staff members are suited neither by temperament nor interest to do an adequate job in this area. Faculty members would be selected for specialized training rather than for academic distinction and would not be given professorial rank. Instead, descriptive titles such as *director* or *consultant* would be used to designate the instructor's area of competence. A differential in salary might be paid to attract capable instructors and to compensate for the requirements of special training and teaching skill.

Students would enter the service division with the purpose of remedying deficiencies in preparation for entrance to the academic or technical division. Entrance would not automatically follow a specific period of study or sequence of classes; it would be contingent on meeting the minimum level acceptable to the other two divisions. Many learners cannot profit from higher education without diagnostic or remedial help. In this group are those who have been educationally, culturally, or emotionally deprived, those who are late maturers or late academic bloomers, and those who were poorly motivated in their early years. Therapeutically trained personnel are needed to work with these groups to help them determine problems, talents, and interests, as well as to provide remedial work in reading, writing, study skills, problem skills, and arithmetic. These functions would be carried out by the service division.

The community-service division

The community-service division relates closely to all three previously mentioned areas. It would undoubtedly be the last of the divisions to be organized in a developing institution. In many smaller colleges, its responsibilities might well be carried out by one of the other divisions. It is described here as an entity to emphasize the responsibility of the two-year college in answering the need for avocational and cultural activities in an increasingly leisure-oriented society. As a community service, this division would offer instruction in creative and leadership training activities; lectures; drama, music, and art; short courses; and workshops, forums, and institutes based on community needs and interests.

Instructors in this division might be recruited from qualified faculty members in other divisions or from the community. Credit would not be given, but some type of certificate might be utilized to recognize completion of a course. Admission to the division would be completely unrestricted. The dean of the division might expect to spend a considerable part of his time in the community, analyzing its needs and organizing new interest areas.

This division should also meet many other community needs which may be beyond the scope of classroom instruction. Reynolds has listed a number of programs which would be contained in this part of the college:

(1) Mutual aid for meeting college-community needs:
    (a) Cooperative art, music, and other cultural programs
    (b) Cooperative development of health services
    (c) Development of safety-education programs
    (d) Development of occupational survey of community
(2) Use of the community as an instructional laboratory
(3) Study and research of community problems
(4) Public affairs educational programs
(5) Recreational-activities programs
(6) Community use of college physical plant
(7) Cooperative efforts for community development [26:144–56]

Such a list of activities could be extended ad infinitum; however, each college should, through self-analysis, determine the types of programs it can provide. Given strong administrative leadership and reasonable responsiveness in the community, both public and private two-year colleges can render significant service to their communities.

General education

Up to this point, the general-education function of the two-year college has not been specifically mentioned. There is a mythical antithesis between occupational education and general education that should be exploded. All divisions of the two-year comprehensive institution should be strongly laced with general-education courses, appropriate to the talent level of the students. If the need of the individual to establish and maintain satisfying economic status is a strong motivational factor, it does not negate the importance of communication and sequential-thinking skills. Minds geared to analysis, criticism, and creativity are as necessary to the vocational world as to the academic world.

The two-year college, then, should contain an academic division with a college-parallel program and a technical and vocational science division for the semiprofessions, with some emphasis also on vocational training. In addition, a service division would provide for remedial work, while leadership training in avocational and cultural activities would be offered by a community-service division. The two-year college would thus be more than a screening device for the four-year college. By providing separate educational "lanes" and by permitting students to move back and forth between them, the comprehensive two-year college would enable the education of all youths and adults over eighteen who were motivated to improve themselves through higher education. Vocational, remedial, and community services will never be more than unproductive orphans so long as they remain unwanted adjuncts of the academic or technical program of the two-year college. If they are nurtured with sympathetic treatment in the right environment, they will flourish. An educational frontier can be kept open by the comprehensive two-year college, offering opportunity rather than frustration to millions of learners. It costs less to educate an individual than to support him in idleness. If the colleges provide the appropriate training, there is a place in the manpower ranks for every youth who has self-discipline and a desire to learn.

Development of the Curriculum

Having examined a possible organization of the instructional program, let us now turn our attention to the development of the various curricular patterns which fit into this program. It should be noted that at least three fourths of the educational offerings of the two-year college afford significant opportunity for experimentation. If there is one need that transcends all others at present, it is the need to make the most of this opportunity, to find and free creative staff members to cope with the problem of offering a college education of significance to all who are motivated to achieve this end.

The college-parallel curriculum

The curriculum for the college-parallel division offers the least opportunity of the four for experimentation by the junior college. In view of the fact that the transfer student is subject to the regulations of the receiving college, it is important that he choose his educational objective at the time he enters the community college. His choice should be recorded on his permanent record forms at the time he is admitted, and any later changes should be made only after consultation with a faculty counselor. It is important that all decisions regarding his future should be made in such a way that he knowingly assumes full responsibility for such changes.

The following group of general-education courses would transfer to any liberal arts college:

(1)   English composition (two semesters)
(2)   Foreign languages (four semesters in one language)
(3)   Humanities, including English and American literature, foreign literature, music appreciation, fine arts, and philosophy (two semesters)
(4)   Social sciences, including anthropology, economics, geography, history, political science, psychology, and sociology (two semesters)
(5)   Natural sciences (two semesters in one science)
(6)   Mathematics (two semesters, based upon at least one year of high school algebra and geometry)

Taken as a group, these courses touch upon every field of human knowledge. In preparing for work in a world where highly specialized experts will need to understand each other's fields, these courses are valuable simply because they give such an immense amount of information in so many areas. They transmit knowledge about human beings, society, history, physical environment, cultural heritage, and art forms.

The program also allows broad preparation in the social sciences, humanities, and sciences. With this background, a student can adjust to a large number of vocations. Perhaps fewer than 50 per cent of all college students really know what they want to do. A Harvard Business School survey showed that only 8 per cent of the graduates were doing what they had wanted to do when in college.

If, however, a tentative choice of the professions has been made, there are preprofessional curricula that should be followed, with deviations from the liberal arts program that can be generalized as follows:

(1)   Business Administration—substitute accounting, economics, and college algebra for foreign language.
(2)   Engineering—substitute mathematics (through calculus and physics) for foreign language; the science elected should be chemistry and electives should include engineering drawing, engineering materials, and mechanics of materials.
(3)   Medicine—chemistry through organic, one year of physics, one year of botany-zoology or biology.
(4)   Law—no required list of subjects: electives recommended in history, English, political science, and economics (to include principles and practices of accounting).
(5)   Teaching—no required list of subjects: some states recommend electives in psychology, speech, and American history.
(6)   Science—mathematics through calculus, two years in the major science, and one year in a related science.

The technical program

If current predictions are to be taken at face value, the United States is on the verge of entering into what might well be termed the age of the technician. Department of Labor statistics reveal that, in the decade 1950–60, over-all employment increased by only 14.5 per cent. At the same time, the professional and technical grouping increased by 50 per cent. By far the larger gains were recorded in the ranks of the technicians. Electrical and electronic technicians increased a whopping 679 per cent, while substantial though smaller gains were shown throughout the field.

It is currently estimated that 700,000 new technicians will be needed in the decade 1960–70. An opportunity exists for the two-year college to make a sizable contribution—if it can successfully solve the problem of combatting the low status frequently assigned to nontransfer offerings.

A technician may be defined as any person who assists with the applied aspects of a trade or profession. Such people are not ordinarily involved in the development of new theory; rather, they apply existing knowledge to immediate practical problems. Frequently they begin as assistants to professional persons, as foremen in manufacturing plants, or as supervisors in construction or processing industries. Their theoretical education, while more limited than that of professional persons, is substantial. For this reason, and because of their sound general education background, they have great job flexibility and opportunity for general advancement.

The U.S. Office of Education recognizes two general classes of technology: engineering and nonengineering. A breakdown of the nonengineering area includes: health services (nurses, dental technicians, dental assistants, X-ray technicians); agriculture and forestry; applied and graphic arts; business and commerce; home economics; law enforcement; hotel and restaurant management; and other miscellaneous occupations.

The engineering technology student pursues a course of study very similar to that mastered by the engineering transfer student. In addition to college-level math and science, the engineering technologist pursues some specialty courses; these are designed to provide practical preparation so as to make him employable at the end of two years. Courses are commonly offered in such areas as civil, chemical, electrical, electronic, mechanical, and architectural engineering.

The industrial technology course is a lower-level course, with more emphasis on practical skill. Consequently, students in this area take fewer math and science courses and more laboratory work. Furthermore, the math and science courses they do complete are specially structured rather than patterned on those of the transfer program. Programs may include such areas as electrical, electronic, and mechanical technology.

The American Association of Junior Colleges lists eighty-six programs in specialized areas. These include many occupations which require specialized education and training. [12:504–34] Several examples will suffice to demonstrate the curriculum patterns employed in technical programs and to give some indication of their content:

ELECTRONICS TECHNOLOGY [3:50]

First Year

	[Hours]		[Hours]
Engineering drawing	3	Communications (English)	3
Communications (English)	3	Electrical circuits	6
Electrical circuits	6	Trigonometry	3
Health education	2	Slide rule	1
College algebra	3	Physical education	1
Physical education	1	Social science	3
	18		17

Second Year

	[Hours]		[Hours]
Advanced electricity	4	Advanced electricity	4
Basic electronics	6	Advanced electronics	6
Physical education	1	Electronic systems	3
General physics	4	Physical education	1
Social studies	3	General physics	4
	18		18

This general curriculum is typical of programs in electronics technology; however, there are many variations among colleges, based upon the objectives of the college, local occupational demands, and the adequacy of faculty and physical resources. Los Angeles Trade-Technical College differentiates between electronics engineering technology and electronics technology both in the number and the content of courses required for graduation. In addition to the basic required courses in English, speech, physical education, health education, and history or political science, the college requires the completion of thirty-three courses amounting to eighty-three credit units. Graduation with an associate degree in electronics engineering requires a total of seventy-two units. The program required of students in electronics technology consists of thirty-two courses totaling fifty-six credit units. The associate degree in this field requires a total of seventy-two units. [6:134–39]

The Fashion Institute of Technology provides an outstanding example of the specialized two-year college serving the needs of the clothing industry in a large metropolitan center. Each curriculum is based upon the specific technical requirements of the occupation and also includes required courses in the liberal arts. The curriculum in merchandising areas is typical of the programs offered in the college:

FASHION BUYING AND MERCHANDISING SEQUENCE [5:43]

Liberal Arts	[Hours]	Major Area	[Hours]
English	6	Fashion marketing	4
Mathematics and/or		Retail buying	3
science	6	Advertising and promotion	4
Social studies	9	Merchandising	
Health education	0	mathematics	2
Elective	3	Executive leadership	3
		Courses in fashion buying	
		and merchandising	9

Related Areas	[Hours]
Fashion Art	4
Apparel design and	
production	3
Textile science	3
Related textiles	2
Electives	3
Total	64

These are some of the items to be considered in initiating a technical program:

(1) The curriculum must be related closely to the requirements for skills, knowledges, and understandings of the occupation or group of occupations.

(2) The curriculum must be developed with the advice, counsel, and support of an industry or a profession. Unless employment can be insured for all those who receive the associate degree, the program should not be undertaken.

(3) A curriculum must be sensitive to occupational changes and should not be too specialized.

(4) Neither the traditional lower-division university curriculum nor the usual vocational-industrial curriculum is adequate in content or objective.

(5) Nature, content, methods of instruction, and purposes of a technical curriculum should seldom, if ever, exactly follow lower-division pre-professional curriculum patterns. Lower-division engineering courses, by themselves, do not constitute adequate preparation for the technician.

(6) The curriculum should be primarily occupation-centered. Transfer value should be of secondary importance. The technical curricula should be designed and conducted as ends in themselves.

(7)   Depending upon the level of the technical program, traditional academic organization of mathematics and science courses may not be realistic. Depth and scope of mathematics and science must be tailored to occupational needs. These courses must have problem-solving objectives and should place less emphasis on abstract concepts than traditional academic courses do.

(8)   Achievement levels and content should be based on job requirements rather than on a specified number of units and courses.

(9)   Craft shops and tools are needed to provide experience on practical problems. Laboratories are also needed for testing, research, and experiments.

(10)   Community leaders must share responsibility with educators for identifying manpower needs and planning programs to meet them.

(11)   The increasing number of part-time and evening students must be accommodated.

(12)   Technical programs will cost more than college-parallel programs because they require more laboratory hours, a lower students-to-instructor ratio, and more expensive equipment and facilities.

Vocational skills and manpower retraining

In addition to the technical programs described above, the two-year college has the responsibility in the area of vocational training for offering short courses and two-year cooperative work-study courses that will contribute to the manpower needs of society. When occupational training includes a large proportion of cognitive work, including regular academic courses in mathematics and science, it should be in the technical curriculum. When less than half the training is cognitive and the mathematics is a part of shop courses, it should be part of the vocational curriculum and under the direction of the placement director, who reports to the dean of students. No program should be undertaken unless there is a job awaiting the student upon the satisfactory completion of the course. Because there are often area or state analyses of long-range manpower needs, much reliance will have to be placed upon cooperation with the federal government.

The Manpower Development and Training Act of 1962 provided for the training of unemployed and underemployed men and women whose job skills are obsolete or insufficient. The training had to be in new skills in demand in the labor market. Heads of families and youths nineteen to twenty-two years old are paid training allowances in the form of cash payments, living allowances, and travel pay, for training periods of up to fifty-two weeks.

As of April 12, 1963, there were eighty programs [33] approved in forty-eight two-year colleges for the following occupations:

Automatic screw machine operator	Forester aide
Automobile mechanic	Machine operator
Chemist assistant	Medical secretary
Clerk stenographer	Nurse (practical)
Clerk typist	Office machine serviceman
Diesel mechanic	Sales person
Draftsman	Sheet metal worker
Electronics	Tractor operator
Engineering aide	Welder

Other programs that are represented with some frequency in community colleges are agriculture, carpentry, computer programming, data processing, electrical technology, homemaking, linotype composition, metal working, and printing.

The comprehensive nature of the two-year college allows movement back and forth among curricula in exceptional cases. Certain outstanding students in the vocational curriculum might transfer to technical courses.

Certain conditions must exist if vocational education is to be developed as a part of the community college: [34]

(1) The community which supports the college must be clearly committed to the idea of providing occupation-oriented programs for those students who are not planning to go on to a four-year college and for adults who are already employed in the community.

(2) The administration and the faculty of the college must fully accept, as a major task of the institution, the goal of preparing students for employment.

(3) The internal administrative structure must be such as to facilitate the development of occupation-oriented programs.

(4) Administrative and supervisory offices in the organization must be staffed with specialists who understand occupational education and who have the responsibility for the development and operation of the program.

(5) Provisions must be made in the administrative structure for continuous curriculum development. Programs must be continuously evaluated, revised when necessary, dropped when they are no longer needed, and supplemented or replaced as new needs arise.

(6) Policies regarding student selection must be carefuly developed and rigidly adhered to. Admission into occupation-oriented programs should be based upon realistic standards. These standards would not be the same for all programs.

(7) Placement services no less intensive than those provided for college-bound youth must be made available to employment-bound youth.

(8) The community college must have an adequate financial base. Federal funds are necessary to supplement state aid, student fees, and local taxes.

(9) The community college must provide adequate facilities.

(10) The community college must maintain and further develop community relations, especially with the economic interests of the community.

There are innumerable examples of vocational programs in two-year colleges. Perhaps this aspect of post-high school education is most fully developed in California, but there are many fine programs in other states. An example of one such program is found at Del Mar College:

RADIO AND TELEVISION SERVICING [4:58–59]

Unit I: Introduction   (50 hours)
History of radio communication, radio mathematics, radio and television waves
Simple radio receiver

Unit II: Basic electricity   (210 hours)
Components of radio and TV receivers, use of hand tools, nature of electricity and direct current, magnetism and DC measuring instruments, alternating current

Unit III: Basic electronics   (277 hours)
Vacuum tubes, power supplies, audio amplification, vacuum tube and crystal detectors, oscillators, transistors

Unit IV: Basic radio   (283 hours)
Receiver principles, servicing receivers, other AM receivers, F-M receivers, radio waves, transmission lines, and antennas, new developments in radio receivers, test equipment for radio servicing

Unit V: Television and TV receiver servicing   (558 hours)
TV familiarization, cathode-ray tube and circuit, vertical-sweep circuit, horizontal-sweep circuit, high-voltage circuits, servicing sweep circuits, syncon circuits, video circuit and service, automatic gain control circuit and service, audio servicing, power supplies, tuners, test equipment and servicing, diagnosis and repair of TV receiver

Unit VI: Transistors   (120 hours)
Transistor familiarization, current gain in transistors, transistor amplifiers, transistor receivers

Unit VII: Mechanics of Hi-fi and stereophonics   (120 hours)
Turntable mechanics, tone arms and pickups, simple amplifiers, speakers and batteries

Unit VIII: Hi-fi and stereophonic servicing   (120 hours)
Hi-fi circuits and mechanisms, stereophonics—circuits and mechanisms

Unit IX: Shop practice   (62 hours)
Techniques of trade, practical service considerations, organizing, planning and estimating shop work, service work

Generally, vocational programs of this type are organized on the basis of clock hours spent in the classroom or laboratory and upon the tested level of proficiency of the individual student. This reflects the tradition established in apprentice programs and the relationship between such programs and federal support. This type of organization is a direct descendant of federally sponsored apprentice programs which are based upon contact rather than academic credit hours. The method of instruction based upon hours of teacher-student contact is quite practical in that course content and student practice can be related directly to the objectives being sought in the curriculum. Should changes in content necessitate revisions in classes, these can be made with little difficulty by changing the number of hours spent on each subject. Another reason for structuring the programs in this way is that some states have specific clock-hour requirements for licensing for some occupations.

Exploratory and remedial courses

A one-year program of exploratory and remedial courses will achieve greater effectiveness with students of limited ability and background if administered or coordinated by the student-personnel division. Let us resolve the conflict between faculty and student personnel by placing under the direction of the dean of students a vocational, exploratory, and remedial curriculum for those not qualifying for or fitting the college-transfer, the technical, or the service curricula. The exploratory curriculum, a maximum of one year in length, would lead to a certificate for those who did not transfer to one of the other programs within the year. The certificate would represent twenty-four to thirty credit hours that might be chosen from the following areas:

(1) Integrated counseling and psychology course (as described by Glanz [11] at Boston University Junior College)
(2) Remedial English and math courses (as described by Meister [21] at Bronx Community College)
(3) Reading and study skills course (as described by Radner [25] at Staten Island Community College)
(4) Exploratory occupational courses (taken with the approval of advisor)
(5) Exploratory transfer courses (taken with the approval of advisor)
(6) New curriculum of independent studies: student selects programmed problems from one hundred different areas of social sciences, humanities, and sciences (as described by Wilcox [35] at Harvard). Blocker and Plummer [22] have identified thirty problem areas in the social sciences that could be used for independent study.

There are several logical implications of the college certificate program:

(1)   The college-transfer curriculum is relieved of unprepared students.
(2)   The student personnel staff teaches the integrated guidance psychology course; the academic faculty thus gets a faculty image of student personnel workers.
(3)   The invitation to failure of the "open door" policy is eliminated: there is a termination goal in the college certificate.
(4)   An analytical study of the student's choice of problems and his progress in measuring them would add a potent interest and motivation for real goals. As guidance can give information on individuals for curriculum goals, so can curriculum give information to guidance for individual goals.

Those enrolled with a goal of remedying deficiencies for later entrance to the college-parallel or technical program would be students above the median, with an I.Q. of 100 or higher, who have been educationally or culturally deprived in their early years. Also included would be people who are late academic bloomers or people who have been poorly motivated in their previous educational experiences.

Students in all divisions would "cross over" for courses in other divisions as appropriate. One of the great advantages of the comprehensive two-year college is its ability to adapt programs to students' needs and its readiness to allow them to move back and forth between divisions.

A SAMPLE UNCLASSIFIED CURRICULUM

First Semester

	Hours
Reading laboratory I	3
Speech laboratory I	2*
Applied psychology	3
Problem-solving in the social sciences	3*
Exploratory elective, technical, or vocational	3*
Physical education I	1*
	15

Second Semester

	Hours
Writing laboratory I	3
Speech laboratory II	2*
Educational and vocational diagnosis seminar	3
Refresher mathematics	3
Exploratory elective, technical, or vocational	3*
Physical education II	1*
	15

* These courses could be used for some associate degrees and certificates of completion.

At the end of the year, students completing the general curriculum would receive a college certificate; some graduates would be advised to advance to the college-parallel, technical, or vocational programs.

Reading and writing laboratories

The reading and writing laboratories are designed for students with significant deficiencies in vocabulary, reading comprehension, writing, and study skills. Initial emphasis must be placed on an adequate screening program, in which students are tested for vision, perception, and study and reading skills.

The laboratories would be for those whose reading is significantly below post-high school level (approximately ninth- to eleventh-grade levels). Students who indicate severe reading disabilities (approximately sixth- to eighth-grade reading levels) would enter the adult high school to work toward meeting a minimum level of competency (ninth-grade level). Many educators underestimate a student who is somewhat handicapped in reading skills. The average American adult reads at approximately a seventh-grade level. Class time should be divided about equally between formal lectures on techniques for improving reading and writing skills and laboratory activities utilizing multilevel instructional materials permitting self-direction and self-pacing for each student.

There is another, smaller group of almost adequate readers who need a program emphasizing greater speed and flexibility. This group could use the laboratory and materials on a part-time, voluntary basis.

To produce a permanent and significant change in the reader's total complex of skills and abilities, a program must be directed toward *modification,* the substitution of more effective functional, perceptual, organizational, and associative abilities for old ones. The program must deal with a broad range of skills and abilities in a carefully planned sequence, and it must be flexible in its adaptation to individual needs and different rates of learning. It must utilize a wide variety of techniques and materials, for there is no single medium sufficiently versatile to encompass all aspects of reading development.

The following basic principles of reading improvement are suggested:

(1) The student must understand that he can improve his reading skills and that the responsibility for doing so rests with *him.*

(2) The student should learn by means of standardized tests—or, if necessary, from informal inventories—how well he reads. After an appraisal of his reading requirements, he should select *for himself* the specific skills he needs to achieve.

(3) Each individual should be given an opportunity to attain these skills at his own rate and in accordance with his own plan while he

does his regular academic work (if he is not seriously retarded in basic skills).

(4)   Instructional materials should be simple, direct, and specific and should be applied in the student's daily reading requirements.

(5)   The student should understand how physical, psychological, and environmental factors may have lowered his reading performance and how these injurious factors may be modified.

(6)   The student should evaluate his reading skills both at the beginning and at the end of the laboratory or training period.

Although these principles aim at self-analysis and self-direction on the part of the student, the instructor undoubtedly plays a vital role in creating the atmosphere, enthusiasm, and encouragement which are necessary for a successful program. The first vital ingredient of any successful program or service is the teacher or director, upon whose shoulders rests the responsibility for adapting the program to the needs of his students. In his daily supervision of the progress of the students, the teacher must make corrections and adjustments according to individual rates of learning. For this reason, every effort should be made to employ a fully trained person for this position.

Under the auspices of the Ford Foundation, the Bronx Community College undertook a program of special guidance and instruction in English and mathematics among New York City high school graduates denied admission to college. [21]

About 65 per cent of the students in the program, after five months of tuition-free guidance and instruction, are continuing their higher education. Much evidence of unreleased academic potential emerged as an opportunity was given to overcome previous deprivation.

Highly motivated students not in the highest stratum of verbal and quantitative abilities achieved startling scholastic progress. Thirty per cent of the group, below the thirty-third percentile in verbal SCAT (School and College Ability Tests) scores, moved up to the middle third; 33 per cent in the middle third in verbal ability moved up to the top third. Students permitted to undertake a single college-level course, simultaneously, held their own.

Despite the special treatment, it became clear that further exposure to higher education would not be fruitful for some students. More could have been achieved with a program of two semesters rather than of one.

Educational and vocational diagnosis

After a semester of applied psychology that would cover psychological principles of human behavior and their application to daily responsibilities and working relationships, there would be a second semester of educational and vocational diagnosis. The course would include the following:

(1) Forecasts of job and educational opportunities
(2) Evaluation of students' interests, needs, expectations, aptitudes, and limitations
(3) Case studies in vocational and educational planning
(4) Observation of at least two different occupations in the community
(5) Individual analysis of the demands, skills, rewards, and limitations of three choices of vocation
(6) Individual conferences for educational planning of vocational choices

Diagnosing the vocational and academic abilities of low- and modest-aptitude students is a task of great complexity and requires professional diagnostic abilities—among them, the ability to predict student capabilities on the basis of probability tables. [36] Counseling psychologists with depth training in therapeutic psychology and sociology are needed. Because of their extensive training, these teachers may have to be paid more than academic subject-matter teachers.

They will try to help the student discover his talents and interests for vocational, social, and personal growth. This involves diagnosis of the individual's ambitions and limitations. Information must be found on vocations for which the individual is fitted, in which he will be successful, and for which there is a demand.

Here lies one of the unique functions of the junior college: to offer opportunity rather than frustration to below-median students.

The community-service program

There is a gradual fading of the line between membership and nonmembership in the community college in the areas being served by the college. The high number of part-time students in such colleges indicates that individuals do not perceive formal education as a process which is concluded with graduation from high school or college. On the contrary, education is viewed as a life-long process, as evidenced by evening classes, adult education, and refresher courses.

One of the potentially serious problems in society is the rapid increase in the amount of leisure available to individuals of all ages. Far too many individuals have never developed adequate interests or skills which would enable them to use their leisure time constructively. The two-year college can meet this need by making its courses available to all who desire them and by organizing additional noncredit courses to fit special circumstances.

The comprehensive development of the community-service division requires new and bold thinking about the broader purposes and applications of education. Certainly, there are numberless educational experiences of value which do not necessarily take place in the classroom. Perhaps the most important function of the community-service programs is the development of related interest groups which will encourage identification of common interests in the community, thus counteracting the fragmentation of society.

The development of the program requires constant and effective communication between the community and the college. College-community communication requires a firm commitment by the administration and the faculty to the concept of community service. Second, the program must blend college and community resources and personnel, both formally and informally, to insure their maximum utilization.

Classification of Students

The key to the successful implementation of the four curricula lies in identifying and attracting students who can benefit from the level of instruction proposed. An admission process scientifically designed to prevent incoming students from enrolling in courses for which they are not prepared will strengthen both the curriculum and the instructional program.

Williamson [36], at the University of Minnesota, calls for statistically competent student-personnel workers to determine probability tables for separate curricula. Hills [15], of the Georgia Board of Regents, used regression equations to work out college-expectancy tables (see Table 8-2).

Faculty members and counselors need carefully developed prediction tables which include high school grade-point averages and test scores if they are to aid students to make realistic educational and career decisions. Although such measuring techniques are not infallible, they give the student a reasonably accurate assessment of his chances for success in collegiate work. For example, a student with an index of 200 on Table 8-2 would have eleven chances in one hundred of making a C average in a liberal arts program.

The disappointing results of efforts to predict curricular success are attributed by Thurston [30] to the excessive numbers of underachievers and overachievers in the junior college population. She also challenges academic achievement as the sole measure of student success in the junior college. An analysis of grading practices by De Hart, at Foothill College in California, showed the inconsistency of grading within sections of a

TABLE 8-2. Expectancy Table for Estimating Academic Performance for the Freshman Year of Entering Students at the University (all students, male and female: N = 1268) *

Index 2 V + M + 4 H	C or Better	B or Better	A	Proportion Admitted as Freshmen
400		93	49	
380		85	33	
360	98	73	20	
340	96	58	10	
320	90	42	5	100
300	81	27	2	
280	68	15	1	98
260	52	7		95
240	35	3		87
220	21			30
200	11			1
180	5			
160	2			0
140	1			
Per cent of 1960 freshman achieving	58	21	1	

* NOTE: V = Verbal score on SAT
        M = Math score on SAT
        H = High school achievement in academic subjects

given course. He suggested that efforts to predict success or failure will be seriously hampered until greater consistency in grading is achieved.

Student-personnel workers need to develop tables for the "hand-minded" as well as for the "word-minded." Biggs [2] found, in a study of thirty-four California junior colleges, that 70 per cent used tests in screening students into various levels of English courses, but he found that only one college had developed and used tests extensively for student placement in technical and vocational courses.

One of the sore points for junior college faculty is the "open door" admissions policy. Hutchinson [16] found that 1000 faculty members in twenty-five Florida junior colleges (69 per cent) favored restrictive admission to college-transfer programs. Medsker [20] found that more than 75 per cent of college staffs favored minimum-ability and aptitude tests for admission to certain standard freshman courses in such fields as mathematics and English.

Classification systems

Related to the problem of matching talent with programs is that of assessing various types of talent. Not all varieties of creativity and ability are susceptible to easy evaluation through standardized group-testing programs. New classification systems are prerequisites to better curriculum planning.

One classification system is to group the I.Q. scores on the WISC (Wechsler Intelligence Scale for Children) as follows: [1:135]

Group I: 120 or above —10 per cent
Group II: 115 ± 5   —15 per cent
Group III: 105 ± 5   —25 per cent
Group IV: 95 ± 5   —25 per cent approximately
Group V: 85 ± 5   —15 per cent approximately
Group VI: 80 or below —10 per cent approximately

A similar classification system could be based upon percentile scores on standard national high school achievement and ability tests:

Group I: 80th percentile and above
Group II: 60th–79th percentile
Gorup III: 40th–59th percentile
Group IV: 20th–39th percentile
Group V: below 20th percentile

The college-age population can be classified into Groups I–V from the WISC or from standard high school achievement and ability tests. Group I would include those students able to work in the highest ranges of graduate and professional study or creative research in the top major universities. Group II would include those who could profit from four or five years of college in the areas of liberal arts, teacher education, business administration, engineering, home economics, or some other profession for which a college degree is either a requirement or an advantage. Group III would include prospective technicians. There is an insatiable demand for men and women who have scientific and technical knowledge but not necessarily a four-year college degree. Group IV would consist of skilled and semiskilled workers. Group V would include the unskilled workers that will always be needed in any society.

The first four groups certainly can profit from higher education. Persons in Group V can also profit from additional education if they have unusual motivation or a special interest. There is also another group to be considered in higher education: those who will be able to profit from higher education only after diagnostic and remedial help. This, the *reclamation group,* is comprised of people needing a second chance. In this group are potential late academic bloomers, the culturally deprived or the poorly motivated. [23]

What talent picture do these groups represent? First, there is graduate school and creative talent. This group would be drawn from those who fall no lower than the 80th percentile in high school achievement and ability tests. Percentile rank alone, however, would be an arbitrary criterion. Correlations are running about 0.45 between college achievement and percentile rank based on national high school achievement tests or high school grades. Additional criteria are being used and developed—for example, creative ability.

The second group includes those with talent for business administration, teaching, engineering, and other professions that require four or five years of college. This group would fall no lower than the 60th percentile on high school tests of achievement and ability, except in special circumstances (resulting from the fallibility of testing in allowing for cultural deprivation).

The students falling into these two categories constitute approximately one third of all high school graduates. If they seek service from the two-year college, they should be admitted to a program that offers work parallel to that given in four-year colleges and universities.

An extension to include an additional 20 per cent of the college-age population would place the lower limit at approximately the 40th percentile on high school tests of achievement and ability. It is from this range and above that technical talent is drawn. All high-I.Q. people will not enter the professions. How about the bright girl who would rather marry than go to graduate school? She may take a technical program to have a salable skill and to increase the family income. Such people will raise the I.Q. level of these programs. The technical group of the college-age population includes a possible one third of the comprehensive two-year college's students.

Another third of all potential college students, including adults seeking cultural improvement and people of all ranges of ability who need rehabilitation services and vocational training, would enter the service or community-service divisions of the comprehensive two-year college. Cultural and vocational improvement is a desire held by a large majority of those over eighteen who have not gone to college. Also, many students in the community college can, through remedial work, become candidates for the academic college or the technical college.

Curriculum Patterns and Instruction

In order to realize the full potential of each curriculum, instructional procedures and techniques in the two-year college must be modified and adapted to the motivations and abilities of the students. Tyler has pointed out that junior and community colleges must examine their teaching methods carefully, rejecting those traditional methods that are not specifically appropriate and developing more effective approaches. He stated that traditional methods may not be effective because:

(1) All junior college students are not motivated to engage in abstract intellectual activities.
(2) Many students are not equipped with the linguistic, quantitative, and conceptual skills required for advanced academic work.
(3) Many students do not have work habits and personal attitudes and values which are in harmony with the requirements of the educational program.
(4) The out-of-class environment of many students does not reinforce and extend the learning stimulated in the classroom.
(5) A high degree of homogeneity among students and in educational objectives does not exist in two-year colleges. [31:526–27.]

Two-year colleges, in many instances, have made adequate curriculum adjustments to occupational requirements and to the abilities of the students themselves; however, this is only one side of the coin. The patterns of course work and course content require adjustments in teaching techniques which will effectively translate content into terms meaningful

FIG. 8-2. Dimensions of Curriculum Patterns and Instructional Techniques

	Skills	Information	Insight and Understanding	Critical analysis and creativity
Concrete				Abstract
Accelerated (Transfer)			XXXXXXXXXXXXXXXXXXXXXXXXXX	
Degree-oriented (Transfer)			XXXXXXXXXXXXXXXXXXXXXXXX	
Applied (Technical and Vocational)		XXXXXXXXXXXXXXXXXXXXXX		
Developmental	XXXXXXXXXXXXXXXXXXXXXXXXXX			
Avocational	XXXXXXXXXXXXXXXXXXXXXXXXXXXXXXXXXXXXXXXX			

Instructional Techniques	2 1	6 4	13 3	7 11
	8 10	2 7	15 1	13 5
	6 4	1 12	5 11	15 16
	12	8 14	8 14	3 10
		5 15	7 16	12 9
			12 9	8
			10	

1 = Demonstration	9 = Lecture
2 = Directed practice	10 = Observation
3 = Discussion	11 = Panel discussion
4 = Field trip	12 = Reading
4 = Film, TV	13 = Role-playing
6 = First-hand experience	14 = Testing
7 = Individual interview	15 = Writing
8 = Laboratory	16 = Tape recording

to the students. Content can be classified as one of four general types: skills, information, insights and understanding, and critical analysis and creativity. These different levels require different teaching-learning interactions in the classroom.

Curriculum-instruction relationships

The relationships among types of curricula and teaching methods are shown in Fig. 8-2. The accelerated (honors) program assumes high ability in abstract thinking, insights and understanding, and places little emphasis upon information. The nonaccelerated transfer group assumes the importance of the same three classifications with slightly less stress upon critical analysis and creativity. Students in technical and vocational fields will spend more time on skills and information than either transfer group, but less time upon skills than students in developmental programs. The students in courses for avocational purposes may be interested in content—from the most concrete to the most abstract.

The application of this concept of curriculum-instruction relationships may be illustrated in any of the traditional liberal arts and sciences or the applied fields. Figure 8-3 illustrates that English

FIG. 8-3. Research and Development Team (Approximate division of occupational activities on any given project) [28]

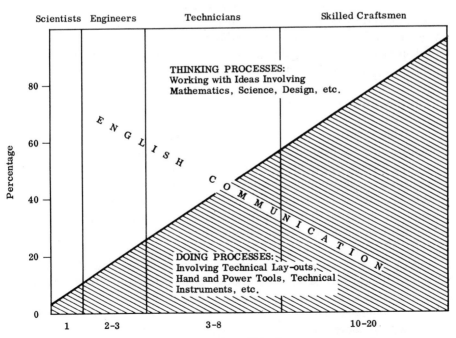

communication cuts across all lines in vocational requirements with more importance for the scientist and engineer and less for other workers on the production team. English, therefore, is a prerequisite for all educational programs, but the content and the techniques employed in teaching it should be adapted to the students and their educational goals. Students who are enrolled in, and have the requisite ability for, transfer courses should be able to profit from teaching which is more permissive and less structured than that designed for students in applied and developmental courses. Honors programs employing seminars, directed reading, extensive and intensive writing, individual conferences with instructors, and similar techniques can stimulate the exceptionally able student to develop his critical abilities and intellectual skills to the optimum level. These students should not be restricted by conventional courses; rather, they should be released and guided to the full realization of their potentialities.

Curriculum content and student motivation

Some teaching methods are tiresome and repetitious for students of high ability. Demonstrations, directed practice, lectures, field trips, and observations do not necessarily stimulate the best in such individuals. Their maturity may make it possible for them to learn primarily by themselves, with very little direction from the instructor. On the other hand, carefully designed individual projects requiring extensive reading, writing, laboratory work, group discussion, individual interviews, and role-playing seem to offer promise for sharpening intellectual skills and creativity. The development of individual initiative and direction, coupled with close relationships with faculty members, will do much to stimulate students to become self-sufficient and to achieve their maximum potential. [7]

The teaching of English, or communications (as it is labeled in many colleges), demands one set of methods with students of average college-level ability and another with students in honors programs. Although average students can probably take far more responsibility than they are now generally given in college classes, they do need more guidance and direction than students in honors programs. Both groups should be required to master the mechanics of language—on their own, not in class. They should also have the opportunity to achieve advanced standing in the subjects in which they are already competent. Research has shown that advanced standing motivates superior students because they are allowed to progress at their own rate. [24]

Automated devices, which are just coming into their own, should be used far more lavishly than they are at present. These devices can be used in the classroom and in the library (or "educational materials center"). Such equipment aids the teaching-learning process by making it possible for the student to learn factual information, solve problems, and establish meaningful relationships and concepts for himself, with minimum direction in class. His independent study should be reinforced through tutorial work, seminars, audited courses, and other means, the most important of which is individual guidance from instructors.

> The fact remains that attention to guidance in many institutions lags considerably behind attention to instructional programs, that many faculty members who are quite proficient in their subject areas have neither the training nor the inclination to undertake extensive guidance of students, and that the diversity of student characteristics demands more than perfunctory attention to the guidance function in programs purporting to offer flexibility in rate or depth of student learning. [8:55]

If students in these four groups are to achieve their full potential, there must be a shift in emphasis from the tactics of teaching to the logistics of learning. Such an emphasis would stress scholarship, problem-solving, and critical thinking. [14] This can be done if the college supplies the proper materials and faculty members whose own competencies make it possible for them to motivate learning of the highest quality. A further requisite is that traditional credit hours and class meetings be adjusted to the specific needs of individual students. Although credit hours may be used to communicate information about students from one college to another, such measurements should not be the focus of the learning process. The judicious use of comprehensive examinations would provide the necessary data for grading purposes and, at the same time, motivate students to integrate the knowledge and understanding of various subject-matter areas.

> Institutions which have had longest experience with credit based primarily on competence rather than on blocks of time recommend the use of some combination of comprehensive or field examinations, advanced standing, and credit by examination to encourage more efficient teaching-learning techniques and to develop better learning habits and more purposeful objectives by both students and teachers. This does not mean the abandonment of reports of the quality and quantity of the student's progress toward the completion of his program; what it does mean is that individual courses are treated as stepping-stones in the larger program and not as ends in themselves and that the quantitative elements of student marks indicate levels of competence rather than time spent in class. [29:23]

The primary difference between teaching and learning in the technical and vocational fields is that course content is very specifically occupational-oriented. This means that the material learned by the student is built upon specific referents: the knowledge and skills required for occupational competence. In English, for example, the emphasis in content is upon all forms of communications and the technical language inherent in the occupation. Teaching methods are adapted to the occupational orientation and to the motivations and abilities of the students.

On the highest levels of technology there is a substantial amount of abstract content, while in less demanding occupations content is more concrete. Teaching techniques will stress demonstrations, samples of materials, directed practice, laboratory work, and audiovisual aids. Less reading and writing is required and there is more emphasis upon application of knowledge and skills. The content of English is generally restricted to oral and written communication in the form of speeches on the technical area and report writing. Critical analysis of language and creative writing are not included in these courses. Thus, the content of such courses is narrower than that provided in transfer courses, and the instructor should provide closer direction and supervision of student work.

The direction of learning in the developmental program must be especially close in view of the students' problems of motivation and their lack of study skills. These students need specific material which begins on their individual level of development and moves them toward mastery of basic reading, writing, and reasoning skills. They require regularly scheduled group and individual guidance. Without such close supervision and guidance, there is little chance that they will master course content. This group also requires directed practice, demonstrations, observations, group discussion, and laboratory experience. Courses should be carefully and completely planned so that realistic objectives can be achieved within the time allotted.

Diversity and the Two-year College

In no institution in America today does such a variety of ages, abilities, and interests exist as in the two-year college. Some of its students are enrolled in remedial reading courses while others master honors courses in English and social studies. Developmental and honors students may be combined in other courses. A large and growing number of adult students demand recognition of their maturity from instructors. Some graduates enter topflight engineering institutions; others swell the growing ranks of engineering and industrial technologists; still others do not last beyond the first semester. An instructor in a first-semester freshman course may possibly have to reach and help all three groups simultaneously.

The diversity of the students in the two-year college can be both a strength and a weakness. Not unlike the succeeding waves of immigrants that contributed so much to the making of America, the onrushing waves of enthusiastic, often ill-prepared applicants to the comprehensive community college will leave their mark on this institution. But out of problems come solutions, and it is this cycle that makes progress possible. If the two-year college views diversity as strength and experimentation as inevitable, the promise of higher education for all may yet be fulfilled.

Has the two-year college responded to the challenges of diversity, or is experimentation limited to a relatively few institutions? Johnson's survey of the instructional practices in ninety-five representative colleges in fourteen states led him to state:

> Despite the substantial and relatively comprehensive list of practices identified in this exploratory survey, it is clear that junior colleges, in general, are doing little experimentation in the effective utilization of faculty services. It must be recognized that most of the colleges included in the survey were selected because they had been known to engage in some innovating practices, but even among these institutions most of the practices reported are found in a scattering of the colleges only.
>
> The general picture revealed in the survey is one of significantly less experimentation than would be expected, or certainly hoped for, in an institution which is often referred to as "the most dynamic unit of American education." [17:12–13]

Johnson attributes that lack of experimentation to the fact that it is difficult to find qualified faculty, and the fact that primary attention is focused upon expansion resulting from soaring enrollments. He points out, further, that there are some notable exceptions among two-year colleges: some are carrying out experimental programs with unusual imagination and vigor.

New approaches

Some additional factors have tended to inhibit the development of fresh approaches to instruction and curriculum. First, there is currently little practical university leadership in these areas. Stimulation from leading universities could do much to move the two-year college toward broader concepts of educational programs and techniques of instruction. Second, some states have legislation which virtually eliminates the possibility of experimentation in course content and patterns. Third, many college administrators are more concerned with status and stability for the college than they are with bold experimentation related to content, technique, and student needs. New approaches to education require the education of members of the board of control, the general public, and the faculty. Having yet to attain security and status, many colleges still feel too insecure to strike out into new fields and to risk possible criticism and failure. Fourth, the faculties of two-year colleges are generally composed of educational conservatives whose personal and professional aspirations and needs might be threatened by extensive innovations in educational programs. Last, students are motivated primarily toward successful completion of the mechanical requirements of college work and eventual acceptance as a "college graduate." They, too, resist changes which are inconsistent with their expectations of the college and their need for continuity and stability.

In spite of these limiting factors, the two-year college must continually adapt to new social and educational needs as they appear on the horizon. Adaptations in instruction and curriculum are the areas of greatest opportunity for the college. Perhaps it will meet this challenge in the future.

Bibliography

1. Bigge, Morris L., and Maurice P. Hunt, *Psychological Foundations of Education.* New York: Harper & Row, Publishers, 1962.

2. Biggs, Donald A., "The Present Problems of California Junior Colleges in Enrolling Students in Appropriate Courses," *Junior College Journal,* XXXII (September 1961), 9–12.

3. *Bulletin,* Palm Beach Junior College, Palm Beach, Florida, 1962–63.

4. *Catalog,* Del Mar College, Corpus Christi, Texas, 1962–63.

5. *Catalog,* Fashion Institute of Technology, New York, N.Y., 1961–63.

6. *Catalog,* Los Angeles Trade-Technical College, Los Angeles, California, 1961–62.

7. Cohen, Joseph W., "Education of the Superior Student," *Junior College Journal,* XXXII (September 1961), 53–54.

8. Cole, Charles C., and Lanora G. Lewis, *Flexibility in the Undergraduate Curriculum: New Dimensions in Higher Education.* Washington, D.C.: USGPO, 1962.

9. Edinger, Oscar H., Jr., and Max D. Bell, "Observations on Opportunity," *Junior College Journal,* XXXIII (January 1963), 5–7.

10. Glanz, Edward C., "Personnel and Guidance Work in a New Era," *Junior College Journal,* XXIX (November 1958), 141–45.

11. _____, "Freshman Psychology Course as the Basis of Student Personnel Programs," *Junior College Journal,* XXXVIII (November 1959), 290–95.

12. Gleazer, Edmund J., Jr. (ed.), *American Junior Colleges.* Washington, D.C.: American Council on Education, 1963.

13. Good, Carter V. (ed.), *Dictionary of Education.* New York: McGraw-Hill Book Company, 1959.

14. Hatch, Winslow R., and Ann Bennet, *Effectiveness in Teaching: New Dimensions in Higher Education.* Washington, D.C.: USGPO, 1960.

15. Hills, John R., "College Expectation Tables for High School Counseling," *Personnel and Guidance Journal,* XLII (January 1964), 479–83.

16. Hutchinson, Nan, "Three Images," *Junior College Journal,* XXXIV (September 1963), 12–15.

17. Johnson, B. Lamar, *Islands of Innovation.* Occasional Report Number 6. Los Angeles, Calif.: UCLA Junior College Leadership Program, University of California, 1964.

18. Katz, Joseph, and Nevitt Sanford, "The Curriculum in the Perspective of the Theory of Personality Development," in Nevitt Sanford (ed.), *The American College: A Psychological and Social Interpretation of the Higher Learning.* New York: John Wiley & Sons, Inc., 1962. Pp. 418–44.

19. Lewis, Lanora G., *The Credit System in Colleges and Universities, New Dimensions in Higher Education.* Washington, D.C.: USGPO, 1961.

20. Medsker, Leland L., *The Junior College: Progress and Prospect.* New York: McGraw-Hill Book Company, 1960.

21. Meister, Morris, "Operation Second Chance," *Junior College Journal,* XXXIII (October 1962), 78–88.

22. Plummer, Robert H., and Clyde E. Blocker, "A Unit on Metropolitan Problems," *Social Education,* XXVII (May 1963), 257–58.

23. ———, and Richard C. Richardson, Jr., "Broadening the Spectrum of Higher Education: Who Teaches the High-risk Student?" *Journal of Higher Education,* XXXV (June 1964), 308–12.

24. Radcliffe, Shirley A., and Winslow R. Hatch, *Advanced Standing: New Dimensions in Higher Education.* Washington, D.C.: USGPO, 1961.

25. Radner, Sanford, "The Community College Reading Program," *Junior College Journal,* XXX (March 1960), 379–80.

26. Reynolds, James W., "Community Services," in Nelson B. Henry (ed.), *The Public Junior College: The Fifty-fifth Yearbook of the National Society for the Study of Education, Part I.* Chicago, Ill.: The University of Chicago Press, 1956. Pp. 140–60.

27. Sanford, Nevitt (ed.), *The American College: A Psychological and Social Interpretation of the Higher Learning.* New York: John Wiley & Sons, Inc., 1962.

28. *Survey of Vocational-Technical Needs for the Pasadena-San Gabriel Valley Area.* Pasadena, Calif.: Pasadena City Schools, 1961.

29. Thomas, Russell, *The Search for a Common Learning: General Education, 1800–1960.* New York: McGraw-Hill Book Company, 1962.

30. Thurston, Alice, "Now That We Are Nine Feet Tall: A Look at Junior College Students," *Junior College Journal,* XXXII (February 1962), 334–39.

31. Tyler, Ralph W., "The Teaching Obligation," *Junior College Journal,* XXX (May 1960), 525–33.

32. U.S. Department of Labor, Bureau of Employment Security, U.S. Employment Service, "Estimates of Worker Trait Requirements for 4000 Jobs,"
Dictionary of Occupational Titles. Washington, D.C.: USGPO, 1956.

33. Vaccaro, Louis C., "The Manpower Development and Training Act and the
Community College," *Junior College Journal,* XXXIV (November 1963),
21–23.

34. Wenrich, Ralph, Professor of Vocational and Practical Arts, University of
Michigan, in speech to American Technical Education Society, Milwaukee,
Wisconsin, December 3, 1962.

35. Wilcox, Edward T., "The New Curriculum," *Junior College Journal,*
XXXIII (February 1963), 16–18.

36. Williamson, E. G., "An Outsider's View of Junior College Guidance Programs," *Junior College Journal,* XXX (May 1960), 489–501.

The two-year college, more than other institutions of higher education, seeks to project a student-centered image by emphasizing as its primary function the comprehensive attempt to meet the needs of widely varying groups of students. The argument that guidance is more important in the two-year college than in other institutions of higher education has been substantiated by the heterogeneity of the student body, the variety and complexity of decisions which students must make, and the need for nonacademic services which support and give purpose to the efforts of students. If Bogue's analysis of the problem of student-personnel services is accepted, it is clear that a comprehensive evaluation of guidance services must take place in most two-year colleges if this function is to approach the effectiveness currently claimed for it by authorities in the field. [3:320–27] There is need for critical appraisal of the organization and administration of guidance services, the kinds of services which should be provided, the quality and quantity of these services, financial support, qualification of staff members, and the responsibilities of the academic faculty for counseling and academic guidance. Such an analysis can provide the framework within which personnel services appropriate to the clients of the college and in keeping with its purposes can be provided with reasonable expenditures of time, funds, and effort.

9

the student-personnel program

Context of the Program

In discussing the adaptive responses articulated by the student-personnel program, it would seem fitting to begin by examining student needs and institutional pressures which provide the context within which the program functions.

Student characteristics

The characteristics of the two-year college student have been discussed in detail in Chapter 6, but certain traits bear summarizing because of the implications they hold for student personnel work.

Two-year college students are, on the average, less academically able than the students of four-year colleges and universities. This factor, whether or not combined with nonselective admission policies, results in certain student needs which may include: remedial courses, assistance in developing favorable study habits, counseling to modify unrealistic vocational aspirations, and aid in adjusting to the emotional consequences of failing to achieve a desired goal.

Two-year college students, on the average, come from lower socio-economic backgrounds than do their counterparts in four-year colleges or universities. It is likely that any tuition, however low, will preclude certain students from attending unless scholarship funds and part-time jobs are made available. Even where tuition is not a consideration, students must still find some way of supporting themselves during the period when they have no regular income. Thus it can be said that a large proportion of those students attending public two-year colleges will need financial counseling as well as placement services.

Two-year college students are facing the most critical period of their lives in terms of vocational choice. One of the most frequently quoted statistics pertaining to these students concerns the discrepancy between the number of individuals who plan to transfer to a four-year college and those that actually do. Medsker emphasizes that more than two thirds who enter plan to transfer whereas only one third actually do. [8:97] It would appear that, at the very least, one third of all two-year college students could benefit from vocational counseling. That this need is understated can be clearly demonstrated by an examination of the literature dealing with the vocational aspirations and decisions of two-year college students.

A substantial number of two-year college students will continue their education at other institutions of higher education. Students who plan to transfer to specific institutions need to be guided so that their course patterns insure smooth acceptance without loss of credit. Those who are uncertain need assistance in selecting institutions which fulfill their vocational, financial, and academic requirements.

The students of two-year colleges, considered as a whole, are more similar to other students of higher education than they are different. Although it is common procedure, in discussing the two-year college, to stress its unique characteristics, obvious similarities with four-year institutions should not be overlooked. Like all college students—or, for that matter, all individuals in a particular age group—the two-year college student has certain social needs that must be satisfied. For example, it is during this period that many students find themselves as individuals and select marriage partners. The emotional problems arising out of this process, as well as the requirements for accurate and reliable information, place a heavy responsibility on the student personnel service.

Institutional pressures

The two-year college, in response to perceptions of the role assigned to it by society, establishes certain requirements which must be met by those who wish to use its services. These requirements, frequently derived from the more conservative elements of society and distorted by the process of being interpreted in an institutional context, are not always comprehensible to the students. Furthermore, as one result of the failure to develop a clear image of the two-year college, requirements are not always consistent among institutions. Certain objectives, however, are sufficiently well accepted to permit their being identified as common to two-year colleges.

A frequent function of education in any society is to establish conformity to social norms. The two-year college seeks to direct overt student behavior so that it does not reflect discredit upon the institution. Public displays of affection, excessive consumption of alcoholic beverages, and other types of socially unacceptable behavior are discouraged through various coercive measures.

Another well-accepted general function of education is conservation of the cultural heritage. Various courses, required and elective, are designed to make the student aware of the historical and legislative achievements of his country and state. Ceremonies are planned to emphasize memorable occasions.

Other requirements imposed by the college are likely to include the area of health education, communication, physical sciences, mathematics, as well as others.

The list of requirements imposed upon the student could be considerably expanded by inclusion of such items as attendance, punctuality, achievement, and types of conduct. It should be clear by this point that these requirements may not be perceived by students as being in their best interests or, for that matter, even as being related to their reasons for attending college. A problem arises: How are the demands of the institution to be reconciled to those of the students, and vice versa? The task of mediating between the needs of the student and the requirements of the institution is assigned to the student-personnel division.

Much that has been discussed under this heading represents the eminently respectable conservative position. The liberal position would include those collegiate experiences that enrich and change the life of the student. These would include programs out of the classroom that would encourage the student to become a world citizen, to rise above the prevailing cultural norm, to be an intellectual twenty-four hours a day. This position would place the student-personnel program in the center of the business of citizenship training through the exploration of the study controversy in a variety of co-curricular activities.

Organization of Student-personnel Services

As has been indicated, the student-personnel program can be viewed as a way of mediating between the needs or perceptions of the students and the pressures of the institution. It should be borne in mind that these pressures are simply a reflection, however distorted, of the demands imposed by society on the institution to justify its reason for existence. The institution seeks to accomplish this task of mediation by the assignment of roles to various personnel in the organizational framework.

Depending on the size of the institution, a role may correspond to the responsibilities of several individuals, or several roles may be subsumed under the responsibility of a single individual. As the discussion proceeds, it will become increasingly evident that student-personnel services are closely related to or often a part of other facets of the total educational program. Wrenn emphasized this point:

> Although some educational functions can be clearly accepted as student-personnel functions, others are borderline between instructional and student personnel, or between general administration and student personnel; whether they are appropriately considered a part of the student-personnel program depends upon the manner in which they are administered. [17:iv]

The criterion for determining if a particular role can properly be described as a part of the student-personnel program is the degree of emphasis placed on the satisfaction of student needs as opposed to the resolution of institutional pressures.

Although the organization of the student-personnel program varies according to the size of the institution, some way of mediating between student perceptions and institutional requirements must be provided. The smaller the college, the less is the likelihood that primary reliance will be placed on a specific segment of the formal organization. There is, of course, nothing wrong with the reliance on informal procedures to accomplish certain of the objectives of the student-personnel program. What must be borne in mind, however, is that everyone's business is frequently no one's business. Administrators must not assume that an ostentatious description in the college catalog and a few platitudinous comments regarding the desirability of "every-instructor-a-counselor" at a faculty gathering will take the place of a properly organized and adequately supervised program. Responsibilities which are not specifically assigned frequently go untended. It is highly desirable, therefore, that specific individuals be assigned each of the responsibilities which make up the framework of an adequate program.

One further caution: It is indeed possible for the spirit to be willing but the flesh weak. The best intentions in the world cannot possibly compensate for inadequate professional preparation. Although this truism is respected in the assignment of instructional personnel, it is frequently ignored in the area of student-personnel services. It is true that there are certain parallels between the preparation of instructors of psychology and that of counselors, but it does not follow that every instructor of psychology either desires or is qualified to fulfill an important role in the student-personnel program.

A frequent practice, particularly in smaller schools, is the use of all faculty members as student advisors. Hardee points out that not all faculty members are suited, by temperament or training, for employment in this capacity and suggests three criteria to be used in selecting faculty members for a counseling role:

(1) The interest of the faculty member in counseling
(2) The ability of the faculty member to deal effectively with students in a one-to-one relationship
(3) The willingness of the faculty member to learn the fundamentals of his counseling responsibility [5:50]

The concept that everyone on the faculty should be a student counselor or advisor is sheer nonsense. Assignment of counseling responsibilities to ineffective and untrained instructors casts serious doubts on the adequacy of the entire program. There are several reasons for which the practice has enjoyed widespread acceptance. The assignment of counseling responsibilities to all members of the staff does not require an increase in remuneration or faculty released time. Thus it provides administrators with an easy and inexpensive procedure for satisfying the requirements of accreditation committees and easing their own consciences. There is also a prevailing belief in certain administrative circles that the counseling service should confine itself strictly to helping students adjust to the academic program and avoid concern with their personal problems. It is obvious that untrained counseling personnel will be only too happy to avoid becoming involved in the personal problems of students; professionally trained personnel have been taught that it is not possible to separate the two.

In order for a student-personnel program to exist, then, three requirements must be met. There must be a specific assignment of responsibilities for the implementation of the program. Faculty members must be trained to carry out their assigned responsibilities. Finally, sufficient released time must be provided to individuals assigned these responsibilities. In the following section, several suggested organizational plans for a student personnel program will be presented, along with typical job descriptions that might be considered appropriate. These are intended only as guides; the actual assignment of responsibilities, particularly in small institutions, must be predicated on many factors in addition to an individual's place in the organizational structure.

Functional concept

The formal administrative structure of the student-personnel program has been illustrated in Chapter 7; but a more meaningful understanding of functional interrelationships can be derived from a view of the actual roles carried out by this division of the college.

The suborganization of student-personnel services within the college setting should resemble a pyramid within which are concentrated all functions relating to the nonacademic life of students. Despite the need for coordination, the rigid line-staff model does not offer the most effective organizational pattern. Structuring the services into clusters of related, mutually interdependent activities improves horizontal communication and cooperation without sacrificing coordination. An ideal organization of student-personnel services is presented in Fig. 9-1.

The ideal administrative organization of a college must embody the principles of functional organization in which activities directed toward the achievement of specific objectives are clustered together in rational relationships with one another. Thus, in student-personnel services, as well as in other aspects of college administration, all students outside the classroom should be organized under a single individual and in a specific department or division of the college. As the organizational chart indicates, all nonacademic and nonbusiness functions

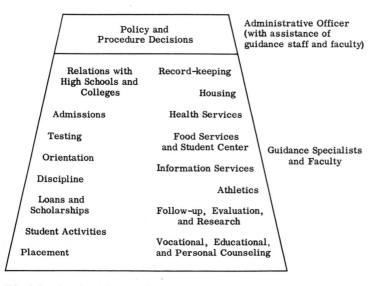

FIG. 9-1. Functional Organization of Student-personnel Services

should be included within the sphere of student-personnel services, because these functions are designed for the direct benefit of students. The processes through which such services are provided remain secondary to their intended effect upon the students.

One of the best examples of poor organization is the removal of the registrar and his functions from the supervision of the dean of student personnel. The assistant dean-registrar in a college of five-hundred or more students should be a professional educator with special aptitudes and training in the techniques of his position. Although it is not always possible for smaller colleges to assign a professionally trained individual to this position, the functions of this office logically belong within the sphere of the dean of student-personnel services.

The processes of student-personnel administration have as their chief purpose the facilitation of the education of students. Records, processes, and routine office procedures are not the product of the offices involved, but merely the vehicles through which students receive the help they need in organizing and implementing their educational program. The fragmentation of functions and the lack of central direction of supporting services can impede rather than support the total education of students. The functions discussed on the following pages are made necessary by the complexity of the educational processes, the specialization of academic personnel, and the size and complexity of the college itself. The disassociation of the instructional program from student-personnel services constitutes a serious problem which operates to the detriment of both areas. Academic personnel may view the student-personnel program as an unnecessary bureaucratic adjunct to the college, lacking in academic respectability and interfering with the basic purposes of the educational process. Communications between teachers and guidance personnel are often confused by this lack of understanding of the problems and objectives shared by the two groups. Although this situation, in part, results from the diverse specializations common to subject-matter personnel as opposed to those working in the area of guidance, the lack of a common background in the psychological aspects of human behavior and the wide variations in philosophical concepts of education contribute to a deepening of the void.

An ideal relationship between these two major educational functions can result only from a merger of thought and action on the operational level, making possible cooperative action and improved support for both facets of student needs. [12] This can be achieved if the academic and student-personnel services are united in the roles of both guidance personnel and faculty. Guidance personnel can better relate themselves to the academic program if they teach a class on a

FIG. 9-2.   Functional Relationships
Between the Academic and Student-personnel Programs

Areas of Specialized Competencies (Guidance)	Areas of Mutual Cooperation	Areas of Specialized Competencies (Academic)
Preadmission and admission	Case conferences on academic and disciplinary problems of students	Classroom instruction
Orientation program		Individual academic advisement
Testing program	Committees for policy and procedural problems	Student evaluation and recommendations
Individual counseling		
	Academic advisement by full-time teachers	
Referral for specialized medical services		Referral to guidance personnel for acute problems
	Sponsorship of student groups	
Supervision of student activities		Research techniques
	Placement of co-op program students	
Record-keeping		
Welfare services	Evaluation of both academic and guidance programs	
Financial aid		
	Institutional research	
Placement		
Follow-up and research		

regular basis. Instructional personnel who are assigned responsibilities for advising students in the areas of their special competencies may more fully appreciate the contributions that can be made by this type of service. The fusion of the two programs is represented in Fig. 9-2.

Financing

With some exceptions, the student-personnel programs in two-year colleges are underfinanced and understaffed. An analysis of staffing charts and budgets clearly demonstrates the inadequacy of resources devoted to the fulfillment of the stated objectives of the student-personnel program. Recommendations have been made outlining a pattern of staffing of guidance services for colleges of various sizes. [7:54] These recommendations are shown in Table 9-1.

TABLE 9-1. Staff Required for Effective Guidance Program in a Two-year College

Personnel	500 Students	1000 Students	2000 Students
Administrator	One, half-time for twelve months	One, full-time for twelve months	One, full-time for twelve months
Professional counselor	One, full-time for twelve months	One, full-time for twelve months	Two, full-time for twelve months
Teacher counselor	Two, half-time for academic year	Four, half-time for academic year	Eight, half-time for academic year
Nurse	One, half-time for academic year	One, half-time for academic year	One, full-time for academic year

The personnel program needs substantially more financial support than it has received in all but a few two-year colleges. In view of the unusual needs resulting from an unselected student body, the costs for an effective program should be from 15 to 20 per cent of the annual operating budget of the college. Thus, if the per student cost was $700 in a college of 1000 students, the personnel program would require from $90 to $120 per student for adequate support. As the college increases in size, the cost per student will tend to decline (the number of people required to perform the same services would decrease in proportion to the number of students).

Types of Student-personnel Services

Any attempt to establish a program of essential services for all two-year colleges is bound to encounter the argument that such colleges differ so widely that the attempt is doomed to failure. McDaniel documents these differences:

Junior colleges differ from each other in important ways. These differences affect their purposes. Some provide facilities for group living and hope to make significant improvement in the personal-social skills and attitudes of their students. Some serve only one of the sexes and hope to make a lasting contribution to the character our culture demands of this group. Some are church-related and have special responsibilities for group living and have special responsibilities for strengthening of religious values. Some are large. Some are small. Some are relatively wealthy. Others are poor.

He then goes on to point out that, despite these differences, certain important similarities also exist, and that among these may be included the attempt to move students

> . . . toward firmer commitments to high ideals, . . . more rational bases for conduct, more understanding, more knowledge, more skill, . . . truer self-estimate and greater ability to cooperate with others, . . . more informed participation in the activities and levels of government, [and] . . . economic self-sufficiency in a job reasonably appropriate to abilities and satisfying to interests. [7:10]

After a careful examination of the differences and similarities among two-year colleges, one is forced to conclude that such differences may affect the emphasis placed on the various student-personnel services, but do not account for their total absence in some cases.

In an attempt to remain unique, the two-year college has frequently avoided the duplication of procedures in effect in four-year institutions. An example concerns the area of academic rank for teachers as discussed by Tillery. [14] It is entirely right and proper to question the unthinking acceptance of procedures prevailing in other areas of higher education. The truth inherent in this statement should apply equally to the unthinking rejection of procedures, simply for the purpose of remaining unique. There is ample evidence that the major efforts of student-personnel programs in four-year institutions are directed to the adjustment and integration of freshman and sophomore students, for it is during these years that students are most likely to drop out or to fail academically and it is in this period that choice of a major must be made and that social adjustment is most crucial. It stands to reason, therefore, that, if many of the problems of entering students are as common to four-year institutions as they are to two-year colleges, benefit could be derived from careful study of the better developed and more comprehensive services generally offered by the four-year institutions.

The services that should be extended by all two-year colleges purporting to offer a comprehensive student-personnel program are discussed in the following pages with a view to what *ought* to be, rather than what necessarily is. The weaknesses of existing programs are well-documented by Medsker:

(1) Many institutions lack policy formulation, planning, and professional direction of the program.

(2) The counseling program in many institutions is inadequate.

(3) Little research is conducted which enables the two-year college to obtain facts about their students.

(4) Two-year colleges make only limited effort to evaluate the personnel program. [8:162–65]

If the student-personnel program is viewed as an adaptive response growing out of the necessity to mediate between student needs and institutional requirements, then it follows logically that variations in programs would arise from an analysis of differing needs of student bodies. It requires no extensive investigation to determine that programs vary much more widely than do needs. One possible reason for this, other than the obvious one of inadequate finances, might be the confusion of administrators and boards of trustees over the difference between needs and problems. As defined by Wrenn,

> A need is a demand of the organism, whether or not acknowledged or understood by the individual. . . . A problem, on the other hand, is something of which the individual is aware, and for which he has no immediate solution. [17:13]

If student-personnel programs were based on needs rather than problems, they would much more closely resemble the services described in the remainder of this chapter.

Admission service

The first contact that a student has with an institution is through its admission officers. Although many private two-year colleges have well-developed admission service with full-time counselors who travel to various secondary schools, the public two-year college—with its tradition of nonselective admissions—has often neglected to consider more than the basic requirements. It is obvious that some procedure must be established to insure that the prospective student meets certain minimum requirements. But, beyond this administrative detail, the admission service also offers an opportunity for benefits to students and institution alike.

The prospective college student is confronted with a series of decisions which have profound implications for his future. The admission officer can, by providing accurate information and well-founded advice, aid materially in insuring that these decisions are wise ones. The student has a right to know the strengths and weaknesses of the institution he proposes to attend. One common procedure for making this information available is through the college catalog. Arbuckle criticizes the misrepresentation that frequently occurs in these publications when social activities are glorified or services are described which exist only in the minds of the college administration. He adds:

> Junior college catalogs usually indicate that the student may be given training preparatory to entering a senior college, or semiprofessional training if he expects to enter the business or commercial world. The objectives are generally couched in such language that it is doubtful whether they mean much to prospective students. [1:51]

In addition to the college catalog, some institutions provide a specially designed student handbook which provides accurate answers to the questions that are most likely to arise.

Another desirable procedure for making information available to prospective students is through close cooperation with secondary school counselors. Such cooperation is most effective when the college provides specially prepared information, in addition to the college catalog. Handbooks for counselors have found ready acceptance in the four-year institution. Brochures, films, and similar media have been tried and found effective in a number of instances. It is also highly desirable for the prospective student to visit the institution of his choice at some time during the admission procedure, preferably with his parents. Student guides can show such visitors around. Besides removing some of the student's fear of the unknown, this procedure can also provide an excellent method for publicizing the college program and facilities.

In addition to needing general information about the college and assistance in selecting an educational program, it is likely that many two-year college students will require information concerning the availability of scholarships, loans, and part-time work. Even the modest tuition fees and expenses that prevail in most public two-year colleges are bound to eliminate some needy students unless they are given special assistance in working out a program to meet their financial needs.

The two-year college faces the problem of determining who, among the ever-increasing numbers of applicants, can best benefit from the training it offers. A comprehensive program for resolving this problem includes the evaluation of prospective students in four areas. The applicant is evaluated mentally by means of aptitude tests. A physical examination provides information concerning his health. Rating forms and letters of recommendation are used to establish some idea of his emotional stability, and a transcript of grades indicates the level of his past achievement.

A second institutional requirement concerns the establishment of admission criteria and the interpretation of these criteria to the members of the faculty. This aspect of the admission program is probably the most frequently overlooked. When a mathematics instructor fails 50 per cent of his algebra class, it is obvious that there is a lack of agreement wth respect to performance requirements. The most promising approach for securing consensus on admission standards is by involving faculty members in their development. When the size of the institution severely limits the degree of participation, special efforts must be made to establish communication between admission officers and other faculty members.

Many two-year colleges pride themselves on the fact that they accept all applicants who meet the minimum qualifications: high school graduation or eighteen years of age. This policy has inspired the title of a very well-known study by Burton Clark entitled *The Open Door College: A Case Study*. Sober second thoughts on this approach have prompted at least one writer to suggest the term *revolving door* as more appropriate than *open door*. Many two-year colleges have followed the lead of large state universities which admit all applicants and then flunk out many of them at the end of the first semester. This policy seems hardly appropriate to the stated goals of most two-year colleges. The only alternative to this procedure is a policy of selective admissions in which students are admitted only to those programs for which there is some reason to believe they may survive. One of the best justifications for adopting this procedure is stated by Wrenn:

> A college that encourages a student to enroll should do so upon the basis of reasonable evidence that the student can successfully meet the scholastic and social requirements of the college.... It is unethical to admit students without regard for their chances of succeeding. [17:420]

It should be noted that, before two-year colleges can answer the question of what qualifications are necessary for success in a given program, they will have to devote considerably more attention to research and evaluation than they are presently doing.

Information service

There are three basic kinds of information which students are likely to require during the course of their attendance at a two-year college. The first concerns vocational opportunities. With less than half of the students of two-year colleges transferring to four-year institutions, large numbers must be given assistance in making wise vocational choices. One procedure for doing this is through vocational exploration. The student is helped to assess his strengths, weaknesses, and interest patterns. He is then provided with occupational information relating to those work areas indicated by his particular pattern of aptitudes and interests.

Another important area in which information will be required is that concerning the policies and practices of potential transfer institutions. A significant number of two-year college students do transfer to four-year colleges. Many among these will require special attention in order that their transfer, without loss of credit and with good chances of success, may be facilitated. A collection of college catalogs to which the student may be referred is essential, but not enough. The two-year college must also maintain close contact with four-year institutions through conferences and a follow-up program to insure the availability of continuous, accurate information on their standards and admission policies.

Finally, the student needs social information. Entering students of two-year colleges have many questions regarding what constitutes socially acceptable behavior in a variety of situations. The popularity of advice columns in newspapers and periodicals attests to the interest shown in these matters. Lacking the more extensive contacts with students that are available to residential and four-year institutions, the public two-year college must seek to exploit every possible area of contact. Social information, attractively displayed and easy to use, can be of assistance in shaping desirable attitudes on the part of the student body.

A brief comment is in order concerning the availability of such information. The information materials need to be centrally located, close to the rooms used by the counseling staff. Ordinarily, the college library is the most central and most easily accessible location. If occupational, educational, and social information is treated like other library materials, its care and preservation is insured without becoming too time-consuming for the counseling staff.

Counseling service

Counseling is the key feature of all student-personnel work. Williamson supports this viewpoint: ". . . [C]ounseling is the most common method, technique, emphasis, and function used in a variety of different services. No other service is universally applicable to all personnel work." [16:183] Student-initiated counseling is most likely to occur in response to a felt need or problem arising in one of four areas.

The student may require assistance in selecting his educational program. Although this is usually a routine function, certain cases may arise in which all the resources of the student-personnel program must be committed. Financial problems, a lack of clear educational and vocational goals, work conflicts, unrealistic aspirations, and similar conditions require the efforts of a trained counselor. If faculty advisors are used in this area, they should be required to have knowledge of interviewing techniques and of the resources that can be made available to the student. The program should be coordinated and supervised to insure that students who can benefit from counseling are referred to members of the counseling staff rather than being left to vegetate in general courses which do little more than perpetuate the confusion which originally prompted their choice. [10]

Students are also likely to seek assistance in selecting a transfer institution. Counseling in this situation consists primarily of matching student characteristics and institutional requirements. A college guide—such as that published by Lovejoy, in which information is given on location, control, enrollment, faculty, fees, housing, fields of study, and scholarships—can provide considerable assistance in carrying out this responsibility. [6]

Students often benefit from the opportunity to clarify their vocational choices. A complete vocational exploration would include the use of tests to determine aptitudes; the use of interest inventories to suggest possible occupational choices; an examination of pertinent literature concerning the nature of the work, working conditions, preparation required, personal requirements, and the occupational outlook; and, finally, an opportunity to talk with people engaged in the occupations under consideration or—even better—actual experience in some related phase of the occupation.

These counseling functions are well recognized by administrators in two-year colleges and are, by and large, approved of in theory even if they are not made possible in practice. The fourth area in which students may initiate counseling contacts, however, is subject to considerable controversy. This is the area of personal problems—involving anything from guilt over premarital sex experiences to psychotic symptoms requiring the attention of a psychiatrist. There can be no well-established line between counseling and therapy. This truism causes the two-year college, with its generally less adequate counseling facilities, more concern than its four-year counterpart. Counselors may be exhorted to avoid personal problems. Such advice fails to consider that problems in other areas are almost always related to personal difficulties and frequently are caused by them. It is a little like suggesting that a doctor correct a heart defect without bothering to consider the requirements of the brain for oxygen.

There are two possible solutions to this problem. They are not alternatives; rather, they are supplementary. The first possibility involves the degree of professional preparation of the person assigned counseling responsibilities. The higher his level of professional competence, the less need there is to be concerned about harm resulting from dealing with problems he is not equipped to consider. The second possibility is the initiation of a referral service through which serious problems may be passed on to those more competent to deal with them. In any event, considerable reliance must be placed upon the judgment of the individual counselor. Care in selecting such individuals would result in less need for useless advice.

The college may initiate a counseling relationship with the student as a result of at least two conditions. In the first situation, failing grades may indicate a necessity for reviewing the student's educational program and study habits. Often this review will result in the identification of deficiencies which, when corrected, lead to the desired improvement. In no area of student-personnel services is there more need for cooperation between counselors and instructors than in the problem of remedying scholastic difficulties. By the time a student has flunked several courses, it may be too late for the college to do more than assist him in adjusting to withdrawal. Early identification of potential dropouts can help to reduce such instances.

A second situation which may result in the initiation of a counseling relationship by the institution occurs when the student violates a college regulation. Counseling theorists have emphasized the desirability of separating disciplinary procedures from counseling procedures. Such a point of view overlooks the potential contribution to adjustment that can be made by disciplinary counseling. According to Wrenn, three purposes are served by this approach:

> (1) [To] provide a permissive situation in which students may talk of themselves without fear of reprisal or violation of confidence and in which they may grow in self-insight
> (2) [To] find and study all of the current and background facts of the case
> (3) [To] help the counselor decide whether the student may learn from the experience and remedy his behavior without referral to a discipline committee for administrative consideration. [17:460]

If discipline is viewed as an attempt on the part of the college to motivate a student to give more mature consideration to his responsibilities rather than to impose punishment for violation of regulations, then it follows that counseling is a most suitable adjunct in this process.

Two additional considerations will serve to round out the discussion. It is obvious that any counseling relationship initiated by the student is more likely to achieve success than one instigated by the institution. It follows, therefore, that maximum publicity needs to be given to the services available, and students whose past records indicate that they can benefit must be encouraged to utilize them.

Admonitions to the contrary, many institutions will continue to utilize faculty advisors to carry the major burden of their counseling program. Such institutions would do well to heed the words of Williamson:

> We do not argue that all personnel workers should be professionally trained counselors. However, it would be to their advantage, in terms

of effectiveness, if they experienced at least rudimentary professional training not only in interviewing, but in counseling interviewing which includes
supervised analysis of the effects of interviewing techniques of various
types. [16:188]

It is desirable for all personnel in the counseling program to have attended professional-level courses in the field. In-service training and
faculty workshops, although valuable, cannot carry the entire burden
for preparing advisors to operate effectively.

Record-keeping service

The necessity for keeping careful records of the student's achievement and progress is well recognized by all institutions of higher learning. What is not so well recognized is the purpose which these records
should serve and the manner in which they ought to be utilized. Too
often educational programs become the servant of bureaucratic procedures when, in actuality, the opposite should be the case. Hardee ex-
presses the only sound justification for the record-keeping function:
"namely, the communication of information in writing between and
among those who know the facts and *those who need to know them.*"
[5:161] Once this conclusion is established, some questions remain to
be answered.

The first issue concerns the nature of the data that are to be collected. This question has already been answered, in part, by the discussion of the admission service. During the admission procedure,
information concerning the student's aptitude, achievement, health, and
personal background will be collected as a matter of routine. To this
information can be added reports of counseling interviews, periodic
grade reports, and other pertinent information that becomes available
during the student's enrollment at the college. In addition to the simple
acquisition of data, some procedure must be followed to insure that
the information is organized so as to facilitate its use. The cumulative
record folder, either the one offered by the American Council on Education or one developed to meet local needs, provides a convenient way
for organizing the material. Many large institutions have found it feasible
to organize their data for processing by machine. Whatever the system
employed, the purpose remains the same: to transmit data as effectively
as possible to all who have a reason for having them.

The information collected during the admission and registration
procedure often has profound implications for the student's educational
program. Physical defects may restrict the activities program or indicate
special consideration in classroom seating. Exceptional ability, if recognized early, can be challenged by supplementary programs or special
class assignments. Students with low ability or academic deficiencies may

require remedial programs. Student-personnel officers have the responsibility for insuring that useful information is made available and, when necessary, interpreted to instructors concerned. It would very likely be much easier to obtain needed information from instructors if they were certain of the use to be made of it and accustomed to being given information in return.

This brings up the second question concerning the record-keeping service. To whom should this information be made available? In answer to this question, general agreement would probably be found regarding the right of instructors and administrators who have dealings with the student to have free access to all information about him (except that obtained in confidential interviews) and the continuing obligation to provide outside agencies with certain types of information. Much less accord would be found with respect to the right of the student to have access to his own file. The writers of this book take the position that the student does have such a right to review the results of testing, health evaluations, and other data which can be of assistance to him in selecting and modifying life goals. Furthermore, it is the responsibility of the college to make this information available in comprehensible form and to provide any counseling that may be required to secure its rational acceptance.

Adoption of a favorable philosophy concerning the degree to which data should be made available is helpful but not sufficient. The location of the information often governs the use to which it is put. If records are carefully guarded by the registrar with an elaborate check-out procedure guaranteed to discourage anyone who lacks the persistence of a Sherlock Holmes, then personnel who have been granted access are unlikely to avail themselves of the opportunity. Ideally, personnel records should be centrally located and sufficient clerical assistance should be provided to facilitate their use. In older buildings, not designed with this requirement in mind, it may be possible to duplicate the more significant records. In no instance should the necessity for safeguarding such records be permitted to become the governing factor to which all other considerations must be subordinated. Records exist to serve students, not to provide registrars with peace of mind.

A third question involves the preservation of records. What material is to be retained after students terminate their relationship with the institution? Increasingly, larger institutions are turning to microfilm as the answer to this problem. More information can be retained on microfilm in much less storage space. If the size of the operation does not justify the expense of microfilming, careful consideration must be given to reducing files as much as possible by disposing of nonessential information. A good case can be made for retaining little more than grades, test scores, and reason for withdrawal (if the student did not graduate). Regular reviews of the retained material and the use to which it is put will result in appropriate criteria for determining the answer to this question.

Orientation service

Orientation procedures of varying degrees of effectiveness are in practice in most two-year colleges. Although some programs are based on little more than traditional practice and a vague idea that something termed *orientation* ought to occur, many programs represent well-thought-out attempts to analyze and meet the needs which arise among students as a result of the transition from secondary school to college.

Student needs met by the orientation program fall into three categories. Students entering college for the first time need to assess their particular pattern of aptitudes and aspirations and to learn how these can be best employed to promote success in the institutional context of the two-year college. Objectives may need to be expanded or modified. Secondly, the student must become acquainted with the facilities and resources of the college and the surrounding community. The public two-year college attempts to integrate its programs with those already existing in the community and thus avoid unnecessary and costly duplication of effort. This objective must be accompanied by an effort to interpret to students the relationships between the resources offered by the college and those existing in the community. Lastly, the orientation program provides an opportunity for students to become acquainted with the activities sponsored by the college and to gain some understanding of how these relate to the total college program.

From the point of view of the college, orientation provides the means by which students may be taught institutional regulations designed to facilitate their orderly integration into the student body. It also provides occasions on which information required for classification and counseling purposes may be readily obtained. If orientation is viewed in its broadest sense, a continuing program can be offered over an extended period to smooth out some of the rough spots that occur during the student's first year in college. In this way, the number of dropouts may be reduced, with a considerable saving to the institution. Perhaps more important, the gains experienced by the individual student ultimately result in considerable benefit to the society as a whole.

Procedures utilized in the orientation program can be divided into preregistration and postregistration phases. Before registration occurs, a number of programs are designed to inform the incoming student of plans and procedures and to encourage him to report for registration. A preregistration program occurring some time during the semester preceding a student's entrance offers an opportunity to complete testing, test interpretation, and educational counseling in an atmosphere less highly charged with tension than that of the period immediately prior to registration. Newsletters to entering students encourage them to persist in their efforts to attend and provide useful information concerning important dates and college activities.

The importance of students in the orientation program cannot be overemphasized. Arbuckle points out: "There is no other personnel service, with the exception of student activities, that can be so effectively organized and administered by students as the orientation program." [1:66] Not only are students most aware of the problems faced by incoming freshmen, but they also are often in the best position to allay some of these difficulties. The "big brother" or "big sister" program in which a second-year student assumes responsibility for one incoming freshman is one example of how students can become involved in the orientation program. Of course, it should be emphasized that not all students are capable of assuming such responsibilities, nor do all desire to do so.

An alternative to preregistration—frequently utilized by residential colleges, whose students may be drawn from a much wider geographic area than those of the public two-year college—is orientation week. Incoming freshmen, and certain carefully selected second-year students, arrive at the college a week prior to registration. Preregistration activities are carried out along with social functions intended to make the student feel at home. There appear to be two extremes in such programs which need to be avoided. First, if the student has too much free time, such problems as homesickness are intensified. But an avalanche of activities exhausts the student and gives him a definite let-down feeling when classes finally begin.

Preregistration activities, although desirable, cannot carry the total burden of helping the student to adjust to the institution. The trend is toward orientation classes, which meet throughout the first semester or the first year for an hour or more each week. These weekly meetings provide opportunities to deal with problems as they occur rather than attempting to anticipate them all during one whirlwind period. Social activities occurring several weeks after registration may meet with more success than those scheduled during the more tense circumstances surrounding the student's initial contact with the college. Finally, a procedure by which students having difficulty are identified and referred to the counseling program before these problems become insurmountable can provide assurance that the two-year college is meeting the responsibilities it has outlined in its philosophy.

Student-activities service

The existence of student activities and the desirability of having the college supervise and sponsor these activities is a subject of little controversy. Not so clear is the relationship that these activities have to the academic program and their function in the total process of education. Periodically, articles are produced decrying the anti-intellectualism of American college campuses and placing the blame squarely on the extensive activities programs—the "frills" without which education would be free to approach the millenium. Because opinion concerning the value of student activities is divided, it would appear important to begin this discussion by devoting some attention to their function in meeting student needs and fostering institutional purposes.

The postadolescent college student stands on the threshold of admission to adult status in a democratic society which has certain expectations for its members. Student activities, patterned as they are along the lines of adult organizations, provide opportunities to learn social skills and techniques for more effective participation in society. Membership in organized groups can result in social acceptance and recognition, which tends to enhance feelings of self-worth and to stimulate additional effort. Finally, student activities teach skills and cultivate interests which promote the more worthy use of leisure time.

From the point of view of the institution, student activities provide a means by which the social impulses of students may be channeled toward constructive ends. Honor societies stimulate scholarship and often provide the college with a willing source of extra labor for a variety of useful projects. Properly administered student activities are models of the democratic process. As such, they represent an invaluable aid in the education of students for life in a democracy. One of the great opportunities in the extracurriculum is to change the prevailing climate of opinion among students through stimulation and experimentation. Discussion and debate can lead to:

(1)   Direction of thought to controversial problems
(2)   Consideration of all relevant evidence
(3)   Acceptance of different opinions
(4)   An understanding of rights and respect for diversity
(5)   A preservation of the rights of the nonconformist
(6)   A working toward consensus
(7)   Fulfillment of the societal obligation to be informed
(8)   The concept of being an intellectual twenty-four hours a day

The emphasis placed upon student activities establishes the use of critical inquiry in the study of controversy. Such participation, carried over into adult life, enhances the democratic way of life.

The values of student activities extend only to those who participate in them wisely. Two extremes may be distinguished which ought to be of concern to the institution. On one end of the continuum is the nonparticipant. Strang distinguishes three ways of getting students into groups: publicizing the groups available, personal invitation, and counseling. [13:247] The problem of the nonparticipant does not receive the attention that it deserves, partly because the functions of student activities are not universally understood and accepted, and partly because such students do not come as easily to the attention of personnel workers as their opposites: the overparticipants. The orientation course offers an excellent opportunity for publicizing student activities and for encouraging participation, both through personal invitation and through the publicity given to the activities of various organizations.

The point system appears to offer a possible solution to the problem offered by the overparticipant. In addition, it provides a way by which elective offices can be more evenly distributed. With this procedure, points are assigned to each elective office in accordance with its importance. Points may also be assigned for membership. Each student is permitted to acquire a maximum number of points. In this way, no student is permitted to hold more than one major office, and some selectivity must be exercised with respect to the degree of participation.

The key to the coordinated control of student activities rests with the student council. Ideally, the constitution of this body should require a review of the purposes and meeting times of all other student groups. If it appears that a new organization will meet specific student needs without conflicting with existing groups, then a charter may be granted. Requiring the student council to pass on requests for social events provides a means for insuring that conflict between events does not occur. Furthermore, the process of getting students to assume added responsibility for the control of their activities lessens the administrative burden that must be carried by the institution while providing students with some insight into the problems involved.

It must be emphasized that students will not assume responsibility unless they are also granted some authority. Frequently, administrators are happy to have students assume the burden of doing most of the work, but wish to reserve to themselves the right of making all decisions. Such a procedure will not work and can only lead to resentment on the part of the students. This is not to say that student councils must be given a free hand. There is a need to educate students to the responsibility for the conduct of student activities which rests with the administration and which cannot be delegated. Nevertheless, it is possible to permit students much freedom in the conduct of their activities provided that areas of responsibility and authority are clearly delineated and that authority commensurate with responsibility is delegated.

In the final analysis, much of the responsibility for the success of a program of student activities in the two-year college must rest with the faculty advisor. Because the student is in attendance only a short time, the advisor has a more difficult task in insuring continuity than is the case in four-year institutions. Under these circumstances, it is often a temptation for faculty advisors to become supervisors. When such temptations arise, advisors would do well to remember that one of the purposes of student activities is to provide students with experience in democratic living. Democracies are noted for their ability to correct errors rather than for a propensity for not making them. By encouraging student leaders to seek his counsel, by setting an enthusiastic example, and by making systematic evaluations, the faculty advisor can insure that the student activity program, far from being a "frill," is making a solid contribution toward the implementation of the goals of the institution. [2]

Vocational placement service

All two-year colleges provide vocational placement service. Frequently, this may be limited to receiving phone calls from prospective employers and pinning notices to a bulletin board. It is quite likely, also, that some students are placed by the efforts of individual instructors who become aware of openings in their special fields. The importance being given to the development of placement services is well illustrated by a recent publication of the American Association of Junior Colleges, *Service Through Placement in the Junior College*. The publication, however, also stresses the failure to provide adequate resources. [9]

Perhaps one of the reasons for the failure of many two-year colleges to develop coordinated placement services can be traced to their generally poorly defined and often unrealistic admission policies. Wrenn points out the responsibility that colleges have for limiting admission to specialized training programs to those who have a reasonable chance of being placed. [17:388–90] The naïve assumption that a student is better off with two years of college, regardless of whether or not society has any use for the skills he learns there, is indefensible because it overlooks the uses to which the same period of time might have been put had the student been more realistically appraised of the vocational market.

The establishment of a centralized placement agency with the responsibility of coordinating student referrals and employer contacts can provide a definite service both to the student and to the community.

This does not imply that the college should attempt to duplicate the efforts of existing public and private employment services. Close cooperation with existing agencies will, however, improve the service that can be offered by all.

The college should assume the responsibility of maintaining files on students and prospective employers. Some system should be adopted for following up the contact by obtaining information as to whether the job was offered and accepted. Periodic checks of student performance can be an invaluable aid in assessing the effectiveness of training programs. It is also likely to result in first-hand knowledge of new jobs as soon as they become available. By keeping track of the availability of part-time as well as full-time employment, the college can aid needy students during their attendance at the institution. There are also valid reasons for making a placement service available to graduates: such a service, whether or not widely utilized, insures students that the college has a continuing interest in their welfare.

Problems in this area occur because the total responsibility is not commonly recognized and, consequently, large gaps develop in the program as a result of lack of coordination and centralization. An effective placement service could be offered by most colleges at little added financial expense, provided that existing resources both within and outside the institution are fully utilized.

Student-welfare Services

All aspects of the student-personnel program may be considered welfare services in the sense that they are designed to meet student needs. For the purposes of this book, however, the term *welfare services* will be limited to those procedures established by the institution for the purpose of providing students with health facilities, housing, and food service.

Health facilities

Of all the potential services of a comprehensive student-personnel program, none has been more neglected by the public two-year college than the provision of adequate health facilities. Although private residential colleges ordinarily have facilities comparable to those of four-year institutions, the public two-year college has, for the most part, justified its neglect of this area on the grounds that the student resides at home and consequently may use those facilities he used before enrollment.

A first requirement for an adequate health program would be the provision of physical examinations under college supervision. If students are to be required to participate in a physical education program, as is general policy, then it follows that the college has the responsibility for insuring that participants are physically qualified. If physicians are employed by the college, there is greater certainty that the examinations given will thoroughly cover important areas. Moreover, athletes participating in strenuous contests should be periodically examined to insure that they are physically qualified. Failure to do so can result in tragedy for all concerned.

A second requirement for an adequate health program would include some type of infirmary service with medical treatment for minor illnesses of an ambulatory nature. A major benefit to the institution in having such a program is that it permits early detection of contagious diseases with the result that preventive measures may be taken before the infection becomes widespread.

A final requirement for a satisfactory minimal program for the nonresidential college would be the provision of instruction in physical and mental health. Of the four areas mentioned, this is the only one that has received any degree of attention in the public two-year college. But, although it is an important aspect of the service, it cannot carry the entire burden. Probably the main reason for its widespread implementation is the fact that it is less expensive than the other three. Perhaps if the funds presently devoted to supporting intercollegiate athletics in some two-year colleges were devoted to improving health services, more than adequate attention could be provided to all who needed it.

To these minimal requirements would be added requirements for facilities for the in-patient care of contagious diseases and other non-ambulatory illnesses requiring continuous attention over a limited period. It should be emphasized that residential institutions, both private and public, have, for the most part, recognized and met their responsibilities in the area of health. It is the public nonresidential institution, primarily, which must awaken to the need and take positive steps to meet it.

Housing

Every college that does not limit its enrollment to students within commuting distance has a responsibility in the area of student housing. Four-year institutions normally require that noncommuting students below a minimum age live in college-approved housing. Although this policy may be designed, in part, to insure that dormitories are paid for, its beneficial aspects are too obvious to require discussion. The inspection and approval of private residences for student housing takes up staff time, but it can insure that students are protected from exploitation and that they will live in a healthy atmosphere.

Residential colleges have many of the same problems as other institutions of higher education with regard to housing. Chief among these seems to be the conflict between running the dormitory as a business enterprise, and simultaneously carrying out appropriate student-personnel functions. Because the two-year college lacks the available supply of dormitory counselors represented by graduate students in the university, the selection and training of supervisory personnel is likely to be pretty much of a hit-or-miss proposition. Some colleges encourage faculty members to undertake the job in addition to their regular responsibilities, while others simply accept the best available applicants for the low salaries that are offered. In neither instance do the results resemble anything like a well-integrated program of dormitory counseling. Often, supervisors become little more than glorified babysitters, with the major emphasis upon enforcing stringent regulations and little attention given to attempts to promote responsibility and growth. A partial solution to the problem would include the use of second-year students as dormitory assistants and the integration of the housing service with other elements of the student-personnel program.

Food service

The problems involved in the preparation and serving of food can be a major morale factor even in the nonresidential institution. Although many colleges of this type maintain cafeterias which serve meals during certain hours, a concession frequently is granted to a private concern and the college limits itself to supervising costs and sanitation.

At its best, the dining room offers an opportunity for teaching social graces and providing a calm pleasant atmosphere in which conversation and good food can be combined for the pleasure of all concerned. When such an atmosphere does prevail, it can be traced to two factors: supervision of food preparation by a trained dietitian, and careful planning of dining facilities.

Follow-up Evaluation and Research

The effectiveness of services offered by the student-personnel program can be determined only by periodic evaluations designed to determine the extent to which student needs and institutional requirements are being integrated. Medsker points out the present weakness of efforts by two-year colleges in this direction and concludes:

> Chief administrators of two-year colleges clearly have an obligation to bring about a periodically conducted, cooperative review of student-personnel services in which all staff members, together with representative students, evaluate the quantitative and qualitative aspects of the program. [8:165]

Certain procedures are particularly useful in fulfilling the need for evaluation. Dropouts constitute a critical problem for the two-year institution. Follow-up studies designed to identify causes for dropping out can be used as a basis for developing special programs and other preventive procedures. The follow-up of transfer students provides evidence of the standards being adhered to by the college in the area of admission procedures and academic preparation. And the follow-up of employed students can promote improvement in training programs as well as facilitate the placement of future graduates. Studies of the relationships between admission criteria and academic achievement can be of assistance in the establishment of more realistic policies.

In addition to the objective indices represented by grade-point averages and success on the job or in a transfer institution, the potential contribution that can be made by student and faculty opinion should not be overlooked. In a very real sense, a service can be no more effective than the reputation it enjoys. The soliciting of student and faculty opinion can help to identify areas of misunderstanding or confusion and can result in a clearer interpretation of the nature and purposes of the services.

The specific contributions of student-personnel workers to the development of instruction and curriculum will be viewed by the faculty as more effective if considerable effort is given to institutional research and to the interpretation of findings to the faculty and administration.

The contribution to the curriculum can be extended, according to Tyler, by a systematic appraisal of the learning being provided. [15] Ruth Strang has long said that research is a major function of student-personnel services. D'Amico and Martorana found six hundred research and information reports on the two-year college in periodicals from 1950 to 1960. [4] There were very few articles in the areas of instruction and curriculum development. Only 9 per cent of the articles were written by junior college faculty and special-service personnel. Yet it is this group that has the most advanced training in research techniques, is most directly involved in serving the educational needs of students, and is most aware of the need for research studies for improving programs and instruction. What load adjustment, what rewards are necessary to get student personnel and faculty to meet their mutual responsibilities in research?

Some problems

Although two-year colleges assert that their uniqueness is, in part, based upon the guidance function, many problems and shortcomings continue to exist in this area of service. The qualities that students bring to the two-year college create special problems wh᠁   must be met by the institution through its personnel program. These problems have been listed by Priest as:

(1) Financial problems
(2) Redirection of students toward realistic goals
(3) Effective vocational counseling to overcome the prevailing negative public attitude toward occupational training
(4) Creation of a more challenging collegiate environment for [the] student, especially during the first semester of study
(5) Development of leadership abilities in students within two years
(6) The definition of the role of the faculty advisor
(7) Development of school spirit and traditions [11:303–6]

These are some of the problems which the student-personnel program must meet. In order to do so, certain administrative and organizational issues must be met and solved:

(1) Can the college provide sufficient financial support for an adequate guidance program?
(2) Will the college be so organized that both specialized guidance personnel and faculty members can contribute to the guidance program in a professional and effective manner?
(3) Will the college be so organized that professional guidance personnel will have an opportunity to contribute to the total pattern of education of students?
(4) Can faculty members adjust to the need for in-service training which will give them the knowledge and skills necessary for effective student advisement?
(5) Can the two-year college find the resources necessary for effective evaluation of guidance programs through institutional research, follow-up studies, and other appropriate methods of study and analysis?

Bibliography

1. Arbuckle, D. S., *Student-personnel Services in Higher Education*. New York: McGraw-Hill Book Company, 1953.

2. Bloland, Paul A., "The Role of the Student Organization Advisor," *Personnel and Guidance Journal*, XLI (September 1962), 44–49.

3. Bogue, Jesse, *The Community College*. New York: McGraw-Hill Book Company, 1950.

4. D'Amico, Louis A., "A Decade of Research and Informative Reports on the Two-year College," *Junior College Journal*, XXXII (January 1962), 292–98.

5. Hardee, M. D., *The Faculty in College Counseling*. New York: McGraw-Hill Book Company, 1959.

6. Lovejoy, Clarence E., *A Complete Guide to American Colleges and Universities*. New York: Simon and Schuster, Inc., 1961.

7. McDaniel, J. W., *Essential Student-personnel Practices for Junior Colleges*. Washington, D.C.: American Association of Junior Colleges, 1962.

8. Medsker, Leland L., *The Junior College*. New York: McGraw-Hill Book Company, 1960.

9. Mons, Milton C., *Service Through Placement in the Junior College*. Washington, D.C.: American Association of Junior Colleges, 1962.

10. Morton, Richard K., "The Junior College and the New Student," *Junior College Journal*, XXXI (April 1961), 434–36.

11. Priest, Bill J., "The Most Significant Problems of Junior Colleges in the Field of Student-personnel Services," *Junior College Journal*, XXIX (February 1959), 303–6.

12. Robinson, Donald W., "The Role of the Faculty in the Development of Student-personnel Services," *Junior College Journal*, XXXI (September 1960), 15–21.

13. Strang, Ruth, "Problems and Procedures of Student Activities," in C. G. Wrenn (ed.), *Student-personnel Work in College*. New York: The Ronald Press Company, 1951.

14. Tillery, Dale, "Academic Rank: Promise or Peril?" *Junior College Journal*, XXXIII (February 1963), 6–9.

15. Tyler, Ralph W., "The Teaching Obligation," *Junior College Journal*, XXX (May 1960), 525–33.

16. Williamson, E. G., *Student-personnel Services in Colleges and Universities*. New York: McGraw-Hill Book Company, 1961.

17. Wrenn, C. Gilbert, *Student-personnel Work in College*. New York: The Ronald Press Company, 1951. Copyright 1951, The Ronald Press Company.

The two-year college is an innovation of the twentieth century and, consequently, has not developed much insulation from the swiftly changing cross currents of the society which gave it life.

Closely related to its social, economic, and political environment, the two-year college is still in the emergent stage. Being young and relatively untried, it does not enjoy the stability of traditions generally associated with other institutions of higher education. Yet lack of tradition can be a distinct advantage when used as an opportunity to develop in response to current needs and thinking. It must be recognized, however, that this lack of stability generates a multitude of problems with which the institution must grapple if it is to succeed in achieving its objectives.

Throughout this volume, the authors have endeavored to identify issues and to suggest directions. It is appropriate at this point to summarize our recommendations under three general categories: (1) educational roles, (2) organization and control—internal and external, and (3) financial support. In interpreting the following comments, the reader will do well to bear in mind that the position from which the authors view the two-year college is predominantly liberal and unquestionably pragmatic. We are in complete sympathy with the efforts of the comprehensive

10

the future
of the two-year college

community college to bring higher education within reach of all segments of the post-high school population. At the same time, we feel the necessity of sorting out those concepts that seem to offer the most promise for the development of a rational and unified theory of two-year college education.

Educational Roles

Fundamental to any discussion of the educational roles of two-year colleges is a differentiation of the missions of the various kinds of institutions in this category. It is difficult, if not impossible, to discuss the two-year college as a single entity; therefore, the classification given in Chapter 2 must provide the foundation for this discussion.

Four types of two-year colleges were identified: the public comprehensive community college, the private junior college, the technical institute, and the extension center, or branch, of a college or university. The over-all educational missions of the latter three are reasonably well defined and accepted within the framework of higher education. Private junior colleges define their educational role in terms of denominational affiliation, basic philosophical position, tradition and custom, and specified educational functions. Although these differ from institution to institution, they generally conform to a pattern involving selectivity of students and relatively restricted curricula designed to meet the stated objectives of the particular institution.

The technical institute has specific functions clustered around the general objective of occupational preparation of quite a specific nature. Branches and extension centers of universities provide access to the baccalaureate degree, adult education, and community services. Here again there are wide variations among colleges, depending upon the historical development and traditional patterns of educational services established in previous years.

The over-all mission of the public community college is somewhat more nebulous, and it would be presumptuous to assume that a standard formula or format is currently being applied to all such institutions in the various states. The authors' belief that the mission of the public two-year college is to educate all individuals of post-high school age or achievement level to the limits of their abilities is predicated upon the assumption that educational programs appropriate for changing societal needs and a heterogeneous student body can be formulated.

This position does not entirely satisfy educational conservatives, for it fails to define educational programs and students in terms of the traditional concepts of post-high school education. In spite of this opposition, the fact that education has become the primary vehicle for social and economic mobility will force the acceptance of the comprehensive concept of the public community college. It may be noted that educational programs leading to professional certification in the fields of engineering, business, veterinary science, nursing, and education were not defined as "collegiate" during the nineteenth century. Now they enjoy high status and acceptance in universities throughout the nation. Thus, it can be seen that the needs of society actually dictate the breadth and scope of educational programs. In the absence of adequate institutional responses, society will create new organizations to carry out the required services.

The "open door" policy

This leads us to the issue of the "open door" admission policy. It is clear that the manpower resources of the United States must be fully developed both qualitatively and quantitatively. The day has long since passed when a highly selective elite could be depended upon to meet social and economic needs. As the number of individuals desiring education beyond the high school increases, society must assume the responsibility for providing for those individuals who possess the necessary motivation and self-discipline the programs designed to prepare them for responsible positions within the social order.

In order to do this, the two-year college must carefully define its functions and, within this framework, develop various curricula leading toward its objectives. With the new programs must come the development of an admission policy which will help new students select programs for which they have some reasonable chance of success. This can be partially accomplished through the development of prediction data for separate curricula (probability tables) which, when carefully interpreted to students, may result in the selection of courses and curricula compatible with their abilities. The college must also be prepared to enforce requirements that deny students admission to programs for which they are not qualified. At the same time, students with average or below-average academic abilities must be given an opportunity to achieve their potential. The selective admission of students to specific curricula is commonly accepted in public community colleges today, as is evidenced by the two-year nursing program. Individuals are not admitted to this curriculum unless they meet certain minimum requirements on standardized tests and have achieved acceptable grades in high school. This procedure has not had an adverse effect upon nursing programs; rather, it has enhanced their status and widened their acceptance. This type of selective admission needs to be extended to other demanding curricular offerings, most notably in the area of liberal arts.

The continuing problem of unrestricted admission to public community colleges involves not only an educational question but also the attitudes of the college administrators, the community, and the lack of clear recognition of the limitations of financial support and college size. A substantial number of public colleges with access to a limited number of students have maintained the "open door" policy in spite of the lack of educational programs appropriate to the abilities and interests of the students being admitted. Small colleges with limited resources are often overeager in their efforts to stimulate larger enrollments. On the one hand, the administrator faces real financial problems; on the other, he knows that the college cannot possibly offer distinctive curricula appropriate to the wide span of abilities presented by his students. Community attitudes also foster such unrealistic situations with the demand that all high school graduates be given an opportunity to enroll in college-transfer courses. The argument here is that parents pay taxes for the support of the college; therefore, their sons and daughters have the "right" to attempt regular collegiate work. The result is a high level of attrition among freshmen in public community colleges. A more healthy situation would be for the college to define its educational roles, to make clear that it can sustain only a limited number of programs. Admittedly, this requires careful planning by college administrators and effective communication with students, parents, and community leaders; however, the continued development of public community colleges requires a more realistic delineation of the possible, rather than the ideal.

Types of programs

The issue of the "open door" leads naturally to a consideration of the question: What educational programs should be provided by the various types of two-year colleges? The scope of the private junior college is relatively restricted, by reason of its role and its purposes, to some combination of religious emphasis, personal and social development, college-transfer courses, and a few occupation-oriented programs. College and university branches and extension centers will undoubtedly continue to provide courses leading to the baccalaureate degree, graduate-level courses, short-range adult-education programs, and limited community services. The public community college, given adequate resources, should provide accelerated or honors transfer programs, baccalaureate programs, technical and vocational courses, developmental courses, and courses in various avocational pursuits. Fundamental to the development of these five interrelated functions is the richness of the resources available to the institution. There has been a tendency on the part of many community colleges to expand programs at a rate detrimental to the welfare of existing educational responsibilities. Rather than expand their educational programs, colleges should first upgrade their existing services to uniform levels of excellence. A priority list must be developed to provide for the orderly accomplishment of their objectives. Decisions regarding new programs should not be reached at upper administrative levels until the faculty has been involved in the decision-making process. Because faculty members have an interest in maintaining the excellence of existing programs, their consent is not likely to be obtained for offerings which are inferior.

This kind of realistic approach to the question of comprehensive educational services will mean that many small public colleges will not be truly comprehensive. Colleges with large student populations or located in metropolitan areas will have the resources with which to provide all types of course work, guidance, and community services. It must be recognized, however, that the ideal of comprehensive educational programs is well beyond the reach of many institutions and that it would be folly for them to attempt such expansion or to claim that they can fulfill the entire broad range of post-high school educational needs.

Approximately half of the public community colleges are large enough and have enough financial support to provide comprehensive curricula in college-transfer, technical, and vocational areas. These colleges have enrollments of nine hundred or more students. It is entirely possible that many of the smaller colleges will be located in areas in which they can develop cooperative programs with other institutions and, by judicious planning and organized community effort, provide at least certain educational services in addition to the traditional transfer program. Certainly these colleges, in cooperation with their communities, can implement appropriate community-service programs built upon the cultural, artistic, and avocational interests of the community. It is not necessary for every college to control and finance these aspects of the educational program. As a matter of fact, the pattern of financing in many states makes this impossible. With aggressive and farsighted administrative leadership and faculty-community cooperation, many such services can be provided at little direct cost to the college. This pattern of development seems to be most logical and reasonable in the absence of financial support for programs which do not generate academic credit hours as defined by state regulations.

The suggestion that the two-year college has a responsibility for the initiation of remedial and developmental courses for students who cannot qualify for transfer, technical, or even vocational studies beyond the high school arouses anxieties on the part of college faculties and is often misunderstood by laymen. Is it the responsibility of these institutions to provide curricular offerings which are clearly not collegiate in character and which may encompass content characteristically included in secondary (and even elementary) schools? It has been made clear in Chapter 8 that the authors believe there are certain practical limitations to the services the community college can effectively offer. It is doubtful that public community colleges can provide meaningful course work for individuals in the lowest 20 per cent of the population as measured by intellectual ability and academic achievement. These individuals, in all probability, do not have the basic capacity to learn beyond a most elementary level. It may well be necessary for society to develop special arrangements for institutions specifically designed to meet the needs of these citizens. However, it is our belief that the public two-year college—whether it be a branch, a technical institute, or a public community college—has a responsibility to provide developmental curricula for individuals with some potential for education beyond the high school. These individuals should have an opportunity to demonstrate their ability to grow intellectually to the limits of their innate capacities and motivations. We have suggested that such remedial courses should emphasize basic skills in language (reading, writing, and speaking) and mathematics, since these two general areas are fundamental to any further study.

Developmental programs do not necessarily depreciate the over-all quality of the educational activities of the institution. The mere fact that they are given on the same campus and, in some instances, by the same faculty does not necessarily affect the quality of other courses. On the contrary, such courses frequently result in the removal of students lacking the proper background from regular academic courses, thus freeing the academic instructor to proceed at a higher level than would otherwise be possible.

A word of caution may be appropriate here. Some students of the two-year college have stated that it has a custodial function. This assumption needs to be examined carefully. Current economic shifts and resulting lack of entry jobs—i.e., those requiring little previous experience—have stimulated some legislative action designed to keep young people out of the labor market for one or two additional years. Unskilled individuals are given opportunities to develop needed skills which they can use to find a useful job and occupational competence. This is a needed and laudable objective; however, it will not be achieved if the individuals involved have little or no motivation to complete the requirements of the courses in which they are enrolled. Social action, in the form of educational opportunities, must be balanced by individual motivation if educational experiences are to be meaningful to the student. Without such motivation, there will be little or no learning.

The public two-year college cannot simultaneously be a quality educational institution and a custodial institution. As society generates larger numbers of individuals who cannot meet minimum levels of competence, specialized institutions must be created to deal with the problem. These may be combinations of work camps and schools, or they may be organized in other patterns. The point is that there are some limitations to the ability of any one organization to handle all social problems. These limitations are apparent in comprehensive urban high schools, where individuals of very low mental ability are put with those of normal and higher ability.

If the community college is to fulfill the many responsibilities already assigned to it by society, it cannot also be the custodian of the unfit and the incompetent. Although society will, in effect, say, "Here, you take this person, we do not know what we can do with him," there are limits as to how far the college can go and still remain an effective educational organization. The college can make its contribution to social needs by providing comprehensive educational opportunities and effective guidance for students, but it cannot—even with unlimited financial resources—cure all the mistakes of parents and society.

A related question concerns the responsibility of public two-year colleges for providing a second chance to students who have attempted college work and failed. Here again, as in the case of developmental programs, there can be little argument but that some post-high school institutions must be sufficiently flexible in their educational policies to permit certain individuals to try again. The importance of such opportunities was clearly demonstrated after World War II, when large numbers of veterans returned to college campuses throughout the country. Many of these individuals had been mediocre or failing students before entering military service. After achieving a certain level of maturity, the majority of them returned to school with adult attitudes, clearly defined objectives, and high levels of motivation. At that time, colleges and universities were eager to give them a second chance and their faith in these marginal students was more than justified by the number who succeeded in meeting or even exceeding institutional expectations. Although the college must maintain a certain degree of institutional integrity and level of quality, this does not justify denying individuals a second chance in an appropriate educational program. Society cannot afford to cast aside individuals who may, given the opportunity, achieve a higher level of personal, academic, and occupational competence than they had in late adolescence; rather, society should encourage all individuals to learn to the limits of their abilities.

Another question closely related to the preceding one is the "halo" effect of the transfer program. Mass media in the United States have made a great point of college graduation as a minimum requirement for social and economic status, completely disregarding the fact that many individuals do not possess the skill or motivation to fulfill the requirements of any baccalaureate program. It is unlikely that the two-year college, in and of itself, can raise the status of vocational and technical programs in the face of current social attitudes toward college degrees. There are some steps, however, which the college can take to develop these programs and to find qualified students for them. It is estimated that approximately 40 per cent of the individuals who are qualified to continue their education do not enter a college after high school graduation. It is from this group, the culturally deprived and the technologically unemployed, that the college must recruit students for vocational and technical training. To this group any college program represents an avenue for advancement. If the program meets economic and social needs, it will achieve status and win acceptance from those individuals being served as well as from society in general.

Guidance services should be carefully organized in relation to comprehensive curricular offerings. In this way, when the student faces failure he has realistic alternatives among which to choose. In the last analysis, society itself will define the status of any educational program, but the college can stimulate a more realistic appraisal of technical education if it produces successful graduates.

Perhaps the most appropriate and immediately effective action which would contribute to the more general acceptance of technical and semi-professional programs is the development of broad national requirements for various types of occupations. The most comprehensive example of the impact of detailed educational and skill requirements is found in the paramedical occupations. All such occupations, which support the medical and dental services in hospitals, state institutions, and private practice, are defined and licensed by state laws and regulations. The relative status of these specializations is thus clearly related to other groups in the profession. The licensing procedure makes possible clear definition of specific jobs and educational programs required for individual qualification and acceptance by the group. Although less well structured, the specialties within business also are based upon generally accepted educational requirements and skill levels.

Improvement of instruction

A related educational question, which arises as a result of enrollment pressures, is whether or not post-high school institutions will move rapidly but carefully toward the utilization of technological advances for the improvement of instruction. It is a commonly accepted assumption that the two-year college provides more individualized education for its students than is available in large, diversified four-year institutions. This assumption no longer bears the light of careful scrutiny because larger junior colleges, both public and private, often have classes as large as or larger than those found in four-year institutions. This is probably a trend which cannot be reversed; however, careful reappraisal and analysis by faculties and administrators can do much to avoid destructive depersonalization of instruction in large classes. As has been suggested in Chapter 8, curricular and instructional adaptations utilizing carefully selected course content and appropriate instructional techniques can do much to shift the responsibility for learning to the student without undue negative consequences.

The personalization of instruction can be achieved, in spite of large classes, through adaptations in class sectioning. Large lecture sections can be combined with small seminars or laboratories, and a closer and more meaningful relationship between formal instruction and guidance services can be developed. In addition, a reappraisal of the assignment of professional personnel and the acquisition of additional clerical and semiprofessional personnel would do much to shift the burden of extraneous responsibilities from the teacher to other hands. These procedures, along with individual institutional adjustments, would permit the organization of large classes while retaining desirable quality in the teaching-learning situation.

Adult education

Perhaps the most neglected educational role is that of providing avocational outlets and experiences for individuals of all ages. If the phrase *education is a lifelong process* is to have meaning, colleges must provide appropriate programs of interest and value to high school graduates and adults alike. It is clear that we are entering an era of greater leisure, while there seem to be fewer and less meaningful outlets to satisfy the personality and creative needs of individuals. Although this responsibility cannot necessarily be carried solely by the college, formal programs should be open to adults. In addition, the institution should attempt to cooperate closely with other cultural and civic organizations which can contribute to the self-realization of individuals in the community.

Unfortunately, this responsibility has been shunned and even disparaged by some state legislatures and agencies. In recent years a number of states have decreased or eliminated appropriations for adult-education programs. It is the belief of the authors that as many citizens as possible should be exposed to new cultural and intellectual experiences and stimulations if they are to deal effectively with personal, social, and political problems in a complex society. In order to achieve this ideal, the college must be recognized as an instrument of social policy, one function of which is to make available relevant experiences to as large a segment of the population as is practical.

Subsumed under the whole question of educational resources for the use of leisure are the more specific problems of the aging population. The increased life span has resulted in a higher proportion of elderly people in our society. With mandatory retirement ages, a large number of individuals find themselves with no focus of interests or activities though still enjoying good health. In a work-oriented society, it appears that many of the older persons view a regular job as an indication of personal worth. In a society in which the need for the older members to work for pay is decreasing, the concept of social usefulness takes on an entirely different dimension.

One of the more evident needs of the elderly is for a more meaningful role in the community. There is also a need for a clearer concept of a useful social role for older persons. A challenge to our society is to develop for the aged activities which will provide them with satisfaction, self-respect, and a sense of participation.

These individuals provide a great, untapped reservoir of experience with unlimited possibilities for the education of the younger and less experienced members of the community. The use of some of these elderly people in community activities and educational pursuits as advisors, part-time teachers, and consultants could greatly enrich community life and provide essential personal satisfactions to those involved.

External Controls

State control

An issue with far-reaching implications concerns state control of public colleges. There has been a marked trend toward increased state control and direction of colleges as the amount of state financial aid increases. In some states, such as New York and Florida, minute details regarding the construction of physical facilities must be approved on the state level. In other states, control is not as comprehensive and detailed.

There are some zones of activities in which state control and coordination are essential if there is to be any logical relationship among post-high school institutions and a minimum of consistency among the programs being provided by individual colleges. For example, it is the responsibility of the state to develop a master plan for higher education. Within such a plan should be provisions for the construction and expansion of community colleges based upon population distribution rather than upon political opportunism. The state should also be responsible for defining the over-all mission of two-year and four-year colleges so that there are complementary, rather than competitive, programs among them. The state should also insure minimum standards of quality in the programs being supported by state funds, as well as the relevance of these programs to other state-sponsored educational resources and to the changing economic complexion of the region. Thus, general patterns of education, with some specific direction and stimulation from state legislatures and agencies, should evolve from the state level. Perhaps most important of all, the state should insure that the costs of unnecessary duplication among institutions of higher education are avoided.

Local control

Without disparaging the role of state agencies, a strong case can be made for continuing local control of a number of important aspects of college policy-making, administration, and teaching. It should be the prerogative of the local board to plan, within minimal safety requirements, physical facilities as developed and recommended by the administration and faculty of the college. It seems inconceivable that a state officer working many miles away is better qualified to design buildings than the professional staff members who will be teaching in them. Other policy questions, such as curriculum patterns, staff selection and retention, personnel policy, and instructional techniques, should be left to local control. Although such a course of action may make for post-high school education which does not fit completely within a logical framework, its advantages far outweigh the superficial efficiency of highly centralized state control and direction.

There is little doubt that the size and complexity of higher education have reached the point where state master planning is essential if reasonable economies are to be effected and the wide variety of educational needs are to be met. Master plans serve the purpose of defining a pattern for the implementation of social policy with regard to education. The application of such recommendations should be carried out on the state level and implemented, in the case of the community college, by locally oriented boards of control. In this way, local boards can operate within the general guidelines set down by over-all state policy and plans but, at the same time, add a unique flavor growing out of local conditions and needs.

Federal influence

Related to this problem is the question of federal influence through earmarked federal funds. Federal direction of higher education has increased enormously since World War II and promises to continue as a major factor in educational planning in the future. There is little question that colleges must have federal support if they are to contribute significantly to national, social, and economic needs. On the other hand, the earmarking of funds for specific sectors of education has had the unfortunate effect of discouraging balance in curricular offerings and available financial resources. The most constructive use of federal funds will take place through individual state master plans, for some states need to develop in certain directions while others need to move toward different objectives. Federal aid should be designed to improve the quality of education while preserving essential variations of regional importance. Should federal aid indirectly induce conformity among all colleges, much of the essential flavor of higher education in the United States would be lost. For educational conservatives, who dearly love this particular argument, it should be pointed out that no such trend is presently evident among state universities receiving large amounts of federal funds.

Professional organizations and boards of control

Professional organizations must also be considered as important external influences. If these organizations retain a reasonable degree of flexibility and adaptability to changing social and economic conditions, they can be the bulwarks for the healthy development of community and junior colleges. Because their orientations are basically educational rather than political, they can act as important counterbalances to state or national domination of post-high school institutions. The patterns of education which will characterize colleges evolve, in most instances, from such professional organizations, and it is essential that they retain a strong influence in college administration, curriculum, and instruction.

Another aspect of college control involves the legal structure of the local board. The authors believe, without reservation, that public and private colleges and technical institutes should have local boards of control and clearly defined financial resources separate from the public schools and four-year colleges and universities. Despite arguments to the contrary, states which have combined public schools and community colleges have found serious difficulties in this type of organization. The trend is toward the separation of colleges from K–12 districts and it is entirely possible that, within a few years, the separation will be complete in most states.

The authors also believe that branches of public institutions are not the best solution to mass post-high school education. Although there is a dearth of empirical evidence, there are indications that two-year branch colleges do not offer broad curricular opportunities, that they shift the financial burden to students, and that they do not have adequate facilities to support an educational program qualitatively comparable to that offered on the main campus. Although branches do provide valuable educational and community services in some instances, the development of a statewide system of locally controlled community colleges will, in the long run, more adequately serve the needs of all potential students.

The area vocational school, a newcomer on the educational scene, has grown out of recent federal legislation. There is reason to doubt the wisdom of the development of additional post-high school educational institutions; rather, the functions of area vocational schools should be combined with those of comprehensive community colleges in a state system in which all citizens would have access to the institutions. The emergent area vocational school and the functions it is designed to serve require careful definition of secondary and post-high school functions. These definitions should be provided in state plans so that the educational objectives being sought can be divided between comprehensive colleges and comprehensive high schools, thus eliminating competition for federal funds.

Internal Organization and Control

Because two-year colleges vary widely in their patterns of organizational control, it is difficult to identify issues in this area that have broad general applicability. It is possible, however, to relate several issues to the groups that participate in or are influenced by internal decisions.

The first of these concerns the relationship of the institution to its board of control. The principal activity of the board has been defined as the determination of policy. It is primarily the responsibility of the institution's chief executive officer to insure that individual board members do not interfere with, or exercise undue influence on, the internal execution of board policy. At the same time, the lines of communication between the board and the internal organization must be well defined and allowed to function freely. One major objection to the K–14 type of organization is that the chief executive of the college reports to the superintendent and is thus insulated from contact with the board. Similar insulation from policy-making bodies is also the rule in the case of branches of four-year institutions. Such insulation can result in a marked impairment of the institution's ability to respond to the requirements of the local community.

Zones of responsibility

A second issue involves the definition of the zones of responsibility for faculty members and the college administration. Currently there is a trend toward the adoption of university patterns of institutional control in many community and junior colleges. This trend has some advantages, but it also carries some serious complications and potential long-range problems. Is the administrator to retain a position of strong leadership and influence in the college? Or—as has been recommended by some professional groups—are the board and faculty to develop policy and administrators to play a secondary role in its implementation?

There has been a tendency in recent years to confuse "democratic" administration with the diffusion of defined authority and responsibility among the members of the organization. Participation in administration by the professional staff is necessary for institutional progress, but such participation must occur within a framework of leadership and through some direction by individuals who carry the responsibility for achieving institutional objectives. Administration is not a passive process consisting of routine custodial activities. The viable organization is characterized by knowledgeable and aggressive leadership cooperating with a well-qualified faculty to achieve mutually acceptable organizational objectives. All members of the professional staff have significant contributions to make to the improvement and operation of the college, but each role is incomplete without the complementary roles of all other individuals.

A common weakness in the organization and control of many institutions is the extent to which students are excluded from participating in decisions which have as their focal point the welfare of the student body as a whole. The median age for students attending two-year colleges is very close to the legal voting age. The same student that the two-year college protects will very soon be making decisions at the polls which may have important consequences for his alma mater. It stands to reason, therefore, that duly elected representative student organizations should play a significant role in appropriate areas of the decision-making process.

The community college must maintain a delicate balance between institutional integrity and effective interaction with changing external conditions and needs. It cannot perform its functions, as defined by society, if it isolates itself from its environment. The administrator serves as a director of the organization's energies, a mediator, and a bridge between the organization and the area being served. These essential functions cannot be carried on exclusively by groups without meaningful leadership.

Finance

Basic to all other problems facing the two-year college is the amount and pattern of financial support. Although this remains a perennial question, having been thoroughly discussed in relation to all levels of education for the last forty years, the fact remains that other problems considered in this volume will remain unsolved in the absence of adequate financial support. Nor does it help particularly to point out that this problem is not limited to the two-year college.

The cost of education

The first issue to be considered is this: Is the current level of financial support for annual operations costs in colleges high enough to insure quality programs of education? The answer is "No!" There is no doubt that the annual average expenditure of approximately $550 per student in two-year colleges is much too low to meet the needs of complex, modern educational programs. In the past, there has been a tendency for community college administrators to claim the ability to educate students at a lower cost than that prevailing in four-year colleges and universities. Considered from the point of view of the student who may be spared the costs of room and board, this assertion may very well be true. From the institutional angle, however, it is demonstrably false. The cost for post-high school courses, per se, is approximately the same whether the course is provided on the resident campus of a university or in a community college. The type of physical facilities, classroom and laboratory equipment, supplies, personnel costs, and administrative expenses are not essentially lower in two-year colleges *if there are no significant qualitative and quantitative differences in the programs being offered students.*

If two-year colleges are to provide comprehensive programs, they must have the same level of financial support as is provided for the junior divisions of public colleges and universities. The myth that there is high-quality inexpensive education must be destroyed. Because junior college students are unselected and present a wide range of abilities, attitudes, and motivations, it is probable that the cost per student should be higher than that in four-year colleges. Furthermore, the two-year college does not have available the relatively low-cost teaching personnel available to universities in their large numbers of graduate students. In contrast, the two-year college must employ full-time career teachers whose entire personal and professional lives are centered upon the college with which they are associated. Their salaries must, therefore, be higher per contact hour than those of graduate assistants and teaching fellows on the university campus. Because this single budget item accounts for at least 65 per cent of the annual operating cost of the college, it is apparent that the college—in the absence of adequate financial support—must take one or more of several courses of action:

(1)   Raise the student-teacher ratio
(2)   Increase the size of classes

(3)   Limit supporting services (guidance, maintenance, clerical services)
(4)   Limit course offerings
(5)   Limit supplies and equipment for teaching purposes

Such stopgap measures are all too often the norm in both public and private two-year colleges today.

The cost per student today should be in the neighborhood of $800 to $1000 per student in comprehensive two-year colleges, and from $700 to $1000 in colleges having narrower educational programs. At current cost levels, this sum would provide adequate financial support for the necessary components of high-quality educational programs in most colleges. Although minor geographic differences in these costs might be justified, the current wide regional variations cannot be defended. The cost of superior educational programs is not significantly different in various parts of the United States. When such differences exist, there is a consistent flow of better teaching personnel from low- to high-paying regions, for differences in support tend to be reflected primarily in salary levels. There is little difference in the cost of educational supplies and equipment, for such materials are produced and sold nationally.

It must also be recognized that the cost of technical and vocational programs will be higher than those in the liberal arts if the necessary supplies, equipment, and qualified personnel are secured to support them. These programs require specialized personnel with high-level educational and occupational qualifications. Furthermore, such programs cannot be taught without close liaison with professional and occupational groups in the community. All these factors require trained staff members, clerical support, and physical facilities and equipment which are quite costly. For example, one of the most widespread technical programs today is data processing. The cost of supplies and equipment for these courses is substantial. If enrollment in these courses is limited, as it frequently is in technical programs, the cost per student becomes very high.

The distribution of educational costs

This brings us to another issue: How should the cost of higher education be distributed among students, local, state, and national sources? The question may be divided into two segments: annual operational costs, and capital outlay for buildings and equipment. The distribution of operating costs to the student ranges from little or nothing in California public colleges to almost complete support through tuition and fees in some private colleges. The pattern of support for operating costs in private colleges is unlikely to change substantially in the future. The student desiring the services of this type of institution must obviously pay almost the entire cost of his education. The problem of student tuition in extension centers and branches controlled by public colleges and universities is another matter, however. In some states, there is clear discrimination against students in extension centers and branches: they are required to pay markedly higher tuition than campus students. There is no rational justification for this differentiation, because both groups supposedly receive the same quality of educational services.

Approximately 15 per cent of the annual operating costs in public community colleges should be supported by nominal tuition charges, with the remainder being divided between the state and the local community. The minimal tuition charge would tend to eliminate individuals who have no serious interest in education. Furthermore, there is at least some slight status attached to goods or services that cost money. That which is free is not generally valued in our society. This argument assumes, however, that provisions will be made for students without financial resources so that economic limitations will not bar them from college.

Although the local community should contribute substantially to the support of the college, in view of the services it receives and the economic advantages of having such an institution, the largest share of the cost should be borne by the state. The present distribution of expenditures, with the principal burden falling on the local community, does not encourage the expansion and enrichment of educational programs. State government is, at present, the largest single contributor to public four-year colleges and universities. Because trained manpower is mobile and a distinct economic asset for the state, there is no logical reason for continued lack of major state support for operational costs in public two-year colleges.

The same argument applies to the federal government. Federal contributions to higher education are not insignificant, and there is every reason to anticipate increased participation in the immediate future. A formula which retained effective token support from the individual student and the local community while shifting the major burden to state and national agencies would do much to insure high-quality comprehensive education in the community colleges.

It is probable that the most effective method of distributing state aid to two-year colleges would be one based upon some adaptation of the minimum-foundation program currently applied to elementary and secondary education in an increasing number of states. The advantages of this type of flexible support—based upon the ability of the local community to contribute—are obvious.

The expense of construction and equipment is also distributed improperly at present. In many states, the local community is required to provide all such facilities. This practice has inhibited the rapid development of needed colleges. There is general agreement that the property tax has, in many communities, reached extreme limits with corresponding reluctance on the part of voters to support further increases. Because state and federal agencies have pre-empted most other sources of tax revenue, they must assume the responsibility of providing funds for campus construction so that this burden may be lifted from the overburdened local governmental units. The principle of state responsibility for capital costs has long been accepted in relation to public four-year colleges and universities. Many states also contribute substantially to building costs in the public elementary and secondary schools. If two-year colleges are to realize their enormous potential, the principle of state responsibility must apply equally to them.

Leadership in Higher Education

Universities in the United States have a tremendous stake in the further development of public and private two-year colleges. If two-year institutions are to serve the majority of freshmen and sophomores in academic and technical programs, they need strong and continuous university leadership not presently available in many states. The time is not far off when universities may find that the majority of their upper-division undergraduate students come to them from two-year colleges. If an adequate supply of capable students is to be insured, universities must face the responsibility for giving leadership to the "feeder" institutions. With a few notable exceptions, universities have overlooked this responsibility.

One area in which responsibility must be exercised involves the adequate preparation of teachers. In the past, teaching personnel have been trained specifically for the elementary or secondary schools, and on the Ph.D. level for research and teaching in the four-year institutions. If community colleges are to assume the broad responsibilities outlined in preceding chapters, it is apparent that there must be certain adaptations in preservice and in-service training of teachers for this particular segment of higher education. Instructors in two-year colleges are neither university professors nor secondary school teachers. They require a preparation that is broader than that ordinarily found among university personnel yet deeper than that necessary for secondary school teachers. Both kinds of preparation should be included in upper and graduate divisions for individuals planning to teach in two-year colleges. Ideally, instructors should approach their first two-year college teaching assignment with proficiency in two closely related fields. In addition, they ought to have a real understanding of the functions of the community college.

Universities also need to develop more adequate channels of communication with two-year colleges so that effective articulation of educational programs on a planned and rational basis may be assured. Too often universities implement innovations without notifying the two-year colleges supplying undergraduate transfer students; the result is discontinuity in the student's educational experiences, reflecting unfavorably upon the two-year college. Although two-year colleges can cooperate with respect to this problem, it is basically the responsibility of the university to lead the way in coordinating the development of those educational programs which have transfer implications.

Although some community colleges have very effective institutional research programs, most have done little effective work in this field because they are too small to afford the expense and personnel involved. If the two-year college is to adapt to the changing environment, provide quality education, and evaluate its educational product, well-designed institutional research is essential.

In view of the limitations of the two-year college, it seems apparent that universities have a responsibility to cooperate in conceiving and carrying out meaningful institutional research projects. Qualitative improvements in two-year colleges depend to a large extent upon the development of such cooperative relationships.

Conclusion

There is a saying that there is nothing new under the sun. The implication of this bit of folk wisdom is that seemingly novel situations have antecedents buried in the distant past and not infrequently represent a recurrence of a long-forgotten problem. The two-year college has not burst suddenly upon the American scene; it is a logical outgrowth of changes in social, political, and educational thought over the past half-century.

If the two-year college appears new and unique, it is because at present it occupies the center of the educational stage, holding forth great promise while concealing its weaknesses behind unclear role definition. In the twentieth century, higher education has emerged as a predominant requirement for enjoyment of the good life. The four-year institution, like the classical high school, cannot serve the needs of the heterogeneous population that has come to view higher education as a necessity and a birthright. Consequently, another institution, the two-year college, has evolved to attempt to meet this need.

What ought to be borne in mind by professionals and lay advocates alike is that the two-year college will not, by itself, induce the millennium, nor will it be the last educational institution to evolve from a complex society that has already seen the rise and fall of many others.

When a new institution arises, it must find a place for itself in the total framework of its environment. Consequently, it is not uncommon for those whose interests are bound up in its development to make extravagant claims about the problems it plans to solve. They may even come to believe these claims, especially when the claims are legitimated by state or federal laws. In the final analysis, however, the new institution will not solve all problems; rather, it will gradually come to concentrate on areas in which it can most effectively function.

The question, then, is not really one of how the two-year college can solve all the problems currently facing undergraduate college education but, rather: Which among the multitude of problems can it most effectively resolve and what ought to be its role in the over-all framework of higher education?

The development and broadening of technical programs may very well be the two-year college's most significant single contribution to higher education. More important even than such development and broadening can be their popularization. Although the technical institute offers preparation of high quality, its limited general education offerings and its obvious vocational orientation make it ill-suited to cope with the major problem confronting technical education today: the recruitment of well-qualified students. There is in education a pecking order of status preparations. At the pinnacle rest the liberal arts, followed by various professional curricula, then down through the technical programs to vocational and developmental offerings. Within the technical area, a subhierarchy exists, depending upon how closely a particular curriculum relates to its professional counterpart. Thus, professional nursing programs find high degrees of acceptance. The same thing cannot be said for all the engineering and industrial technologies or for many of the other technical courses.

The comprehensive community college, with its recognized and prestigious transfer program, is in a much better position than the technical institute. Efforts must be made to reach the group of qualified students who do not, at present, continue their education and to steer them into appropriate technical areas. At the same time, many of the students currently entering liberal arts and other transfer programs need to be channeled into the technical program. Although it may be difficult, it should not be impossible to convey the message that successful technicians generally lead far more satisfactory and socially useful lives than baccalaureate flunk-outs.

The preceding comments have indicated the necessity of upgrading and enhancing the two-year college's efforts in the technical area. With respect to transfer programs, and most especially the all-pervasive liberal arts curriculum, quite the opposite is required. Junior college education has its share of conservative administrators who prefer to define post-high school education strictly in terms of the four-year model. A substantial proportion of faculty members pattern their teaching on the university model and are only too eager to flunk those students who have difficulty conforming to it. Many boards lack an understanding of the needs of students or citizens who fail to react in terms of conventional middle-class standards.

The need, then, is to redefine and interpret to the public the place of transfer programs within the total context of the college's offerings. A selective admission policy will do much to change the popular concept that students ought to be permitted to fail such courses before considering more realistic alternatives. It is very possible that, if one third to one half of the present enrollment in transfer courses destined to fail or to become discouraged and quit had been required to start college experience in an appropriate program, society might have many more technicians than is currently the case. Although the two-year college at present devotes 75 per cent of its effort to programs leading to the baccalaureate degree, a proper redefinition of its role would undoubtedly channel more than half its resources into the education of technicians.

Of course there are those prophets who see the two-year college ultimately educating as many as three fourths of the undergraduate lower-division students. This prediction would seem to negate the preceding assumption. The fact of the matter is, however, that the first two years of college today are undergoing a transition not dissimilar to that previously experienced by the secondary school. Although the college population has undergone enormous expansion in terms of absolute numbers, there is reason to believe that the qualitative expansion has not kept pace with the quantitative increase. In other words, a substantial proportion of the entering college population today would not have qualified for admission even to the less selective institutions thirty years ago. Because four-year schools can afford to be selective, the problem of coping with students who have little preparation and insufficient motivation will fall largely to the two-year institution. To increase transfer offerings and to admit unqualified applicants would be the height of folly. Students should be required to work up to transfer programs rather than be allowed to enter such programs and be counseled into technical areas only when it becomes clear they cannot succeed. It is in this very practice, at present widespread, that much of the problem concerning the relative status of transfer and technical curricula lies.

Another major issue that may be raised with respect to the question of role definition concerns the degree to which junior college resources should be committed to the so-called developmental area. There is currently much emphasis on the salvage function of the community college which entails rather extensive diagnostic and remedial services. Just why many junior college student-personnel workers feel certain that they will succeed in this area, where the secondary schools have failed, is somewhat obscure. Although the college must provide diagnostic and remedial services to salvage individuals whenever possible, it is very doubtful that late bloomers will ever exist on campus in the profusion with which they appear in the literature. Consequently, the diversion of limited college resources to this area will probably always bring a rather limited rate of return. It should be emphasized, therefore, that the technical and transfer areas need to be given preference. This constitutes no major recommendation, because it is the current practice in almost all institutions. What would be novel, however, would be an honest evaluation of this service and the reporting of such an evaluation to the general public. A more frequent practice is to make extravagant claims which, in effect, cannot be supported.

In a heavily urbanized society, the junior college cannot ignore problems that, although peripheral to role definition, nonetheless have direct bearing upon the effective implementation of any defined program. Public community colleges now being organized in major metropolitan centers must face such issues as whether campuses should be located in depressed central areas or on the generally more respectable peripheries. If such institutions define as their responsibility the provision of opportunities for the culturally or academically disadvantaged, programs must be adapted to achieve this goal.

A related issue concerns the proper degree of college involvement in such problems as unemployment and the upgrading of cultural life and interests. The public community college would seem to have considerable potential for coping with such complex problems.

In the final analysis, the two-year college will not necessarily be judged by how many things it attempts but, rather, by how many things it successfully accomplishes. The two-year college will do well to note this point.

index